An Eagle's Sky:

My Life as a Birdman

By

John Stokes

Copyright 2013

Table of Contents

Chapter 1

Early Lessons

I have a bird's eye view of the land. It is a clear, warm spring day. The sun has been up for an hour now and I can smell dogwood flowers and freshly cut grass. This is not unusual for this time of the year, but considering the fact that I am three thousand feet in the air flying over Lookout Valley, it is remarkable. As I glide above this vernal landscape, I forget for a moment my human form and think about what it is like to be a bird. I feel the freedom of being able to go where one wishes. In the moment, I have the ability to disconnect from the earthbound world and the problems sometimes associated with it. Below me, below us, are two Red-tailed Hawks. Perhaps this is a pair and maybe they are searching for a place to build their nest. I wonder if **Osceola** *sees them. I glance over my shoulder and sure enough, he is looking down, watching the birds as they pass below us. Soon, the hawks fly out of sight.*

It has been 12 years since he has flown. The Incident, the shooting, left him crippled and unable to fly. Still, I know he has the desire to become airborne. Over the years, we have shared many things like heartbreak and defeat and have overcome seemingly insurmountable obstacles and life changing events. Osceola has helped me through all of this. Our lives have been intertwined. But now, it is time to give him something back in payment for all he has done for me. The ultimate gift I can give is flight. For a second, we lock eyes. We come from different worlds but are kindred spirits and share the love of the sky. I turn my head and re-focus on our flight. I feel the surge of the dogwood scented thermal updraft and bank my hang glider into a turn. We start to climb and before too long, we gain a few hundred feet of altitude. My mind drifts…

I am John Stokes. This tale probably had its beginnings when I was less than one year old. I am one of those people who have memories of my infancy. I have had a lifelong fascination with birds. This fascination, check that, this obsession, perhaps began with a bird mobile that hung above my crib. I always reached for the plastic cardinals and jays as they orbited above my head. When I was old enough, I finally reached the mobile and pulled it off its holder. As far back as I can remember I have been intrigued by the avian world. So much that I probably knew the names of the more common species of birds before I knew my ABCs.

I was born in New Albany, Mississippi, but spent the first ten years of my life in Meridian, Mississippi. This is not a birdwatcher's paradise by any stretch, but there were plenty of bird species to catch a curious kid's attention. The first birds that I really came to know were some English Sparrows that nested in our clothesline poles. In the spring, I saw these sparrows taking nest material such as grass and paper, into the horizontal arms of the poles. I built a nest of grass on the limbs of a nearby apricot tree, hoping the birds would use it instead. When the sparrows arrived with some nest material, I flapped my arms and chirped and pointed at my nest, hoping the birds would notice it. Needless to say, the sparrows ignored my offering, perhaps thinking that this odd little human may have fallen on its head a few times too many.

As soon as the sparrows started incubating, I dragged a stepladder that was tall enough for me to peer into the nest with a flashlight. Usually, the incubating adult darted out of the pole as I made my ascent. I then saw the brown speckled, half-marble-sized eggs. One by one, I took the eggs out, carefully examined them and replaced them into the nest. As soon as the babies hatched, I was there with the light. I wouldn't touch them because I believed the misconception about the parent's ability to smell my human scent and would cause them to abandon their offspring. My belief in the myth probably saved many a young sparrow from my over-scrutiny.

At the age of five, I began my first serious study of birds. Each day I checked the nest to monitor the babies' progress. Each day the youngsters were larger than the day before. I also noticed that when I tapped the pole, the nestlings' mouths popped open, expecting to be fed. Eventually, the sparrows made their first flights. Perhaps what fascinated me about birds was their ability to fly. When I saw these young birds trying their new wings, I watched with envy. I wanted to do the same. How free they were! I observed the fledglings follow their parents from one tree to the next and how I longed to fly.

I was amused by another bird, the Turkey Vulture. We had a few of these large scavengers that occasionally flew over my neighborhood. In the early 1960s, the TV Western was the rage. Shows like *Rawhide* and *Gunsmoke* drew a large number of viewers. I recalled a particular show where a guy was staked out in the desert. Obviously, he had done something to wrong his captors. They had left him there in an ultimate "Time Out" to contemplate his actions. As the relentless sun slowly roasted the hombre, some Turkey Vultures appeared overhead and began circling, anticipating a western feast. Seeing this, I surmised with my young brain that by playing dead in my back yard, I could entice my local vultures in for a closer look. One day I stretched out in the middle of my yard for what seemed an incalculable amount of time (probably about ten minutes). I hoped that some vultures would fly over and by chance, two did. They began circling above me, but soon left. As they were leaving, I thought I heard one say to the other,

"The boy looks dead and smells dead, but he's not dead yet!"

I never got the vultures to come down and for my effort, I was rewarded with a extreme case of chiggers. Watching the vultures soar overhead until they climbed out of sight only increased my desire to fly.

My father, Gilbert, was also interested in flight, and this spurred my curiosity as well. In fact, during WWII, he was originally attracted to the Navy. He wanted to be a naval fighter pilot, but the vision test halted his dreams. He had 20-20 vision, but he was color-blind, something he didn't know until he took the test! He was later drafted by the Army and was assigned to the Infantry. He went through basic training and boarded a ship bound for Japan. He was to participate in the U.S. invasion of Japan, but luckily, Japan surrendered three days before his group was to land. The fleet was diverted to the Philippines where he was eventually assigned to the Motor Pool, a job he did well, but not the one on which he had his heart set. He eventually met a young woman named Maria Lopez. Things progressed nicely and they were married in 1947. They had their first child that year, only to be stillborn. After returning to the states and New Albany, Mississippi, they had their second child, my sister Susie, in 1949. I came along in 1956 and my younger sister Mary was born in '58.

My father continued his interest in flight, although he never pursued a private pilot's license. He was always taking me to the airport to watch planes take off and land. He kept me supplied with various flying objects such as wooden gliders, rubber band powered planes and eventually a gas-powered line-controlled Piper Cub. I think I was a little too young to fly the model. On my first attempt and first revolution, I promptly smacked it into an oak tree.

The plane never flew again. Later, my Dad bought me a P-40 Flying Tiger, but predictably, I never got to fly it. Still, it was great fun watching my father's satisfaction going round and round making the plane climb and dive.

My first attempts at personal flight came at the age of five or six. At the time, there was a television show called *Ripcord*. I was obviously influenced by TV shows. In this series, the heroes skydived and parachuted to rescue the lady in distress or to foil a bank robbery. I thought that this was the coolest thing! These guys jumped out of a plane, free fell with their arms extended (like a bird flying), pulled their ripcords, and parachuted to their mission. I thought that this looked pretty easy. The parachute container to me looked like one of my mother's purses. The parachute itself looked like a bed sheet. I had these items at hand. One problem I had was altitude, or the lack thereof. On the TV show, the guys jumped out of an airplane, something I didn't have. However, I had a huge sweet gum tree in my backyard that seemed lofty enough to provide ample freefall time. The plan was simple; get my Mom's purse, put a sheet in it, climb the tree, jump out, then as I was falling, reach into the purse, pull out the sheet, hold on and float to Earth! I had seen this in a cartoon, so it had to work! It was a revelation.

Sooo, I got my Mom's purse, the sheet, my best gripping "tenny shoes" and with the confidence of a Army Ranger, I proceeded to climb the tree. I got as high as I could, walked out on a limb, and launched myself into the wild blue yonder. Quickly, I was introduced to three things: 1) Gravity, 2) Sudden Deceleration, and 3) my Guardian Angel. Not two seconds after I jumped and before I could reach the sheet, I hit a limb with some netlike branches. The branches caught me, promptly knocked the breath out of me and gave me a wake-up call with reality. I could have been hurt or killed that day, but God and the Universe apparently had other plans for me. If I were going to fly, it would have to be by different means.

Chapter 2

My First Birds

My great-grandmother Polly gave me my first pet bird. It was a Budgerigar, or more commonly known as a parakeet and her name was Dixie. She was prominently displayed in our house in our planter area in between the living room and den. I was about four years old. Sadly, Dixie didn't last long in our house. Her cage was suspended above a planter partition by a spring that was connected to a nail. One day, the nail apparently came loose and Dixie's cage came crashing to the floor. The impact probably caused her to have a heart attack, as Dixie flopped and fluttered briefly on the floor of cage. She quickly expired. I was saddened by this and by coincidence, my Grandma Polly soon died. To top it all, about this time, I almost choked on a piece of steak. I kept asking my father if I was going to die, and he assured me that I was going to be okay. These events made me very aware, at an early age, of my own mortality.

When I was about seven, I got another budgie. The bird was green, a male, and I named him Sam. He was the first bird that I trained. He flew from his cage to my finger. If I patted my head while he was flying, he landed on my head. We had Sam for several years. One day, my Mom went outside to check the mail. She had forgotten that Sam was riding on her head and when she opened the mailbox, he flew away. I was at school when this happened. Had I been home, I might have been able to retrieve him. My mother felt terrible. She said she would get me another bird, but for several days I went outside, held up my hand, and whistled for Sam. Nothing. Hopefully, someone else found him and gave him a good home. I didn't get another budgie for about a year. I guess I secretly hoped that Sam would return home.

The next pet birds we got were some chicks at Easter. It used to be common to give children chicks, ducklings, or rabbits at this time of the year. We got three, one each for my sisters and one for me. Each was dyed a different color. I picked the red one. We actually had pretty good luck raising them. I guess my parents knew what to feed them and they were kept warm in a box with a light bulb. No telling how many thousands of these young animals died over the years that were not cared for properly. Thankfully, this practice of giving young animals for Easter is fading fast. Our chickens made it to about three-fourths grown in size and suddenly disappeared. We never knew what happened to them until about six years later. We had moved from Meridian and were back visiting our old neighborhood. We had stopped at our friends' house, the Basses, who lived behind us. Mrs. Bass asked me if I remembered those chickens that we got for Easter one year. I said yes. She asked if we wondered what had happened to them. I told her that I thought a cat had gotten them. She said,

"Yeah, and the cat's name was Mr. Flowers!"

I was a little puzzled. Her elderly father, Mr. Flowers, lived with her until he died. It seems that one day the three chickens had wandered over to the Basses porch. Here, they met their untimely demise at the hands of the ninety-year-old man! Mrs. Bass said that he caught them, rung their necks and cooked them. If you think about it, the sight of a ninety-year-old, frail, pale, white-haired man choking chickens was a sad sight indeed!

The next birds we acquired were two baby Peking Ducks (the domestic form of the Mallard). We named them Homer and Jethro. Homer died about a day after we got him, but Jethro did very well. We had a large back yard that was presided over by our very gentle

11

Collie, Dancer. She quickly accepted Jethro and at night, the duckling snuggled into her fur to keep warm. Apparently, Jethro had not imprinted on his parent ducks, which usually happens before it is two weeks old. Nearly all birds imprint. Whatever the young bird sees during the imprinting period; be its parents, a human, or in this case, a dog, this is what the bird believes it is for life. It became apparent to us that Jethro thought he was a dog. When Dancer went down the fence barking at a passerby, Jethro did his best to quack-bark. Jethro also ate out of the same bowl as Dancer. One day, my Father brought some food for Dancer and Jethro immediately began to eat. Dancer quickly showed this upstart duck-dog who was at the top of the pecking or in this case, nipping order. With a quick nip to the head, Dancer sent Jethro scurrying under a hedge. Afterwards, Jethro waited until Dancer had her fill before venturing close to the vittles.

One morning, before I left for school, I saw Jethro sitting under a hedge and was acting rather peculiar. I noticed that he would not get up when I called. I ran over to see what was wrong, thinking that he was either sick or injured. As I got closer, he reluctantly rose to his feet revealing a large white egg.

"Jethro's a girl!" I yelled.

I picked up the still warm egg and took it into the house. My parents and sisters were amazed and my dad said,

"Well, I guess she is now Jethrine!"

This was cool to me, since the Beverly Hillbillies show was popular at the time. The character Jethro had a twin sister named Jethrine (which everyone knew was Max Baer in drag). We occasionally let Jethrine sit on her eggs, but more often than not, we collected the eggs and my Mother used them whenever she made cakes. The duck eggs added richness to the cake that wasn't attained when chicken eggs were used.

Chapter 3

Nashville

At ten years old, my family moved to Nashville. My father had been working for Royal Globe Insurance Company as a Safety Engineer. In this profession, he inspected buildings that were insured or about to be insured by the Company. For about six months prior to moving the family, my Dad lived in a boarding house. He wanted to make sure the job was going to work out before moving us to a new city. The job seemed to be stable enough, so the decision was made to relocate. We waited to finish the school year and although it was tough to leave our house and friends, it was a new adventure. Before we moved from Meridian, we had to give Jethrine to the local City Park. The park had a huge duck pond with about fifty ducks (no doubt many of these were survivors of Easter). It was sad to give her away, but our new house did not have a large back yard and Jethrine's protector, Dancer, had recently died during surgery to remove a tumor. Dancer had lived a full life of thirteen years. She was very patient with kids (as I would ride her like a pony when I was smaller) and with Jethrine. With Dancer gone, we felt that Jethrine would be safer and happier at the duck pond. Who knows, maybe she became the protector of the other ducks, since she thought that she was a Collie.

At the end of the school year we made our move. I had just finished the fourth grade and was looking forward to being in the fifth grade. I was also anticipating going to public school for the first time. I attended a Catholic school until we moved, so going to school without first having to go to church would be different. Also having a civilian as a teacher again would be fun. I think that Catholic school nuns who taught in the 1960's had the supreme agenda to make their students holy. They sure did their best to scare the hell out of us!

Nashville was a much larger city than Meridian, with more things to see and do. We moved into a three-bedroom house with a basement that also included one pregnant cat. We had never had a cat before because unfortunately Dancer would have killed it. Before long, the cat had kittens. It was quite fun to have all of these playful felines in our midst. Nashville proved to be a wonderful experience. We lived in a nice middle class neighborhood with a lot of kids about my age with which to play.

My sister Susie found a job working at Pauline's Pet Shop. This was a superior job in my book! I was always excited to go with my mother to pick up Susie from her job. I got to see the variety of animals Pauline had for sale, which included a number of birds, fish, reptiles and even monkeys. Being fascinated with animals, it was always hard for me to leave when it was time for Susie to get off work. It was perhaps at this time that I got the desire to work with animals. Money would not be as important as the knowledge I would acquire.

The summer seemed to go on and on, but school soon started. This was a first for me; I was the new kid in school. At my previous school, St. Patrick's, we had new kids every year because we had a nearby naval base. I actually looked forward to being the new guy. September, 1966, I went to Tusculum School for my first day in fifth grade. My teacher was Dorothy Weight. Mrs. Weight was an All-American looking teacher, straight out of Leave It To Beaver, probably in her late twenties with short brown hair. Her classroom was decorated with the usual flags, maps, globes and chalkboards. But what made her room unique was an abundance of houseplants and assorted pet animals; a couple of hamsters, a turtle, an anole (commonly, but wrongly called a chameleon), a 10 gallon tank full of tropical fish and two Zebra Finches. Each week, Mrs. Weight assigned several students the tasks of caring for the menagerie. I was anxious to get my turn at caring for one or all of the animals.

Since I have always been an outgoing kind of person, I made friends very quickly. The first kid that befriended me was Alvin Jones. Alvin lived on the way home, so I walked part of the way with him. One thing I liked about Alvin was that he was funny. He was a little chubby and when he laughed, he jiggled and shook. He also had a pet chipmunk named, uh, Alvin. He asked me one day if I wanted to see him and I naturally said yes. I had never seen a real chipmunk up close and Alvin turned out to be pretty cute. I went home and told my mother about Alvin's pet chipmunk. I remember my mother asked with her accent,

"Janny, what ease a cheepmonk? A croos between a chimpanzee and a mankey?!?"

I explained that it was a rodent that lived in holes in the ground and ate a variety of nuts.

"Ooouuh, it sounds like a rat to me, yuck!" my mother replied with a shiver.

She told me to tell Alvin to keep it at his house and everything would be fine.

I really liked my new school. It was quite a different experience than the parochial school I had attended. Everything was a little less regimented and I did not miss getting up early to go to church before school. A subject that was taught at Tusculum that was not offered at St. Patrick's was music education. I first thought I wanted to play the drums, but I soon gravitated toward the trumpet. My parents bought my first trumpet that year and I quickly learned how to make sounds on it. What emanated from

15

my trumpet could not be called music, at first, but more closely resembled the mating call of a bull wapiti! Pretty soon, I learned to do simple scales and a few simple songs such as "Mary had a little lamb". In this case, however, if Mary's little lamb had heard my rendition, it would have probably found a nearby cliff from which to fling itself. I did get better.

The seasons passed rather quickly that year and winter arrived. We actually had some measurable snowfall and this was only the second time in my life that I had seen snow! It was quite fun to sled for the first time and my neighborhood had plenty of hills that made this possible. Christmas that year was rather magical. We were in a new city that had a lot of decorations and a huge Christmas parade. Santa was good to us that year since my mother was working a part-time job at a department store. This gave our family additional income and, no doubt, employee discounts on toys. It was a great year, but my life was about to change.

In January, 1967, my father learned that he was to be transferred to Royal Globe's Memphis office. He broke the news to us at dinner one night and it left the family a little in shock and saddened. We were just getting used to Nashville as our hometown and the only thing I knew about Memphis was that Elvis lived there. We began packing our belongings and the moving van arrived to cart the larger items. My last day of school was a tough one. I said good-bye to all of my new friends and made one longing, last look at my schoolroom. What an inspirational place it turned out to be! Before the last bell sounded, Mrs. Weight called me up to the front of the classroom and wished me a farewell from the students. She also handed me a present. It was about the size of a pack of index cards. I opened it, and to my surprise, it was a bird identification field guide. Mrs. Weight had noticed that I read a lot of bird books from the school library and wanted me to have a bird book to use and remember Tusculum Elementary School. That act

16

was one of the defining moments in my life! That little field guide propelled my interest in the bird world to a new level. It may have even inspired my career. To Mrs. Weight and Tusculum School, I am forever grateful! We left for Memphis early the next morning. As we drove by Tusculum School, with my bird guide in hand, I said a silent good-bye. I turned and watched the school with tears in my eyes until we drove out of sight. What was waiting for us in Memphis?

Chapter 4

The City of the King

We arrived in Memphis and got a room at a Holiday Inn in the Frayser section of town. Frayser was a predominately middle class suburb of Memphis that was known for being a little backwards. In fact, on the Wolf River bridge that separated Frayser from the rest of Memphis, someone had hand-scrawled a sign, which read, "Now entering Frayser. Set your clocks back 30 years!" To us, it was another new, large city with a lot of different things to do. We stayed at the motel for several days while the house we were to rent was being prepared. One of the first things I noticed was that there was an abundance of children, just like in Nashville. We also lived on a "cove" or cul-de-sac as it is known elsewhere. This was great for all the children to play in since it was not a through street.

At this point, I became known on the block as the "Birdboy". All the children knew that I had an interest in birds, and if someone found an injured or orphaned one, they usually brought it to me. One boy from the next block down even brought me four half-grown starlings that were orphaned when his father cleaned the eaves of his house. For about two weeks, I fed the nestlings worms that I managed to find under bricks and logs and crickets that I purchased with my allowance from the local bait shop. After two weeks, thankfully, the starlings were flying and were ready to be released. Before I gave them their freedom, I came up with the idea to put different colored rubber bands on the legs of each bird. This was so I could keep track of them after they were set free. Well, the birds were released and the next day I found a leg, complete with a yellow rubber band, on the ground, next to a pile of feathers. One had met its demise at the claws of a hungry cat. The bird I "banded" with the blue band was never seen again, but I did see the red and green-banded birds for about two weeks afterwards. I even saw the red-banded one feeding on crickets after my neighbor had cut his grass. My first banding project was a success! Thinking back, I wish that I not had put anything on those birds' legs due to the chance that one may have gotten tangled. Live and learn.

During this time, even though I was called Birdboy, I could have easily been called "Birdkiller". Like many boys my age, I had a BB gun, and yes, I shot birds! I didn't, however, shoot them in a malicious way. I shot them more in a way that John James Audubon did...to study them. This didn't make it right, though, but it was the only way I could get really close to study them. Some binoculars might have saved a few sparrows' lives. I did feel very badly when I shot them and wished that I could have returned the life I had taken. (Later in my early professional bird career, I started a bird rehab program that returned many shot birds back into the wild). This phase didn't last long. One day, while shooting at a Blue Jay, I missed the bird but killed a window instead. This I had to replace out of my pocket and I also received a stern lecture from my father.

My father did take me "hunting". I put hunting in quotations because we never shot anything other than cans or bottles. These excursions into the woods did cultivate my interest in the natural world. I have been very fortunate that the Stokes family has a wooded tract of land in northeast Mississippi near New Albany. This land totals about 254 acres and is mostly oak and hickory wooded hills. There are several natural springs and a spring fed pond. This land is still owned by the Stokes family, although after my Grandmother's death in 1985, it was divided among her children. I always looked forward to going to the "Woods". On numerous occasions, my Dad and I hiked around the property and he told me of the family history of the place. He showed me the old home place where my aunt and two of my three uncles were born. At times, he took me down to the spring where the salamanders lived and where, as a boy, my father showered during the summer.

We went down to the "bottoms" of the Tallahatchie River. He showed me the old channel where the Tallahatchie flowed before it was channelized by the Corps of Engineers. Somebody within the Corps came up with the less than bright idea of taking meandering rivers and straightening them into rapidly flowing ditches. This was to help with flood control, but the legacy has been some of the worst soil erosion in North America. There is hope, however, that the latest plans will allow for the rivers to meander again. Very rarely can Man improve on Nature.

During one of our trips into the woods, I had my first encounter with a hawk. I was walking up an old road trail when a Broad-winged Hawk landed on a tree limb about 30 yards ahead of me. I raised my air rifle in a knee-jerk reaction and pointed it at the bird. The hawk was totally unafraid and had I fired, I doubt I would have done much damage to it. I was fascinated by this rusty-breasted bird! I lowered my rifle and continued staring at it. As my dad approached, the hawk took off and flew over the hill. I told my father that I had seen the bird. He asked me if I had shot at it and I replied that I had not. He said "good" and that they were protected by law. He always emphasized safety and obeying the hunting laws. He also told me to never waste anything and to never shoot anything unless I had intended to eat it. A number of years later, my desire to hunt was killed with a single shot.

Chapter 5

The Boy Scouts

Another life-changing event occurred when I was in the sixth grade at Denver Elementary School in Memphis. Every year, the local Boy Scout Troop had its annual sign-up day for boys who had turned eleven. I was only mildly interested in the Scouts. I didn't know much about the organization and didn't know anyone who was a Boy Scout. With some reluctance, and with plenty of prodding from my father, I went to see what this was all about. Troop 301's Scoutmaster, Homer Burkett, was at our school's cafeteria that evening with handouts and the typical speech on why I needed to become a Boy Scout. Mr. Burkett was a large, loud and robust man. He was a former cook in the Navy who was part Italian, part Native American. He weighed close to 400 pounds, but this was not 400 pounds of jiggly, non-athletic fat. He carried his weight well and could easily outrun any boy in the troop. He also had a great sense of humor.

I decided to give the Boy Scouts a try. I went to my first troop meeting a few weeks later and was assigned to Eagle Patrol. The patrol leader lived closest to me and made it convenient to go to patrol meetings. My first campout took place some two weeks later. We all met at Mr. Burkett's house Friday after school. I had been given a list of things I needed to take on the trip; a sleeping bag, a poncho, a mess kit with a knife, fork and spoon, waterproof hiking boots, matches, several changes of clothes, a sweatshirt, a light jacket, and a cap. I had all my stuff packed into a small canvas backpack. My Dad got off work early so he could take me to the drop zone. We arrived at the scene and were first greeted by a traffic jam. We had over seventy boys in the troop and with just about as many cars on a two-lane street off-loading boys and their gear. The National Guard would have had a hard time keeping order!

My Dad finally found an unoccupied spot four houses down where he parked the car. He accompanied me to the swirl of running, grab-assing boys that loosely orbited the Troop's bus, affectionately called the "Gray Ghost" because it was grayish-white in color. He told me to have fun as he pressed a five dollar bill into my hand. He checked with one of the adult leaders on when we would be arriving back on Sunday and then waved to me as he weaved his way back to the car. As I surveyed the assembly, I couldn't help but think of army ants that had surrounded some hapless creature. Some of the older boys were on top of the bus loading gear into the rack. Other were tossing gear up to the boys on top of the bus, but the majority of the kids were burning off their pre-pubescent energy by running, yelling, tackling, and tripping. I chose a quieter spot near the bus door. I met the first boy in my troop who did not go to the same school as me. His name was Robert V. Bickers, Jr. He introduced himself and sang a little ditty that sounded roughly like his last name..."Bic-a-bock, a-Bick-a-bock, a-Bick-a-bocka, baaaaaybeee, yeah!!!" I said my name was John Stokes. I didn't have a song to go with my last name. Through the years in Troop 301, Robert became my most trusted friend. He was the Spock to my Kirk and even resembled the logical, pointed-eared alien (except, he didn't have pointed ears).

Robert was in Bat patrol. Bat patrol was the coolest patrol in 301. It always had the best food on campouts, the best camping spots, told the most jokes and had the most fun. This was due mostly to its patrol leader, Mark Mosely. Mark was a natural leader. He oozed cool. He didn't raise his voice, blew off things that bothered other boys and always made good decisions. I wanted to be in Bat patrol! Eagle patrol was run by Mike Halford, a seventeen year old semi-jock who really didn't seem like he wanted to be in the Boy Scouts. Mike was a bit of a smart ass who cared little for authority (as a lot of people back then, since this was at the height of the Vietnam War). He was a reluctant leader who seemed to view his job of patrol leader as one might look at a pimple; an irritation he hoped would soon go away! Our so-called patrol meetings lacked organization and resembled ongoing episodes of The Three Stooges. I looked for Halford to be on this campout, but someone said that probably wouldn't show up and that he rarely went on any of them with his "Why bother"?!? attitude.

However, our Assistant Patrol Leader, Mike Gatlin was there. Mike was an intelligent fellow who had suffered deforming injuries to both arms when he was younger. He fell from a tree and landed on his palms instead of his feet. Both the ulna and radius of each arm were crushed like beer cans and resulted in Mike's arms six to eight inches shorter than normal. Mike took a lot of crap from many of the boys because of this and it gave him a bit of a complex. Mike always seemed to be on the defensive and generally picked on anyone smaller than he was, including me. It didn't bother me too much and I usually had something smart or funny to respond to his aggression, but never did I make fun of his deformities!

Finally, all of the boys arrived, all the gear was loaded, and off we went. The noise inside of the "Ghost" was incredible! Imagine seventy boys all talking, most screaming, at once. Mr. Burkett had to pull the bus over several times screaming,

"You boys shut up! The sign is up!"(holding his right hand up with three fingers pointed skyward.)

23

This meant BE QUIET! He said he couldn't hear the traffic around him. The noise probably gave him a splitting headache, too! Well, we were quiet for a while, but the noise gradually increased to unsafe levels. Fortunately, after an hour on the road, most of the boys had fallen asleep. In less than two hours, we arrived at Camp Currier in Mississippi. There were already a dozen or more troops set up, as this was the Fall Camporee. The Camporee was a fun competition between all the troops that lasted for two days. Our troop did okay, with Bat Patrol being the best from 301. Surprise, huh? I had fun and the weather was nice and crisp. On the way home, I remember being tired and ready to take a shower. Our busload of boys smelled like a giant bag of bar-b-qued pork rinds. I felt like a charcoal briquette. All in all, this first campout was great!

Throughout the many years I was in the Scouts, I learned many things. I learned to build a fire with just one match. I learned to stay warm when camping in sub-freezing weather. I learned to tie knots that wouldn't slip. But most importantly, I learned a lot about nature. The merit badge program, which certain ones are required to advance in rank, focuses a lot on the natural world. The one merit badge I looked forward to getting was Bird Study.

I finally got the chance to take the course one summer at Kamp Kia Kima near Hardy, Arkansas. This was a perfect place to learn more about birds. Hardy is located in the eastern Ozark Mountains and has a diversity of bird life. There were only three of us in the course and we met every morning at five o'clock to watch the birds as they became active. I learned the songs and calls of birds that I had only seen in books. I learned to look for birds in certain habitats. After a week, I had learned enough to earn the badge, the one I was most proud to receive. It was with this merit badge that I became more interested in the birds of prey. I had seen several species at Kia Kima; the Red-tailed, Red-shouldered, and

24

Broad-winged Hawks, the diminutive American Kestrel and the Black and Turkey Vultures. After my Kia Kima experience, I looked for raptors on every camping trip. By the time I was fourteen, I set a personal goal to work with eagles and other raptors. I didn't know how I was going to reach this goal, but it was one I felt that I must try to attain.

I eventually became an Eagle Scout. So did Robert Bickers, Jr. and Mike Gatlin. Mike Halford dropped out of Scouting to play football. In 1984, my former Scoutmaster and a man who inspired and influenced the lives of many young men, Homer Burkett, died of a massive heart attack while elk hunting in Colorado. I attended his funeral, as did many of my former troop mates. Before the casket was sealed, I asked Mr. Burkett's son-in-law to place something in with Homer. It was a tail feather from one of the Bald Eagles at the Memphis Zoo. When he saw what it was, he didn't hesitate. I simply told him that Mr. Burkett had helped me become an Eagle and this was my way of honoring him. As I said a silent thank you and good-bye, he slipped the feather inside Homer's jacket. He was now soaring free.

The Scouting experience has added more to my life than any other experience. It taught me the values of teamwork as well as self-reliance. It taught me about being fair and considerate. I learned invaluable lessons about Nature that helped shape my career. But mostly, it gave me a set of values that I continue to live by today. I've been accused of being too much of a "Boy Scout", something some people may find offensive. I just simply smile and say, "Thank You!"

Chapter 6

Hawks, other raptors and "Pigman"

As previously mentioned, by the time I was fourteen, I had set a goal to work with eagles and other birds of prey. I began to acquire my goal by learning everything I possibly could about these birds. I spent a lot of time at both my school and the local public libraries. Anything pertaining to eagles and raptors I had checked out on a regular basis. I knew that a majority of these raptors were in trouble due to a number of factors; all human-related. Many of the species were having difficulty reproducing due to eggshell thinning caused by pesticides such as DDT. DDT was used extensively on crops to kill insects and due to agricultural runoff, DDT and its breakdown products entered the food pyramid at microscopic levels. At the top resided the predators such as the Bald Eagle, Osprey, Peregrine Falcon and Cooper's Hawk.

All of these birds were in serious decline. The Bald Eagle was also assaulted on two other fronts; loss of habitat and illegal shootings. In fact, at this time, the Bald Eagle in 1970, was at its lowest number in the lower 48 States-only 417 nesting pairs were found. The Peregrine Falcon was at such critical low numbers that only a few pairs existed east of the Mississippi. The environment was in bad shape. I felt a little helpless. What could I do to help these birds? I saw one opportunity through Hunt-Wesson Foods. This company had a program where it bought Bald Eagle nesting land in Wisconsin. All the general public had to do was send labels from cans of their products. For a certain amount of labels a parcel of land was set aside in the participant's name. A certificate was issued to the participant declaring this to be so. I encouraged my parents to buy this company's food products so I could send in the labels. My family ate a lot of Hunt-Wesson foods for a while and I proudly amassed a number of certificates! At least I felt like I was doing something to help the situation.

Fortunately, the environmental movement that began in the late '60s was well underway and DDT was banned from use in the U.S. in 1972. I would hate to think what the natural world would be like today if those far-sighted "Hippies" had not been able to voice their opinions! It has taken a number of years for the affected raptors to recover and only recently has the Bald Eagle and the Peregrine been taken off the Endangered Species List.

At sixteen years of age, my infant raptor career got a bit of a nudge in the form of my driver's license. Being a little more independent allowed me to visit the natural world a little more often. I was fortunate to live within a twenty-mile drive of one of the largest state parks in Tennessee, the Meeman-Shelby Forest State Park. This park comprises over 14,000 acres and borders the Mississippi River on the west. About half of the park is river bottomland forest while the other is loess soil wooded hills. Part of the park is included in a wildlife management area in which hunting is allowed. I spent a lot of my spare time in these areas. Usually after school, I made the 30-minute drive out to Shelby Forest. Sometimes I carried a fishing rod, sometimes a shotgun and occasionally my friends Mark Woods or Bobby Berry would go along, too. We all shared a love of the natural world, with hunting or fishing being an excuse to be out there. There were many times that I didn't even fire my shotgun or catch a fish, but I did learn a lot about the forest and its inhabitants on these excursions. A couple of times, I was lucky enough to see a migrating Osprey catch a fish at Poplar Tree Lake. This was a rare sight too, in that

DDT had seriously reduced the Osprey numbers, which has also rebounded since the ban of DDT.

On my drives out to Shelby Forest, I occasionally saw a few Red-tailed Hawks. I usually saw this adaptable bird either soaring or sitting in a tree next to the road. Sometimes when I saw a hawk in a roadside tree, I stopped to get a closer look. Most of the time, the tree-perching hawk took off as soon as I stopped. But, on occasion, one lingered long enough for me to get a good view. I later found that the Red-tailed Hawk is one of the wariest hawks. This is possibly due to fact that this bird was long persecuted as a "chicken hawk", a reputation that it doesn't deserve, since it rarely eats chickens and is primarily a rodent eater.

At this time, in the early Seventies, the Red-tail was also reduced in population. Not to the extent of the Bald Eagle, but reduced none the less. This was probably due to illegal shootings and the afore-mentioned "chicken hawk" syndrome, where the only good hawk was a dead one! No wonder it was wary of humans. Still the Red-tail hung on and became a model of raptor perseverance and resilience. Over the years, I have learned a lot from this bird. I have rehabilitated close to a thousand of them and have been amazed by how tough they are.

In high school I took all of the biology courses that I could. Along with the courses came the usual dissections. In my Senior year, in my Biology II class, I earned the nickname "Pigman". One of our dissection subjects in this class was the fetal pig. We peeled away the various layers of skin, looked at the muscles and skeletal system, and finally the internal organs. All of this was performed on the left side of the pig. After a few days, we finished with our pigs and our instructor, Coach Dillingham, said we could do with the pigs what we wanted. He obviously meant for us to throw them away.

I went to throw mine in the trash and noticed a length of twine in the can. I got the twine and tied it around the shoulder area of the pig. My high school was not air-conditioned and it was a warm spring day. My Biology classroom was on the third floor and below us was a typing class. After I secured the line on the pig, I lowered it out the window. The windows in the school opened outward and when one was fully opened, it was nearly horizontal. One of the windows below me in the typing class was fully opened and provided a platform for what became a macabre tap dance! As soon as I heard the piglet's hooves touch the glass, I started bobbing it up and down, with the hooves clicking a ghoulish rhythm. Screams soon emerged from the typists as the partially dissected, partially decomposed porker rattled a crazy dance. The screams alerted students in the classrooms across the way. As I continued bobbing the pig, the screams got louder and more students from the opposing building stood to see what was taking place. By the time the porcine marionette show was in full swing, there were about 300 students pointing and laughing.

Mr. Dillingham was amused by the show and suggested that I take the pig down the hall to Mr. Boone's Psychology class. Windows in the classrooms also opened into the hallway. One of Mr. Boone's hall windows was opened, so I tossed the pig through the window. Screams and laughter erupted and suddenly someone yelled,

"Mr. Robey's coming!"

Mr. Robey was the Principal and was generally a no-nonsense guy. I grabbed the string and hoisted the pig back out the window. I made my way back to my room, disposed of the pig in the trash and sat down, fearing the worse. Within 20 seconds, Mr. Robey knocked on the door. Coach Dillingham answered,

"Yes, come in Mr. Robey".

Robey said in a southern drawl,

29

"Someone said dat dare's sum kinda ahb-ject hangin' out one of yo' windas. Ah've come he-yah ta see fo' ma sef!"

Dillingham replied, "Nothing been hanging out any of my windows! All of my students have been studying for a test!"

As he said this, he looked at me and winked. He continued,

"It must have been another room!"

Robey, somewhat puzzled, bought it! He apologized for interrupting us and went on his way. As soon as he was out of earshot, everyone in the room burst into laughter! Coach Dillingham looked at me, laughed and shook his head saying,

"You owe me one, Stokes!"

I definitely did! The rest of the week, I heard the buzz around the school about the dead animal that tortured the typing class and I answered to "Pigman" for the rest of the year!

Chapter 7

I discover hang gliding

I graduated from Frayser High School in May of '74 and worked a summer job at the Texgas gas station. I called myself a Petroleum Engineer. In reality, I was an attendant. It was a fun job and I made enough money to pay for my college tuition for that year. In August, I began my freshman year at Memphis State University. Earlier, I had turned down two music scholarships. I didn't want to be a high school band director for the rest of my life. I planned to major in Forestry or Wildlife Management. However, I was like several thousand freshmen that year who doesn't truly know what he or she wants to do with their college career. I still wanted to work with eagles, so I figured that Wildlife Management or Forestry would eventually get me to that goal. I went to school full-time and worked at Texgas three days a week.

On one of my in-between class breaks, I was in the university library and went to the periodical section. I was looking for something to read to burn up some time and I found a *Reader's Digest* that looked interesting. One of the listed articles was entitled "*The Flyingest Flying*". This sounded intriguing. As earlier mentioned, I had always wanted to fly. I even went up in a small plane a few times. The view was nice, but the flying was not what I had experienced in my dreams of flight. No, it was more like riding in a VW Beetle with wings.

As I read the article, I realized that this might be the type of flying for which I was searching. The article described a type of flying people in California were doing. They attached themselves to large kites and ran down sand dunes and grassy hills to become airborne. They were gliding like birds! The kites were apparently easy to build and a number of manufacturers were in business across the country. As I read on, I could hardly contain myself! Where could I find a hang glider around here? My answer came a few days later. I was back in the library and was in the periodicals, again. This time, I happened upon numerous copies of Ground Skimmer Magazine, the publication of the young United States Hang Gliding Association based in Los Angeles. These magazines were to me like M&Ms to a chocoholic! I could not believe my fortune! I made note of several "kite" manufacturers in my region and sent for brochures. I quickly had several in hand, including one from Cloudman Glidercraft in nearby Nashville. Nearly all the gliders were similar and varied in price from 300-450 dollars. It was cheaper to buy a kit as opposed to ready to fly and all the gliders came with a harness, either a swing seat or prone model. I thought,

"Hey, I can build the kit form and save myself fifty dollars!"

I contacted Cloudman Glidercraft and asked how much shipping would be from Nashville. Thirty-five dollars. Not bad. In the long run I would save ten dollars buying the kit. Through the winter I saved my money. By Spring, I would be ready to buy my wings!

I kept myself focused on the hang gliding idea by reading and re-reading the Ground Skimmer magazines. There were a lot of good articles on launching and landing, turning and home-building gliders. By the time I got my glider I would be ready to fly it! I also asked around if anyone knew any hang glider pilots. No one did. The usual response to my queries was "Are you crazy!" No one understood this longing I had for the sky and it seemed that I would be alone in this quest for flight.

Chapter 8

1975

During the winter of '74-75, I saved as much money as I possibly could. First, I had to save enough to pay for my spring semester of college. Second, I had to save around $350-400 to purchase a hang glider kit and to pay for the shipping from Nashville to Memphis. These days, $350-400 dollars doesn't seem like a lot, but I was only making $2.50 an hour at the gas station. As each month passed, my saving account grew. By the time it reached $300, I could hardly stand it! I began my search for some suitable training hills from which I could fly. The terrain around Memphis consists of small, rolling hills. I lived in a section of town that had the most of these small hills. I found a spot behind my former junior high school, Georgian Hills, as my first training hill. It had a nice slope (at least from what I knew), and had a long, flat area at the bottom for landing. There was also another hill nearby that faced the opposite direction for those days that the wind blew the other way. I was set. All I needed was the glider.

By April 1975, I finally had enough money to buy a 16-foot standard Rogallo hang glider kit from Cloudman Glidercraft. The standard Rogallo hang glider is still what most people today think of as a hang glider. The Rogallo wing was invented by Dr. Francis Rogallo who was a NASA scientist involved with alternate methods of spacecraft landings. In the Mercury program, the capsule landed in the ocean and was retrieved by helicopters and frogmen from a nearby carrier. NASA was looking into alternate ways to bring the two-man Gemini capsule back to Earth. The best working alternative was a foldable delta wing that could be steered by the astronauts. The capsule could then be landed on skids on one of the dry lakebeds in California. It was a much cheaper method to bring a capsule home, but the idea was scrapped after a few years.

Dr. Rogallo's collapsible wing was shelved, but "Rog" released the patent for his design. By the early 1960, an Australian named John Dickenson had made a Rogallo wing ski kite. Most people flying ski kites at this time used the flat kites. These were somewhat unstable and dangerous. Working from just a photograph, Dickenson constructed the Rogallo kite out of aluminum tubes, aircraft cables and a nylon sail. He first built a half-scale model and eventually a full-sized one that proved to be very stable. Dickenson was eventually contacted by Dr. Rogallo, who gave him his full blessing on his design. About the same time, Dickenson befriended a fellow by the name of Bill Moyes. Bill was a flat kite enthusiast who performed all around Australia. He had heard about the new wing and was interested in forming a partnership with Dickenson. The two hit it off and Moyes began flying Dickenson's wing. He also began to re-write the record books for altitude gained and time aloft. At the same time, another Aussie named Bill Bennett had bought one of Dickenson's kites and began swapping records with Moyes. Eventually Bennett took his kite shows on a world tour and first came to the U.S. In 1969, he became famous by flying by the Statue of Liberty after being towed aloft by a speedboat. Pictures of this feat went around the world and Bennett became an instant celebrity. Dickenson eventually got out of the business and Moyes and Bennett went on to become hang glider manufacturers.

Meanwhile, in the late 1960's in the U.S., hang gliding had a parallel development to the Aussies. The exception was that the Americans did not start with a tow kite, but developed a foot-launched version of Dr. Rogallo's design. The American "kites" were primarily constructed from bamboo, duct tape and plastic sheeting, nicknamed "Bamboo Bombers". These were flown off the sand dunes and small cliffs along the coasts of California. By the early 1970's, the Bamboo Bombers gave way to the aluminum framed, cable braced, nylon sail gliders that John Dickenson had developed in Australia eight years earlier! By the time I bought my standard Rogallo, hang glider pilots in the U.S. were flying off mountains and staying aloft for several hours. I was eager to set my own personal records.

By mid-April, my glider had arrived. It had a white Dacron sail and came with a primitive prone harness, which allows one to fly in the horizontal position, rather like Superman. These early prone harnesses were referred to as the "Blueball" harnesses because if any time was spent in the air, the pilot, if he were male, usually had a funny walk after landing. The sail was ready to mount and the tubing was pre-cut to the exact length. I did, however, had to drill the holes and install the bushings to bolt the frame together. I also had to cut the cables and install nico sleeves to prevent the cables from slipping. I had never seen a real live hang glider before, so building this one from a kit took several days. By the third day of working after class and before work, the glider was finished. I was ready to take to the air.

My first attempts to get the kite into the air occurred behind Georgian Hills Jr. High. Along with the glider's instructions came a manual on how to launch and land the craft. What I didn't know was that the instructions for launching the kite were for the seated position. Also, the slope I had selected did not slope enough for the glide ratio I had with this glider. Back then, a standard Rogallo had a glide ratio of 4:1, meaning that for every four feet traveled forward, the glider sank one foot. The glider I fly today has a glide ratio of 11:1, and some of the competition models get better than

16:1. In order for a glider to be launched, the hill must slope away at an angle greater than the glide ratio of the glider. The hill I was attempting to fly from maybe had a slope of 5:1. I didn't know this. I tried and tried and tried again to get the glider to fly, but kept crashing down onto the control bar. I finally gave up.

I remembered a hill I had seen near the Frayser Drive-In. It was approximately thirty feet high and twenty-five feet of that was a sheer cliff. This would be my next place to attempt aviation. I invited my parents out to watch me "fly" off this hill/cliff. The hill faced south and I had a southerly breeze blowing at about five miles per hour. My parents had trudged through the weeds and mud and had been waiting for about thirty minutes. I sensed a growing impatience, especially since they were slowly being drained of their blood by hordes of mosquitoes. I was finally yelled that I was ready to go. The launching position I had learned from the manual did not serve me well this day! With one hand on the basetube (the bottom of the triangular frame) and one on the upright tube, I began my stalled launch. My hand positions coupled with less than adequate speed, immediately put me in a left turn. I quickly impacted with the ground thirty feet below and was luckily unhurt. At that point, my Guardian Angel was reactivated to full time status. My dad yelled to me,

"Are you okay?!?" I yelled back

"Yeah, I'm alright!"(my pride was a little bruised).

My father continued, "Okay, we'll see you back at the house!"

They turned and walked back to the car, swatting mosquitoes all the way. That was the one of the few times they ever saw me fly. I did get better.

It's funny how things work. The day after my impact "flight" at the drive-In, I had my glider with me at the gas station where I worked. The contact with the ground left a red mud streak on the left wing and a bent control bar. I usually had time in between customers to do extra things such as sweep, clean the restrooms, wash dirty hang gliders, etcetera. I assembled my glider and had washed off most of the mud. I set it in the corner of the lot to dry. A guy driving by in a white VW Beetle spotted the glider. He did a U-turn in the street and came in inquiring,

"Hey man, is that your kite?"

I said "Yes".

The fellow got out and introduced himself as Rick Boggan. He wandered over to the glider and asked,

"What happened to your control bar?"

I then knew that he knew something about hang gliding. I asked Rick if he was a pilot and he said that he indeed was and had been flying for about six months (an expert back in those days). I told him of my attempts to fly and he concluded that I needed to go to a better location. He said he knew of a nearby hill where he could guarantee I would fly.

Two days later, I met Rick after work. It was a Saturday and he was off from his job as a graphic artist. I worked the early shift that day. We went to the southeast-facing hill which was located off a busy road in a new subdivision. I unloaded my glider from the truck and assembled it. Rick straightened my control bar by applying firm, steady pressure to the bends; something I didn't know could be safely done. By the time I had the glider together, a crowd of nearly one hundred people had gathered. Hang gliding was still very new to the public and it seemed that everyone wanted to see me "jump" off the hill on my kite. I donned my harness and clipped my carabiner into the suspension line on the glider. I was ready to make my run when a policeman walked up. He saw me and said,

"Oh, I thought there had been a car crash!"

He was wondering why all the people had gathered.

"It is okay for me to do this here?!?"

37

I asked of the officer. He replied that he knew of no laws that prohibited people from running down hills with large kites on their backs. He stayed and watched.

"Are you ready, Man?!" Rick asked. I was.

"Well, pick 'er up and level your wings, watch your nose angle", Rick instructed.

I did all that and began my run. I started with my nose too high. I ended up stalling the glider without getting airborne. The crowd let out a collective, "Awwhh!" Rick helped me bring the glider back up the hill. He asked me if I knew what I did wrong and I said, "Yeah". He said,

"I'll watch your nose angle this time by holding your keel and we'll see if we can get you flying."

I hooked back into the glider and checked my harness. Rick held my nose at the proper angle and said that everything looked good. I began my run and the glider lifted me off the ground. Years of dreaming about bird-like flight coalesced in that moment. I was flying! I felt lighter than a feather. I could hear the wind rushing in my ears and a muffled cheer from the crowd. Time was altered. What seemed like a thirty-second flight was only about six seconds long. I landed on my feet. I unhooked from the glider and started jumping up and down like Daffy Duck. Rick ran down the hill, slapped me on the back and shook my hand. The crowd was still clapping and began to disperse. I couldn't believe it! This was the most incredible sensation I had ever experienced! I took my glider back up the hill for another flight and then for another and another. I made five flights that day. I had so much adrenaline from the flights that I was on a natural high. With Rick's help, I had achieved the fulfillment of one of my life's dreams. I had learned to fly. From this point, flying became a lifelong passion and I have never looked at the sky in the same way since.

That summer I continued to fly whenever I could. I also flew off anything that was high enough. I now knew what size and steepness of hill I needed to get airborne. I flew off levies, road embankments, cut in hills and even on a very fragrant slope near a sewage treatment plant. The biggest crowd I drew was at Sardis Lake in northern Mississippi. I probably had about 500 people stopped to see me fly off the earthen dam. I had an interesting encounter with a mostly intoxicated spectator. I was preparing to launch when this ruddy-faced individual wandered up and slurred an exclamation;

"You're one crazy sonofabitch! Have you been to the doctor lately?"

I said I had an annual physical recently. He countered

"No, I mean a shrink! You're obviously f*cking nuts!!!"

His tone had changed from jovial to belligerent. I started to get irritated when I noticed that the slob had zipped the end of his shirt into his fly. This obviously bothered him when I glanced at his dilemma. He wandered off down the hill, cursing and all the while trying to unzip his fly.

I once again prepared to launch when I heard a voice behind me say,

"Excuse me, Sir!"

I turned and saw a uniformed Corps of Engineers officer. He continued by saying,

"I'm sorry, but you can't fly that kite here!"

I asked why and he said that I was contributing to the erosion of the dam! I asked if he was serious and he said,

"Very!"

This really puzzled me as I looked along the face of the dam. There were literally hundreds of people on the dam slope, some were sunbathing, and some were tossing frisbees, footballs and baseballs. To top it all, there was a large tractor-type lawnmower

39

cutting the grass on part of the slope! I saw another, smaller slope facing into the wind and I asked if I could fly over there. He said," No" and that I would have to pack up my kite and leave! The portion of the crowd within earshot started to grumble and someone yelled,

"Let him fly, Pig!"

I could see that the situation was getting ugly and the officer a lot more agitated. I decided to comply before I was arrested for inciting a riot! As I broke down my glider, a loud chorus of "boos" arose from the crowd. The officer stayed until I had my glider on my truck and had pulled away. I felt my first of many years of ignorant prejudice directed at my sport. I've had people give me looks that one might give a leper whom had asked to borrow that person's toothbrush! I don't know how many times I have been told that I am crazy. Now, when I'm told I am crazy, I just smile and agree and think, "If I am indeed insane, then you don't know what you're missing!"

Chapter 9

1975-Part Two

The second life changing event that happened in 1975 was that I saw my first Bald Eagle, in the wild or otherwise. The Memphis Zoo didn't have any eagles on display. I was fortunate enough to live within one hundred miles of a lake that had a wintering population. I had seen on the news that the Bald Eagles were arriving at Reelfoot Lake in northwest Tennessee. The reporter said that on a good day, without too much effort, one could see 30-40 birds. He also mentioned that the State of Tennessee offered eagle tours around the lake. I thought it would be pretty cool to see an eagle in the wild, so I called my friends Mark Woods and Don Watkins. Don was an amateur photographer that had been trying to get some good pictures of various birds of prey.

On New Year's Day of '75, Mark, Don and I loaded up and left Memphis at five in the morning. We arrived at Reelfoot at dawn and not being really sure of where to watch for eagles, we went to the State Park's museum. Behind it was a walkway that wound its way through some cypress trees at the edge of the water. We had not been there more than five minutes when suddenly we heard the whooshing of wings. Directly overhead, at treetop level, flew a majestic adult eagle! Its wingspan appeared to be between six and seven feet. It flew to a nearby snag and landed. We watched through our binoculars as it consumed, headfirst, a still-wiggling shad. Soon, more eagles flew overhead and out in front of us.

One scene that is forever frozen in my memory is the sight of an adult eagle passing a fish to its trailing offspring. We had spotted the two birds heading directly for us. We all froze, knowing that any movement might spook the birds. I thought they would have turned away, but the adult and its brown-bodied young kept coming towards us. Right before they were overhead, the adult dropped a fish to the immature bird. The youngster did a half-roll and snagged the prize before it fell too far. The adult flew back towards the open water and the immature bird landed in a cypress tree to eat its meal. All in all, we saw over forty different birds, mostly adults. We had simply two things in our favor; dumb beginners' luck and a great place to view eagles. This was the beginning of my eagle-watching career. I knew that I had to somehow work with these birds! Until then, I could always visit Reelfoot in the winter.

Autumn of '75 found me enrolled in my second year at Memphis State. Forestry was still my major, but I was still taking the basic courses that the university required. I was back at the gas station part-time after a brief stint as a stocker at a local department store. My life had settled into a comfortable routine of school, work and occasional hang gliding. I was gradually getting higher, slowly getting bolder. I discovered that Memphis had about a dozen or so hang glider pilots. Colonel Frank Dawson, an Aerospace Instructor at Memphis State had started the Mid-South Hang Gliding Club. The club members were gradually finding more places to fly. My mentor, Rick Boggan, quit flying all together. He had been at a mountain flying site, Petit Jean, in Arkansas, and witness the death of his flying buddy, Jim Waggoner. Jim had modified his glider and this modification made the glider pitch divergent; it wanted to dive. The kite went into a tucking dive from about 500 feet up from which Jim was unable to recover and was killed instantly. Rick was one of the first people to arrive at the scene and decided that hang gliding was no longer for him.

Hang gliding, in 1975, was still in the toddler stage and all the pilots flying then were essentially test pilots. In 1974 and 1975, over 75 people were killed in the U.S. alone! Hang gliding was wildly popular and there was very little instruction. It wasn't uncommon for someone to buy a hang glider without ever seeing one (as I did), find a local hill or cliff, and attempt to fly, even in 30-40 m.p.h. winds! Some of these people were lucky or well watched over and succeeded without killing themselves. Others were not and dearly paid the ultimate price for their innocent ignorance. Jim's death also affected me, as I now knew of someone locally who was killed in the pursuit. It made me a little more cautious, as cautious as an invincible-feeling nineteen-year-old can be. It also made me a little more aware of the fragility of human life.

1975 wasn't finished with life-altering moments. In October, I met my future first wife. My sister, Mary, was working at Bonanza Steak house as a cashier. Wherever Mary worked, I usually got some kind of discount or something free. Here, I was able to get a deep discount on a ribeye dinner, so one night I decided to take advantage of my sister's employment perks. While I slid my tray along the dessert track, I noticed a beautiful, petite brunette behind the cheesecakes! She looked up and smiled at me and I thought-WOW! When I got to the check-out, my sister asked if there would be anything thing else. I said

"Yeah, some information about that girl behind the desserts".

She said her name was Debbra Davis. Mary didn't know much about Debbra. She said that she would find out if she was dating anyone and that my ribeye dinner with drink came to $1.49! What a deal-get a steak and maybe a date! Mary came home with the info I needed-Debbra wasn't dating anyone and she also gave my sister her phone number! Lady Luck had a sadistic smirk on her face. The next day I summoned the courage to give Debbra a call. She wasn't home. I once again ate ribeye that night, especially since both Mary and Debbra were working. As I went through the line and past the desserts I said an awkward "Hello" to Debbra. She said,

"Call me Debbie."

I said,

"Okay, Debbie. Will you be home later so I can call you?"

She replied that she would be home by 9:30 and to call her about 9:45. Gosh, it seemed as though she liked me! I was a little shy about asking girls out and didn't have a whole lot of practice at it. (I dated the same girl, Mary Guinn, through high school and a few other girls after that). Nine forty-five appeared on my clock radio face. I nervously picked up the rotary phone and dailed her number, with each number seemingly taking ten seconds or longer to complete. Finally, the last number, and the phone was ringing. A woman answered, and I said,

"Hello, this is John Stokes."

"Oh, Hello, this is Debbie!" she replied.

Our conversation included the usual small talk and our shortened life histories. I told her a little about myself and my family and I finally got around to asking her for a date. She was off the upcoming Friday, so we made plans to go to eat (not at Bonanza) and then to see a movie. I was off from the Texgas that evening, but I'm sure the petroleum retail world didn't miss me.

Friday rolled in sooner than I expected. I went to Debbie's father's house to pick her up for our first of many dates. Everything was awkward, as first dates usually are and I tried my best to smooth things with humor. Well, my jokes bombed as very little laughter came from Debbie's side of the car. Dinner was a little better and I tried a little less to be funny. Luckily, the movie was a place where we didn't have to talk much. The ride back to her house was a little better in that we were able to talk about the movie. We arrived back at her father's house and I walked her to the door. There we were on the porch and I said "Well..."and before I could continue she said,

"I had a nice time". I said, "Good", and gave her a quick peck on the cheek.

"Do you want me to call you tomorrow?" The very pregnant moment gave

birth to,

"Sure, I would like that, but I have to work so call me about 9:45."

"Alright, good, I'll call you tomorrow night". I replied. We said our good-byes and I went on my way home.

One advantage of having a sister working where your date does is the reconnaissance she is able to do. It's like having an FBI informant working for you. The next evening, Mary made it home from work at about 9:30. I was able to debrief her for a full 15 minutes before I called Debbie.

"Does she like me?" I asked.

Mary said, "Sure, and she thinks you are very funny!"

This surprised me since Debbie didn't laugh a whole lot. My 9:45 call was a pleasant one and soon small talk led to bigger talk. One date a week led to three, four, five until we started seeing each other everyday. I met all of her family and was accepted by her four brothers and two sisters. I got along well with her mother, Janette, but really clicked with her father, Dan. He was in his last year in his "Lifer" Navy career. He was a friendly guy that liked animals, autos and sports. Whenever I picked Debbie up for a date, I hoped that her dad was there. We always had some friendly, interesting conversations and he was well versed in a variety of subjects.

Time passed pretty quickly. We had our first Christmas together as a couple. Then our first New Year and our first Valentine's Day. Not long afterwards, I made a life-changing decision. One night I asked Debbie to marry me. It wasn't a well-planned event, I was a little drunk at the time. She said to ask her again tomorrow, but added,

"If you don't ask me again tomorrow, don't bother to call me anymore!"

Well, I was a "man" and couldn't go back on my word. I did ask her again the next day and to my surprise, she said, "Yes!" I now was unofficially engaged. I didn't have a ring to give to her; in fact, I wasn't making enough money at my gas station job to buy one. Plus, I was attending college full time and didn't have time to take on a longer, better paying job. Wouldn't you know it, a man came into the gas station one day who was looking for some mechanically-minded people to work in his shop rebuilding alternators and starters for diesel trucks. His name was Joseph Vickery and he asked me if I knew someone who might be interested. I asked him how much the job paid. The salary seemed to be enough. I said that I would think about it and I got his phone number. That night I spoke to Debbie and talked about a plan that if I quit school and took this job full-time, I would probably have enough money for us to get married in the summer. She thought this to be a great idea.

The next day I called Mr. Vickery and told him I wanted to take the job. I skipped class that day and went to downtown Memphis to see Mr. Vickery's setup. Memphis Diesel Electric was located in a small metal warehouse about ten blocks from the heart of downtown. The place was relatively clean, with the usual clutter of old alternators and starters in piles or in boxes on a number of tables. I met all the employees, three of which were family members: his wife, son and daughter. I knew his son, Paul, from high school and from my neighborhood, but I didn't know much about him. I told Mr. Vickery that I didn't know much about alternators or starters, but I was willing to learn and that I learned pretty quickly. He said that he could teach a monkey to rebuild an alternator. The thought crossed my mind that I hoped that my pay was not in the form of bananas! He said that he needed someone and I seemed to be a good choice. I asked him when I was to start work and since this was Thursday, he said to come in on Monday.

I called Debbie after she got home from school that day and told her that I was going to take the job. The next day, I went to Memphis State and withdrew from the University. It was a tough decision, especially since the semester had just started a few weeks prior to this. I also gave noticed at my gas station job. I apologized to my boss, Larry Buse, who then said,

"There's nothing to apologize for! You've been a good employee and I'm going to hate to lose you, but whenever you have an opportunity to improve your situation in Life...go for it!"

So with Larry's blessings, I worked my last day at Texgas that Saturday. Rebuilding alternators and getting married seemed to be a long way from my goal to work with eagles. Little did I know that I had just gotten on the road that would take me to the zoo!

Chapter 10

A New Direction

On February 23, 1976, I began my first day of work at Memphis Diesel Electric. It was a little awkward for the first few days and I started with a simple thing to rebuild; a solenoid. The solenoid is the part of the starter that when you turn the ignition key on your car or in this case, a diesel truck, it pulls, with electromagnetic force, a small gear. This gear engages the flywheel, which then turns the crankshaft and pistons. At the same time, a glow plug ignites the vaporous diesel fuel and the engine begins combustion. There are very few parts to be replaced on a solenoid, so I quickly became proficient at rebuilding solenoids. The next thing to refurbish was the rotor part of the alternator. This wasn't a fun thing to do, since the rotor had to be placed in a lathe and a metal ring where the brushes make contact had to be shaved and sanded. The shaving part wasn't so bad, but the sanding part was rather dangerous. This required taking a piece of sandpaper cupped in my fingers to match the diameter of the freshly-shorn ring. Then, I had to reach into the spinning rotor, past the spinning cooling blades and sand smooth the metal ring. This required a steady hand since the spinning blades could have easily injured or even severed a finger! I valued my fingers and desired to have them around for other activities such as pointing, nose-picking, eating or anything else that required delicate dexterity. Needless to say, I reduced my caffeine consumption during this time. I eventually graduated to rebuilding alternators and starters. This proved to be quite satisfying since I was taking something that was totally broken down and was getting it to work again. Something I later did in my bird career.

My plans were soon to change. I got married on June 4th and within six weeks, I was laid off. This was quite a blow to my new life as a married man. I applied at the Memphis Zoo, but I didn't have the required minimum of six months of animal job experience. Fortunately, I wasn't out of work for very long. My friend, Mark Woods, was now the manager of the Texgas service station where I once worked. Mark needed someone during the day, so I naturally said that I wanted to work. Work I did, too! I worked as many hours as Mark could give me. I rode my ten-speed bike to work so my wife could use the car. She worked in downtown Memphis at USF&G Insurance and it was convenient for us to ride to work when I was at MDE. The Texgas station was about three miles from my apartment, so I could make it to work in about fifteen minutes. I usually worked the 6 a.m. to 2 p.m. shift, so my commutes occurred right around dawn. One morning, I was cruising down a hill in the pre-dawn light when suddenly, "Pop!" an English Sparrow hit me in the head! I veered around for a few seconds; I was a little stunned, and pedaled my way back up the hill to see if I could find the sparrow. It didn't take me long to find him. He was in the middle of the road, also a bit dingy, but as I made my approach, he flew off! No harm done. I had a slight headache for a few minutes as I rode the rest of the way to work.

I had been at the gas station for about six weeks when one of my former neighbors, Marilyn Pearcy, stopped in for fuel. Marilyn knew that I used to work at this station and was surprised to see me here again. I told her of my situation and she mentioned a job opening in the animal department at Plough (now Schering-Plough) where she worked. The position was that of Animal Caretaker. She was very familiar with my love of animals and though that I might be good at the position. I was a little puzzled

49

why Plough had an animal section and she explained that they tested some of their products on the animals such as Maybelline cosmetics, Di-Gel antacids, and Coppertone sun products. The animal caretaker cared for the lab animals such as rabbits, rats, guinea pigs and mice. I said,

"Well, the last time I applied at the Memphis Zoo, they rejected my application and said that I needed six months of animal experience".

This job would count as animal experience so I told Marilyn that I was interested. Within two days, Phil Rose, Animal Department head, called me for an interview. I went to Plough and met Mr. Rose, a tall slim likeable fellow with a slight southern drawl. He told me of the job duties and that I would have to work every other weekend to care for the animals. He also warned that the animals were terminated at the end of the test period. If I could handle this, I had the job. At the time, I hunted, so I didn't have a problem with killing animals, as long as it was done quickly. I also didn't have problem with working every other weekend. So, for the second time in less than a year, I left Texgas.

I began work at Plough in September, 1976. The pay was comparable to what I was making at MDE. Plus, every other week I would get extra pay for the weekend work. I had to only come in for a few hours, so most of my day was free. This allowed me to spend a little more time with my new wife and also to hang glide more. I was now getting higher and flying longer. I was now flying off a place called River Bend. River Bend was a 150 ft. high bluff along the Mississippi, about thirty miles north of Memphis. The area behind the bluff was being developed for vacation houses. A road ran from the top of the bluff to the bottom and this made retrieval easy. It wasn't uncommon to make ten flights a day and I also got to work on my turns. The Mississippi was only about two hundred yards from the base of the bluff and the bend in the river sometimes produced a pretty impressive whirlpool. So, there was plenty of incentive to make a 90 degree turn right after launching.

The animal lab at Plough was in the basement of the main office building. I guess this was done to isolate the rest of the building from any odors that may have emanated from the animals. This area was even below the mailroom, where the lowest paid workers are generally kept. As it turned out, I was probably the lowest paid person in this Company. I didn't mind this since I did not plan to stay here for the rest of my career. My job was somewhat boring and monotonous. I did look forward to the arrival of the new lab animals. The mice and rats were four to five weeks old when arrived and were very playful! The clean cages with the fresh bedding seemed to energize the little rodents. I delighted in watching these youngsters, but felt a great sadness for them, too. I knew that their short lives would not be filled with much pleasure. Most of the rats were used in LD-50 tests, meaning that 50% of the test group received a lethal dose of whatever product was being tested. Rats cannot regurgitate and make perfect test subjects for products such as pesticides and others that might be accidentally ingested by a child. The mice were generally used for skin tests.

The animals I felt the worst for were the rabbits. They were brought in and placed in what I called "stocks". These wooden troughs resembled the old stocks people were locked into with their heads and arms through holes in a hinged board. The rabbits had their heads place in the stocks and were not allowed to eat or drink anything. Usually, fairly benign products such as eyeliner or mascara were placed in one eye. The other eye was left alone to be used to check irritation against. Occasionally, some pretty caustic substances were placed in the rabbits' eyes. Plough had a muscle-soothing balm similar to Ben-Gay and this stuff ate the cornea off the eye! The rabbits usually, and predictably, reacted violently to this substance. Many dislocated their spines when they struggled to

51

get out of the stocks. Unfortunately, many did not die when this happened and had to be left in the stocks, paralyzed. I hated this whole procedure!

After a few months, I got used to the ins and outs of the animal lab. Still, I didn't like what was done to the animals. Many of these "tests" seemed to be useless in my opinion, but I wasn't the one making the decisions. My job was to keep the animals fed, the bedding in the cages changed, and all the cages cleaned after the animals were gone. The days I hated the most were the days that the animal were "sacrificed". Keep in mind that I was a hunter at the time and I had nothing against killing an animal if it was to be eaten, but this was different. These animals were treated like so many sheets of litmus paper to be disposed of after the tests were finished. To make the situation worse, the animals were not humanely euthanized with either gas or injection, but bashed in the skull with a blunt bar, in the case of the rabbits or guinea pigs, or with the rats, their necks were dislocated. To be fair to Mr. Rose, he always did this quickly and cleanly, but one of the lab workers, Sheila, had a tough time doing it right. She probably weighed 105 pounds, with sand in her pockets, and possibly had the arm strength of an eight year old boy. Couple this with a squirming 10-15 pound New Zealand rabbit and what you witnessed was a screaming, bloody mess. Usually, I had a bunch of cages to clean while this all occurred, but sometimes I couldn't help but hear all the misery that was going down.

I didn't like Sheila very much and I'm sure she didn't like me. I usually tried to avoid her if I could, but sometimes I had to work around her while I was cleaning cages. She seemed to have a cutting-board sized chip on her shoulder and sometimes took out her frustration on the animals. One day, while I was in my cleaning cube, I heard an odd sound coming from the rabbit stocks room. It sounded like someone cracking their knuckles over and over again. I then heard Sheila say,

"Be still you stupid rabbit!"

I then heard the popping sound again, so I peered through the glass in the door leading to the rabbits. As I looked through, I saw Sheila with a small board in her hand. She was trying to put some test agent in a rabbit's eye, but every time she got close to it, it kicked and bucked. She responded by hitting the rabbit in the head with the board she had in her hand. As soon as I saw her do this, I ran into the room and stared her down. She had a look of surprise, then fear, finally anger as I'm sure she saw the anger in my eyes. I wanted to take that board away from her, pop her in the head a few dozen times and then shove it up her skinny a$s! No words were exchanged, but I gave her a look that expressed that if I caught her doing this again, that I was going to turn her into a crimson-headed Popsicle. I may have been in the lowest position in this company, but I was certainly not going to let anyone abuse the defenseless. From this point on, Sheila was my enemy.

Chapter 11

Spreading My Wings

January, 1977. My hang gliding skills had progressed to the point where I was ready to make my first mountain flight. I had flown off River Bend about forty times and became versed at making 90 and 180 degree turns. These were required for mountain flights so I could burn off altitude to make a safe landing in the designated landing field. The time had come to go to Petit Jean Mountain. Petit Jean is a 740 foot "mountain" about 60 miles northwest of Little Rock, Arkansas. It faces northeast and the launch site, at the time, was a flat-topped rock face near some power lines. There was enough room to get a good run before plunging off a 40 foot cliff. The landing field was a large 50 acre cow pasture about half a mile away from the launch and populated with about 100 Angus cows. It was a good sized landing field for a person's first mountain flight. I was ready to go. I could hardly contain my excitement as I made the three-hour trip from Memphis. I was also a little apprehensive. I was going from 150 feet of altitude to 740 feet. The other pilots on the trip assured me that the extra altitude was safer because if anything happened, I would have more time to react and adjust. As we got past Little Rock, the Sun began to rise. We had left Memphis with our three vehicle caravan around 4 a.m. We planned to get to Petit Jean early to take advantage of the smooth morning air. By the time we got to Morrilton, Petit Jean was in full view. I began to get a few butterflies as we started our ascent up the mountain. My wife was along and assured me that everything was going to be okay.

We arrived at the launch site and were greeted by a bright blue sky and temperatures in the mid-forties. In front of Petit Jean flows the Arkansas River. Across the river are a number of huge fields. These, along with the river, combine to make the prevailing winter wind flow very smooth as it climbs the mountain. We unloaded our gliders from the vehicles and I set mine up very carefully. I checked and rechecked every wire, bolt and tube. I inspected the sail of my 17-foot "standard" glider. This was a very simple glider, as were most at the time, so it didn't take long to assemble.

Within twenty minutes, everyone was ready to launch. I decided to watch several people fly before I took my leap of faith. The wind was blowing straight into the mountain at about five miles per hour. This was perfect for launching since it provided enough wind to fill the sail during the launch run. The first two pilots were off pretty quickly and both made a slight dive off the cliff to build a little airspeed. Oliver Gregory was next. He was a pilot who started flying about the same time I did, but advanced considerably faster. Oliver had already flown Petit Jean several times and said that it was an easy flight. I felt that I should have already flown here, too, and that Ollie wasn't that much better than I was. But he was. He was a natural pilot and learned very quickly. My perception that I was at the same skill level as Oliver would get me in trouble a few months later. Oliver had a smooth launch and flew his glider in the seated position. The other pilots, including me, flew prone or in the "superman" position. Ollie had a great flight with a perfect landing and his girlfriend, Jackie, drove his van down to pick up Oliver and the other two pilots. I decided to wait until Ollie got back to the top to ask him for some tips for my flight. After all, he had done this several times.

Ollie and company made it back in about twenty minutes. I readied my glider, put on my "blueballs" harness, and donned my helmet and gloves. I moved my glider to the launch rock and did a hang check to assure my harness was clipped in correctly to my glider's suspension line. I looked around as if this were going to be my last moment on Earth! I jokingly told people they could have various possessions and told Ollie that he could have my Grand Funk Railroad collection of 8-track tapes. I kissed Debbie, partly good-bye and partly for luck and said a quick prayer. Oliver had his hand on the keel of my glider to give me a "keel assist" during my take off to assure the proper nose angle at launch. Ollie asked,

"Are you ready?"

"As ready as I'm gonna be!" I replied.

The butterflies in my stomach could have been a mass of migrating Monarchs. I took one deep breath and said

"When I count to three, I'll go".

Oliver said, "Don't look down, look out at the fields across the river".

This was sound advice as I picked up the glider...

"One, two, three"...I began my run.

The glider dropped slightly as I went off the edge of the cliff. I instinctively pulled in to get the speed up. I was flying with some altitude! This was the most unreal and exciting sensation I had ever experienced. I prayed out loud,

"Please Dear God, let me have a safe flight and a safe landing!"

My prayers were answered. I think I set the Petit Jean speed record on route to the landing field as the trees below me went by in a brownish-gray blur. I set up my approach on the far end of the field and did a series of linked 90-degree turns. One hundred feet, fifty feet, twenty five, ten, five and a perfect landing... on my stomach! I didn't care! I had flown off Petit Jean! I was now a mountain pilot. I had fledged from the nest and survived. I could hardly wait to get back up to the top. As I unhooked from the glider, I heard cheers coming from the launch. I looked up and saw several people waving their arms. I responded by jumping up and down and flailing my arms wildly. I looked up at Petit Jean with a sense of awe and had the feeling toward her not unlike one has for a lover.

My wife drove down from the mountain and gave me a congratulatory hug and kiss. We loaded my glider and returned to the top. Everyone gave me slaps on the backs and handshakes and a few commented on how fast I flew to the field. I said that on this next flight I would slow down and enjoy the scenery a little more. I assembled my glider once again and moved to the launch. I did my hang check to make sure my harness was connected properly. Oliver gave me a keel assist again and my launch was nearly perfect. This time I slowed down enough to actually look back at the mountain. I even noticed the Arkansas River as it wound around the mountain's base. It now stuck me that I was flying! Not that I didn't realize this on my previous flights, but this time I felt so alive! Someone made a snide comment a few weeks earlier that I had a death wish because I was a hang glider pilot. Actually the opposite has always been true. I hang glide because I have a life wish...I want to explore life to the fullest! Hang gliding has allowed me to experience life in a way I could not imagine. As I was flying down from the mountain, I saw the world as a different place. I saw it in three dimensions instead of the linear world I was used to on the ground. Any problems I may have had were left at the launch.

Well, back to reality. It was now time to set up my landing. I was about three hundred feet up and I began a series of linked 90-degree turns to line me up into the wind on the long end of the field. I didn't want the flight to end, but it did so with another belly landing. I would have plenty of time to work on landing on my feet. I walked my glider to the end of the field and began breaking it down for the trip home. I watched several of my fellow birdmen make their flights and landings. Twilight was soon upon us. We loaded our gliders for the trip back to Memphis. As we left the mountain, I couldn't help but watch it recede in my rear-view mirror. I had come to Petit Jean a fledgling and now I was a soaring bird. It had been a good day.

Chapter 12

Euthanasia and eating dirt

My job at Plough had settled into a tedious, boring and sad situation. Now early spring, at least I could look forward to the weekends when I could fly. I had become attached to a couple of lab rats and took them home as pets. One had been dosed with Di-Gel antacid and the other with a pesticide. Both looked relatively healthy and were very playful. I also brought home a rabbit and found homes for about ten more until someone at Plough thought it a bad idea.

One significant thing happened at work. A new department head took over and was calling everyone into his office for ideas and comments. When it came my turn, I introduced myself, feeling that I was meeting the Great and Powerful Oz, said that I was the lowly Animal Caretaker. He said that he was interested in everybody's ideas and opinions. I said that there wasn't much I could change in my section, but it seemed that this Mega-Million dollar company could afford to buy the necessary stuff to put the animals to sleep. He urged me to explain the situation of the current "euthanasia" practices and appeared to be genuinely appalled. He said that he couldn't promise anything, but he'd look into the situation.

About three days later, I was in the cleaning room, emptying the cages of some rats that had been terminated, when my favorite lady, Sheila, burst in with the words,

"I hope you're happy!"

After recovering from shock of her somewhat sudden appearance I asked,

"For what?!?"

"Because of yooouuu, we now have to put the animals to sleep!" she angrily snarled.

Once again, I felt I was in a scene from the Wizard of Oz, but this time, I had thrown the bucket of water in the face of the Wicked Witch. I yelled

"Alright!!!!!"

This didn't make Sheila any happier (as I imagined her melting into the floor). She stormed out, pulling the door out so quickly that it pounded against the concrete wall. A small victory had been won! At least the animals wouldn't suffer through painful deaths any longer.

A few days later, the euthanasia fluid arrived. Mr. Rose took me in and showed me how they were to euthanize a rabbit. About 1.5 cc of the solution was drawn into a syringe and was injected in a large vein in the rabbit's ear. The rabbit simply quit functioning. No longer would there be the barbaric skull-bashing. I felt a little bit more at peace and thanked Mr. Rose for showing me the procedure. Meanwhile, Sheila was in the background, glaring at me. As I left the room, I was humming the song, "Ding Dong, the Witch is Dead!" I stopped short of asking Mr. Rose if he had enough stuff in the bottle to take care of Sheila!

My hang gliding was getting better, too. I had flown off Petit Jean a few more times and had actually started landing on my feet. I also had my glider modified into a higher performing design and was satisfied with the new flight characteristics. Oliver Gregory, meanwhile, had flown off Mt. Magazine, a site in west central Arkansas that is the highest place between the Appalachian and Rocky Mountains. Situated at 2873 feet above sea level, the actual altitude from the top of the mountain to the surrounding valley is around 2,100 feet. Petit Jean is 740 feet above the landing field. I was familiar with the altitude of this mountain, but Magazine was three times higher. But, if Ollie could fly from here, I could, too! I still couldn't admit that Oliver was a better pilot! He was ready for Magazine. I was not. This didn't stop me, though. Ego is a strange creature.

Memorial Day weekend, my wife and I joined the caravan to Magazine. We stayed in a small hotel in Havana, Arkansas, and after breakfast, went to look at the landing field. This is something that pilots new to a site do before flying from the mountain. This allows one to become familiar with obstacles to avoid and to map out a landing approach. The main field was huge and was owned by the Albright family. Mrs. Albright warmly embraced the hang gliding community and the feeling was mutual. I was also shown the emergency landing fields, collectively known as the Shoeprint fields, which, viewed from the air, together they looked like a shoeprint. After surveying all the landing options, we made the 30 minute drive to the launch site. At this time, most of Magazine was still fairly wild. There were a few camping areas, but these were fairly primitive. An occasional black bear, bobcats, and turkeys had been sighted.

We got to the launch and were greeted with a wonderful view. The wind was blowing in from the south, straight into the mountain at about five miles per hour...perfect for my first launch from here. There were a number of pilots already set up and the Memphis contingent quickly joined them. I carefully assembled my glider, and checked and re-checked every part. This would be a high altitude flight for me and would also be the longest glide I would make. It was about four miles to the Shoeprint fields; four long miles over trees and wilderness. One did not wish to come up short and land in a tree in this sea of green.

A couple of Arkansas pilots launched and flew to the landing field. Their flights looked pretty smooth and it took them about 12 to 15 minutes to make it to the field. By contrast, the flight time from the top of Petit Jean to the field below lasted about 2 to 3 minutes. I was nervously excited. It was time for me to launch. The launch at Magazine consists of a rocky slope that drops to a 200-foot cliff. After leaving the mountain, there's about half mile of a tree-covered shelf that then drops away to a series of spines that run perpendicular to the mountain. I brought my glider up to the launch rocks and did a hang check to make sure every part of my harness felt right and that I was properly connected to my glider. I had a new piece of equipment on my harness, a parachute, and I wanted to make sure the container cleared my control bar base tube. I also had a crude pellet-type variometer. This instrument told me how fast I was rising or descending. I swung it into position to make sure I could clearly view it. One thing I was lacking was an airspeed indicator. The most simple of these consist of a plastic tube that air funnels into a small opening. The air then pushed a calibrated disk up to mark on the indicator that responds to windspeed. This type of indicator is still widely used today. It also cost the same, too, about $23, including the mounting bracket. This was $23 I should have spent back then.

Full of confidence, but a little scared, I launched. The takeoff was uneventful as I pulled on a little speed. I made it over the half mile-long shelf and was over one of the spines. The trees seemed to be moving more slowly than I was used to, so I pulled the bar in to prevent a stall. What I didn't realize was that I had more than sufficient airspeed and the trees were moving more slowly due to my "higher than I was used to" altitude. I was literally diving my glider down the top of the spine. Squirrels were probably scared. I looked at my variometer. It was registering 800 feet per minute down! This was twice my normal sink rate. When I realize this, I pushed out on the bar a little and zoomed away from the top of the spine. In the process of the prolonged dive, I had burned too much altitude to make it safely to the main landing field. I did have enough to barely make it to the heel of the Shoeprint fields. I eeked over the outstretched limbs of a 100 foot Oak tree much like a homerun just clearing the glove of a left fielder. I landed safely and was proud to be a Magazine pilot.

I disassembled my glider and loaded it up for the thirty-minute trek to launch. Conditions were still in the acceptable range for me so I quickly, but safely, reassembled my wing. Before long, I was ready to launch again. This time I had a little more confidence and my launch went smoothly. Someone told me to fly straight out past the shelf or "Headwall" as it was called, and look for a waterfall. I did and it was a terrific sight! At this point the mountain really drops away and I got suckered into the "trees are moving too slowly" syndrome. I pulled in on the control bar again and began a prolonged dive along the spine. I was repeating the same mistake as on the previous flight! I looked at my body position and realized that I had the basebar past my knees! One normally flies with the basebar at between the chest and the chin. Once again, I had burned too much altitude to make it to the main field, so I opted for the Shoeprints again. This time I made it over the heel and was headed to the larger "ball of the foot" field. A row of trees some thirty feet high separated the two fields and I was too low to safely turn back to the "heel field" and too low to clear the trees. There were two trees that formed a goalpost situation directly ahead, so I thought of myself as a football. I pulled in to gain a little momentum and aimed for the small gap between the two. My strategy was to zoom over the longest limbs to land safely on the other side. This almost worked, but one limb caught my right side flying wire and spun me into a 90-degree turn. There I was, thirty feet up and in a stall. The glider I flew at that time parachuted nicely and I should have gone for that option. Instead, I pulled the bar in to regain flying speed, but this only aggravated the situation. When a hang glider stalls, the nose will automatically drop, the glider will dive for a prescribed amount of feet and the glider will resume normal flying speed.

When I pulled in, I essentially rotated the nose down at the wrong time. Big time pilot error. In aviation mishaps, greater than 90% of the accidents can be attributed to pilot error. Hang gliding is no different. I was about to contribute to the statistic. The last thing I remember was the ground rushing to meet me. Luckily for me, the glider had begun to pull out of the induced dive. The next thing I remembered was that I was unclipped from the glider and was pulling two of my front teeth back into the proper alignment. I also was spitting out broken parts of two more teeth. Another thing I had was a torn lip. I gently tugged on the right side and I knew from the amount of travel that I needed some stitches.

As I stood there in my sparkly state seeing a lot of electric-like flashes, I stared back at the mountain trying to figure out which mountain it was; Petit Jean or Magazine? I remembered something about a flying trip to Magazine, but I felt like I was in a dream. I thought that even if this was a dream, I needed to get my lip sewn back together. Suddenly overhead, Oliver Gregory appeared. He was on his way to a landing in the main field. I needed help, so I furiously began waving my arms. Ollie looked down and thought I was waving at him for doing a nice 360-degree turn. I kept waving and he figured that something was wrong. He landed nearby and got to me quickly. One of the first things I asked Oliver when he arrived was if I needed plastic surgery on my lip. When I asked him, I pulled my torn lip out to reveal the damage. Ollie responded by saying,

"Oh John, don't do that, you're making me sick!"

As Ollie led me out of the field, the whole situation didn't seem real. By the time we got back to the main landing field, my wife had arrived. I didn't know who she was! She asked if I knew her and I said,

"No, but you sure are pretty!"

I was taken to a small clinic in Havana and I barely recall having my lip sew back together. After about three hours, my head began to clear. Around the bonfire that night, people came up to me and said how lucky I was that I had not broken my neck! They were right. God spared me that day. I had let my ego control my actions. I thanked Oliver for his help and conceded in my mind that he was a better pilot. I reconsidered my flying and it was a couple of years before I again flew Magazine. A few years later, Ollie set the Magazine endurance record with a flight over eight hours in length. He later gave up flying for awhile to concentrate on college. He eventually became an M.D. and is now a Psychiatrist in Chattanooga. About ten years ago he returned to hang gliding. I'm still not to the level of pilot Ollie was over thirty years ago. But that's okay, I didn't have to pay for my lesson with my life and a big change was about to happen. I was to see why I was spared!

Chapter 13

The Zoo calls

In mid June of 1977, I was watching the local TV news and a story aired about the Memphis Zoo. It seemed the zoo was understaffed and was under the threat from the U.S. Department of Agriculture for shutdown. The zoo needed to hire seven more keepers and had to do so within the next two months. This was my chance! The next day, I had my wife go by City Hall and pick up an employment application. I now had the six months animal experience needed and I felt that this was my window of opportunity. That evening, Debbie handed me the application. I said to her that this was the beginning of my new career and she chuckled slightly. She said that I needed to have the application returned within the next two weeks. Something told me to get in back sooner. I filled it out and had Debbie take it in two days later. When she came home that evening, she said it was a good thing she returned it. It seems that they had so many applications for the seven positions that the City decided to reduce the number of days that it would accept applications. Today was the last day for acceptance of applications! Luckily, I had played my hunch (or was it simply fate)!

A couple of weeks went by and I began to think that the zoo was not going to call me. I was starting to look at Plough as more of a long-term job and my way out of here was by going back to college. It's funny how we perceive things. No sooner had I given up on the zoo, did I get a call for an interview. They needed to see me in two days, so I asked Mr. Rose for the time off and he obliged my request. The interview day came and I was excited about finally getting a chance to possibly work at the zoo. I made it to the zoo about 30 minutes before my interview time, so I went to the birdhouse to look around. It was unfortunately closed for renovation, so I wandered over to the petting zoo. I thought that it would be great to work anywhere out here. Ten minutes to three; I had better get to the zoo office. I strolled up to the secretary's desk, introduced myself and told her that I was there for a 3 o'clock interview. At three o'clock, the door to the conference room opened and Asst. Zoo Director, Duane Able came out and asked,

"Are you John Stokes?"

I replied that I was and he invited me in to have a seat. Seated around the table were the Curators of the different departments; Cliff Ross, Bird Curator, Chuck Beckson, Reptiles and Aquarium, Mike Williamson, Mammals and Richard Weeks, Education Curator. Duane asked me if I wanted some coffee or water but I respectfully declined. I was already nervous enough and I didn't want to take a chance of spilling something on one of these guys that might be my future boss.

The interview went well. I was asked about my animal background and Chuck Beckson said that he noticed on my application that I was an Eagle Scout. He said that his sons were in the Scouting program. Mike Williamson asked,

"If you are hired, where would you like to work?" I told him,

"I would be willing to work anywhere, but all of my life, I have really liked birds!"

Beckson and Williamson turned to Cliff Ross and Richard Weeks said,

"There's your man, Cliff!"

I looked at Cliff and nodded and waved. Cliff asked me if had any experience with birds and I told him that in the past I had a few parakeets, a duck and some chickens that were eaten by an elderly neighbor! Everyone laughed! I told him that I was always watching birds and really like birds of prey. I also said that I was willing to learn more about them but also emphasized that I was willing to learn about any animals, at the same time looking at all the curators. I didn't want to blow any chances I might have! Chuck Beckson said,

"Well, even if you are hired and don't get into the Bird section, you can always transfer later when an opening comes up."

I thought, "Just hire me for anywhere here and I'll worry about getting into the bird section later!"

I also said a silent prayer to that I would get this job. Apparently, my prayers were answered before they were even asked! At the end of the interview, all present thanked me for coming and that I would know something, one way or another, within two weeks. Two weeks seemed like a long time to wait on my future, but, as it turned out, I didn't have to wait more than just a few days.

The following Monday afternoon I was in my cleaning room and in stepped Phil Rose, my boss.

"John, can I speak to you for a minute?" he asked.

I said that I was at a point in my cleaning that I could stop. He said,

"I have gotten a call from a fellow named Cliff Ross from the Memphis Zoo. He wanted to know what type of person and worker that you were. I told him that you were a good worker and that the only drawback to your personality was that you occasionally hit the ground too hard on you hang glider!"

Mr. Rose had a look that was a combination of being proud and sad at the same time.

"They want you to work at the zoo, John, and I told Mr. Ross that you would be a great zookeeper!" Mr. Rose added,

"I always felt that you needed to work at the Zoo. This is not the place to be for someone who really cares about animals! It's hard enough for me to work here sometimes!" He continued,

"The job is yours if you want it and Mr. Ross is going to call back here in about an hour to offer you a job in the Bird Department!"

I was a little stunned. For a number of years, I had dreamed of working at the Memphis Zoo and soon I was going to be working there in the Bird department!

Mr. Rose requested, "All I ask from you, John, is about two weeks so I can find someone to take your place",

I agreed to that and he wished me good luck. I went back to the cleaning room and was a little lost. I couldn't believe it! I was going to work at the Memphis Zoo. Within the hour, Cliff called and officially offered me a job. I told him that I had to give Plough two more weeks and he said that he understood. He told me to come in on July 23rd at 8 o'clock a.m. July 23rd would be the first day of my professional bird career.

The last two weeks at Plough went quickly. Everyone, including Sheila, was nice to me. About three days before I left, they hired someone to replace me. The guy wasn't really an animal person and in some ways, this was good. My last day was bittersweet and was actually harder to leave than I thought it would be. I said good-bye to the lab's mascot guinea pig, Bridget, and to Mr. Rose, who wished me good luck. On my way out, I went upstairs and found my friend, Marilyn Pearcy, who helped me get this job in the first place. Little did she know that she had helped me get my start into my dream career. I thanked her for her help and told her to come and see me at the zoo. I left her office and left my name badge at the guard stand. I had been set free and was ready to begin my new life. Life was good on that sunny, summer day!

Chapter 14

A New Career

July Twenty-third. I arrived at the Memphis Zoo at 7:30 a.m. I walked past the gate guard and strolled down past the waterfowl lot to view Monkey Island. I could hardly believe that I was starting my first day as a zookeeper! I was giddy with excitement and was anxious to get to work. Thirty minutes passed quickly so I made my way to the zoo office. Cliff Ross was there waiting and greeted me with,

"Well, John, are you ready to get going?"

I said, "Yep, let's go!"

The first thing we did was to go to the employee lounge to punch my first timecard. We then walked across the zoo to the reserve birdhouse, which was a converted zoo director's residence. It was officially called the "Tapp House", after the head of zoo maintenance, John Tapp. It seemed that Mr. Tapp and his family were the last to live in the house before it was converted into a holding area for birds. I followed Cliff through the front door and was greeted by a cacophony of bird calls. The bedrooms had been converted into cages that housed birds ranging from finches to parrots to a couple of most unusual large birds called Great Indian Hornbills. Joe and Jolene were the names of the hornbills. I grew to really like both of these birds. The first co-worker I was introduced to was Betty Lee Elliott. She was preparing food in the kitchen for the birds' morning meals. This included a mixture of ground dog food/carrots/graham crackers, along with chopped boiled eggs, chopped apples and chopped bananas. Cliff introduced me and placed me in Betty Lee's charge. Betty Lee was in her early thirties and was a former hippie type. She was very laid back and spoke with a California-like drawl. She had straight, long brown hair and wore granny-like glasses. I asked her what she wanted me to do. She said,

"Take this pan of food and put it in the big cage in the second bedroom, man."

I did so and the cage contained a variety of colorful finches. The next to be fed were Joe and Jolene. They both got a huge pan of sliced apples, sliced bananas, whole boiled eggs, crickets and raisins. They loved raisins! Betty Lee haphazardly threw the pan in the enclosure and we went around to the other side to watch them eat. Joe hopped down and immediately started eating the raisins. I was amazed how delicately he could pick them with his two-foot long beak. Joe was also very fond of crickets. He usually ate them next. He was also very considerate of his smaller mate, Jolene. Occasionally, they got into a beak-fencing contest, but when it was time to eat, they got along well. Joe was even kind enough to share the raisins with Jolene and offered her some in his beak. He grunted when he had one to give her. She accepted the raisin with a higher-pitched grunt and this seemed to strengthen the bond between them. As I later got to know both the birds, I was able to hand feed both by using the same type of grunts.

Betty Lee and I next went down to the main birdhouse. It was under renovation, but housed many birds in some of the completed enclosures. In one section called the Center Flight, lived a flock of Chilean Flamingoes, which are related to the vivid pink Caribbean Flamingo, but live in the foothill lakes of the Andes Mountains. There were also various shorebirds and an ancient Wood Stork, named Stan. Stan had been in captivity at least twenty years and was probably several years older than me (I was twenty-one at the time). Most of these birds ate a combination of soaked dog food,

71

flamingo fare, made of ground shrimp and carotene pigment, birds of prey diet, made of horsemeat, beef, chicken and fish, and a liberal amount of crickets and live minnows. The Center Flight had a waterfall, which fed an upper pool, which cascaded into a larger pool. It had a ceiling height of over forty feet and had a number of larger tropical plants such as palms, banana trees, and fig trees. The enclosure was ringed by a gunnite rockwork, which had been painted to resemble real rocks. Also, the rockwork held many spaces for planters, which would eventually hold pots of vines and other appropriate plants. Little did I know at the time that I soon would have a big hand in making this area look like a slice of rainforest.

Feeding time was always something to witness. As soon as the minnows were placed in the pools, the shorebirds and terns went to work. In five minutes, the 300 minnows were completely eaten! Also, the stunned crickets went fast. Within an hour, most of the food in the six large pans had been eaten. We fed most of the smaller birds twice a day, due to their higher metabolism, and the food in the afternoon was completely different from the morning meal. A lot more fruit was fed. The common food from the first meal to the second was grated boiled eggs. We fed chopped apples and bananas, soaked raisins (which began to resemble grapes again), more birds of prey diet, mealworms, cups of honey water and apple and orange halves. We also cared for some birds in the side exhibit cages that were already completed. Included here were some fascinating honeycreepers. These small birds occupy a niche between tanagers, which are fruit and insect eaters, and hummingbirds, which are mainly nectar feeders. For their size, the honeycreepers seemed to be very intelligent and very curious. This is something I discovered about many of the smaller birds. We tend to associate brain size with intelligence. However, with many of the birds that were small in size, there seemed to be an astonishing amount of reasoning ability! Recent discoveries in raven intelligence suggest that these birds may be as smart as dogs!

One of the burning questions I had was did we have any birds of prey? I asked this of Betty Lee and she said that we had a few Barn Owls, a Crested Caracara, an Egyptian Vulture and a Black Hawk Eagle.

"He's really pretty, too!" Betty Lee remarked.

"Where are they kept?" I queried.

"The Barn Owls are at the Tapp House and the rest are in a corn crib cage across from Monkey Island. You'll get to see them later," she concluded.

I couldn't wait! The Black Hawk Eagle sounded pretty interesting. Betty Lee said that he would sit on a glove. Maybe, now I was about to realize my goal to work with eagles. Later in the day, I went down to the corn crib cages and looked at the different birds. The Black Hawk Eagle was very striking. He had lemon-yellow eyes, captured by a black head with a spiky crest. His charcoal, goose-sized body was completed with a long black and gray barred tail. His feet were the same color as his eyes and were equipped with two inch ebony talons. He name was Cortez and had been donated to the zoo a few years earlier. It seems that a military man had gotten him somewhere in Central America. He had been found when he was very young and hand-raised. Cortez was imprinted on humans and did not know that he was a bird! I couldn't wait to hold him! That would come later. I had a pretty full first day and before I knew it, it was time to go home. I went down to the employee lounge to punch my time card and I met a lot of my fellow zookeepers. I looked around and saw a unique batch of people. Here was assembled a lot of people, who, like me, loved animals all their lives and were lucky enough to make a career working with them.

Over the next few days I met several more of my co-workers and the rest of the bird collection. I went down to the waterfowl lot and help feed the birds there and also met some of the macaws that were in residence in the corn crib cages next to the birds of prey. One macaw, in particular, a Blue and Yellow Macaw named Fatman, caught my attention. Cliff introduced me to Fatman and showed me a number of tricks that he had learned. The zoo had a bird show as recently as two years before I arrived, but a lack of public interest forced the zoo to discontinue it. Fatman had been the star of the show and did tricks such as rollerskating, bike riding, rope climbing, and tightrope walking. He still remembered all of his tricks as Cliff went through as series of hand signals that put Fatman through his routine.

While at the corn crib cages, I asked Cliff about Cortez. Betty Lee relayed that Cortez sat on the glove of a trainer. I asked Cliff if anyone had held him recently. He said,

"No, but he's very mild-mannered and would sit on anybody's glove".

I told him that I wanted to start working with Cortez.

Cliff said, "Tomorrow, when you finish your daily routine, I'll get the equipment, and we'll get 'em out".

Wow, I was about to hold my first eagle! Tomorrow came none too soon. Cliff came to the Tapp House and got a couple of eagle gauntlets and a temporary jesse strap. This strap went around Cortez leg to keep him from flying off. It was also very long and served as a leash. As we walked down to the corn crib cages, I could hardly contain my excitement. Cliff unlocked the door, slid it open and walked up to Cortez. He extended his left gloved hand, touch the back of Cortez' legs and he stepped up on the glove. I helped put the strap on the great bird's leg and Cliff asked,

"Are you ready to hold him?" All I could say was

"Yeah!"

Cliff held Cortez in such a manner that I could get him to sit back on top of my glove. I was a little nervous, but Cortez was a pro and stepped back very lightly. Cliff said to hold my hand a little higher since birds of prey like to be on the highest part of the arm. I couldn't believe I was holding this magnificent bird and I also couldn't believe how light he was. He only weighed around five pounds and this was due to his light skeletal structure. Birds that soar or spend a lot of time in the air have hollow bones. These hollow bones are internally braced with a truss type of system that provides support without a lot of weight. The system is similar to some types of bridges that use the maximum support, but with minimum structure. So, of the five pounds that Cortez weighed, less than four ounces of that was skeletal weight!

Cliff left me with Cortez and said if I needed anything to come to the office. Apparently Cliff trusted both of us to do well with each other. What a beautiful bird he was! I marveled at his grandeur and was in awe of his potential power. To me, predators are at the pinnacle of design. As I was admiring Cortez, I began to notice his weight. Five pounds doesn't sound like much, but it was starting to feel like twenty-five! After about thirty minutes I began to unintentionally lower my fist. *A raptor likes to be on the highest portion of one's arm.* Slowly Cortez began walking up my arm and eventually perched on my shoulder. Had I kept my fist height above my elbow, he would have still been on my glove, but now, I had an eagle on my shoulder! Several visitors came by and took pictures while I tried not to panic. What to do? I didn't want to bother Cliff, especially since he told me to keep my fist higher than my elbow. I decided to see if I could get him to step off onto a perch in his enclosure. Luckily Cortez was very gentle. As soon as I got inside his enclosure, I backed Cortez up to a limb and viola', he hopped right onto it. Crisis averted! I took his leather strap off, told him thank you and went back to the Tapp House. Cliff later saw me and asked how it went with Cortez and I said,

"It couldn't have been better!" I should have added to this, under my breath, "that you didn't see me with Cortez on my shoulder!"

Working with Cortez became an everyday habit. After I finished my daily routine in the Bird House, I went down to the corncrib cages and got Cortez. I began to talk to the public about birds of prey with Cortez on my glove. It didn't take long to make some converts. To help me with my raptor facts, I went to the Zoo's library and found a book called *Hawks, Eagles and Falcons of the World,* by Leslie Brown and Dean Amadon. This book became my Bible from which I preached about birds of prey. I found a section on Black Hawk Eagles and read the species description. This listed weights, wing measurements, and in some cases, foot sizes of the sexes within the species. It seemed that Cortez fell within the parameters of a female and a large one at that! I showed Cliff what I had found and upon reading it, he agreed that the former "he" was actually a "she". It took a little bit of a mental adjustment on my part to call Cortez "her", but it was something she knew all along. She just didn't know that she was a bird.

Chapter 15

1978

1978 was a mixed year for me. My wife and I moved from our two-bedroom apartment to a two-bedroom house. This house was in a quiet neighborhood in the Frayser section of Memphis. It had an attic for storage of our now accumulating extra stuff and even held my hang glider (with some fancy wiggling; the glider was 18 feet long). The second bedroom also made a great animal room. I had a couple of parakeets that I made a nice cage and it allowed them to look out one of the windows into the treed backyard. I made a larger pen outside for a rabbit named "19" that I rescued from Plough. Our cat, "Beau", could finally go outside and soon learned the "see and avoid" tactic in dealing with the local dogs. We also acquired a Poohuahua (poodle-chihuahua mix) named Toby. He was pretty intelligent and quickly learned that Beau controlled the area inside the house and the perimeter that was also known as the yard. To add to this mix, I brought home a three day old Barn Owl named "Micro" that I was raising for educational use. He eventually occupied the second bedroom and it became essentially a free-flight pen, complete with decorative newspaper covering the floor.

My job at the zoo was becoming almost an obsession for me. I really loved working there and began to spend more time at work. I rarely got to work past 5 a.m. and was very involved in the final phases of renovation of the birdhouse. We had the side enclosures painted with scenery that depicted the natural habitat of the birds that were housed in them. We had an artist volunteer named Mike

Turri who was a big fan of science fiction, but had a great eye and hand for natural settings. The enclosures he painted had murals that were so realistic that a number of birds, when placed in their new cages, tried to fly off into the artificial sky! Luckily, none of them were hurt and usually figured after a few tries that the distant mountain range or waterfall didn't exist.

After Mike painted the enclosures, I picked the appropriate "furniture" to complement the mural and provide the future occupants with suitable perches and a natural type of habitat. The cage floors were mostly covered with sand so the droppings and old food could be sifted out and also harbored less bacteria. I found several varieties of sand that I was able to blend for different colors for each enclosure. We also used gravel and pine bark nuggets. One of my favorite enclosures was the Barn Owl exhibit. It was designed to look like a cutaway of a barn loft. I found some wood from several old barns and made the entrance to the nesting area through a crack in a board. The cage also had one-way glass that gave the owls a feeling of privacy, but allowed the public to easily view them. Outside of the fake loft was an area that looked like the outside of a barn at twilight, complete with a silhouette of a silo. Hidden in this area was a pool for water and a place for the owls to get their food. The owls did well in this exhibit and when the Birdhouse was opened, the public seemed to like it as well.

My hang gliding avocation was struck with tragedy in 1978. I lost one of my flying buddies. Members of the Memphis club went to a Mother's Day Weekend Fly-In at a place called Flood Mountain, Arkansas, across the valley from Mt. Magazine. Flood is a northwest facing launch, almost as high as Magazine, and faces the prevailing wind after the passage of cold front. I was tempted to go, but the Weather Service had called for clear air turbulence below 3000 feet for the region that Flood and Magazine were located. My friend and fellow hang glider pilot, Don Burris, called me Friday night to ask if I were going to the Fly-In. I told him of the weather report and he said,

"Aw, come on, we are all going to have some fun!"

Little did I know, but that conversation was the last I was to have with him. I respectfully declined Don's invitation and told him I would make it another time.

Saturday was "blown out" at Flood, with winds well over thirty miles an hour. Sunday, was a little better, but the air was still somewhat turbulent. The first to launch was Oliver Gregory. He yelled down that the air was trashy and that he wished that he were back on the ground. Ollie soon caught a thermal updraft and climbed in it over a thousand feet over the mountain. Don was next to launch. He expressed concern that there was a hill near the landing field that might produce some extreme turbulence if someone got behind it. He said that he definitely didn't want to get behind the hill if he got low. It was almost a self-fulfilling prophecy. Don launched and got bounced around for awhile and apparently decided he had enough and went to land. As Don got nearer to the landing field, he got low in an area he should not have been, behind the turbulence-producing hill. To everyone's horror on launch, they watched helplessly as Don's glider was thrashed out of control and finally impacted in the landing zone.

Meanwhile, Ollie had lost the altitude gained from the thermal and was headed in the direction of the main landing field. He, too, witnessed Don's ill-fated flight and saw him go behind the hill. He quickly flew down and landed to help him. He ran through some woods to the site of Don's crash and found him face down in the dirt. He wasn't breathing so Ollie started mouth to mouth resuscitation. Miller Stroud, a Memphis pilot, and Bill Munday from Arkansas, quickly arrived to help. They kept the resuscitation efforts going until the ambulance arrived. Don officially died on the way to the hospital. It was Mother's Day.

I got the call about Don around eight o'clock that evening. Another pilot who decided not to go to the Fly-In, Burt Alderson, gave me the news. I couldn't believe it! Don was gone! We had almost thought of ourselves as invincible and that nothing like this could happen to one of us, but it did. I thanked Burt for the call and then told Debbie. She immediately welled with tears and I began to cry as well. We had all gone dancing just the week before and Don, who was recently divorced, did some goofy disco dance with Debbie, much to everyone's delight and amusement.

"Don is dead. Don is dead",

I kept saying to myself, trying to come to grip with the reality of the situation. It just didn't seem real. We had lost one of our own. Don was buried a few days later in Potts Camp, Mississippi. I didn't attend the funeral. Not to disrespect Don, but I just wanted to remember him the way he was. After this, everyone re-thought their flying. We were mortal. We could die.

About six weeks after Don's death, another incident magnified our fragility. Lyle Cogbill, an Arkansas pilot, was flying at Magazine when his glider was kicked out of a thermal. The glider went into a dive, recovered, went into another dive, recovered from that dive, but this time, it broke both leading edge spars. Lyle's glider started to spiral, much like a helicopter. At this point, he was 1500 feet above the ground and without a parachute. Luckily, the spiral actually produced enough lift that Lyle basically landed unhurt in the trees. He was temporarily deaf after being spun so much, but was in good shape considering the alternative. Both of these incidences made us all rethink conditions and our flying limitations. The manufacturer of the defective glider gave Lyle a brand new glider and a parachute. The pilots who didn't have parachutes, got them. We were determined to not let Don's death be in vain. We had all learned some painful lessons. Not a flying day passes when I don't think about Don. I know he's there, watching over me as I fly.

In June of '78, the Tropical Birdhouse was finally opened on our annual Zoo Day. Guest of Honor that year was Marlin Perkins of the St. Louis Zoo and Wild Kingdom TV show fame. Marlin was the first real celebrity I met and it was pretty cool to shake hands with a guy I grew up watching on the television. Marlin, along with Jacques Cousteau, inspired a lot of people in my age group to seek careers in the natural world. Both of these fellows probably had a lot to do with getting the environmental movement started by bringing the wild world to our living rooms. Marlin officially opened the Birdhouse and all the bird section staff accompanied him through on tour of the new facility. He was impressed with what we had done with the enclosures and expressed delight in the murals and corresponding enclosure "furniture". He really liked the two large "flight" rooms that had waterfalls and tall tropical plants. These flights had no barriers such as wire or glass to separate the public from the birds. Overall, Mr. Perkins seemed to like what we had done to the former zoo greenhouse.

A few months after the Birdhouse opened, the Zoo created three new management positions, Assistant Curator of Birds, Mammals and Reptiles/Aquarium. I was in consideration for the position of Assistant Bird Curator. A number of people applied for the three positions and when the application deadline closed, interviews began. I was considered to be the shoo-in for the Assistant Bird Curator position. My interview went pretty well, and when asked by Asst. Director Duane Able if I had any questions I responded by saying,

"Yeah, why doesn't anyone care about the animals around here?"

He asked me what I was talking about. I was a little mad about the previous winter when we did not put Cortez and the other exotic raptors in for the winter.

"Are you referring to the Black Hawk Eagle?" Duane asked.

I said, "Yes, exactly!"

"Well, we have left that bird outside for several years now!" Duane explained.

I looked over at Cliff and he had a look of, "Why now?!?"

Earlier in the year Cliff and I apparently had a communication mix-up and he thought that they had brought the bird in every year. Duane said they left her out. I went ahead and took Cortez inside, much to Mr. Able's anger. Duane had been right. They did leave Cortez out all year. She had gradually acclimated to the cooler temperatures. I was wrong and my timing to ask about this was terrible. I had blown my chance for the position. It also upset the balance of who got what job. Martin Mahoney, a recent transfer from the Mammal section, got the job I wanted. Dan MacDoogal, a reptile expert got the Mammal position and Walter Douglass, got the Reptile/Aquarium nod. I gained nothing but a lesson in controlling my temper. I had another chance in the future.

Chapter 16

The Memphis Zoo Raptor Rehab Program

Also, in 1978, I started the Memphis Zoo Raptor Rehabilitation Program. I was passing through the zoo office one day, and overheard the secretary talking on the phone. She explained to the person that the zoo didn't take injured hawks and their best bet was to contact a veterinarian. I knew that most of the vets in the Memphis area, with the exception of Dr. Green, knew little about raptors. I talked to Dr. Mike Douglass about the possibility of doing rehab at the zoo. I proposed that if he did the surgery, I would do the actual physical therapy. He agreed and said that he could gain some experience that he could apply to the zoo's exotic bird collection. I was a member of the Memphis Audubon Society and I asked some of the club's officials if the Society would be interested in supporting the fledgling rehab program. They told me that they would have a discussion at the next board meeting and put the topic up for a vote. Meanwhile, I had talked the idea over with Cliff Ross, my direct supervisor, and told him that I had enough time to do both my keeper duties and rehab. He knew this was true. I came in at 4:30 in the morning and usually had all of the birds in my care taken care of by the time everyone else got to work. I also got permission from Cliff to get the zoo's secretary to refer the injured raptor calls to me.

It wasn't long that we got our first Red-tailed Hawk. The Red-tailed Hawk is the most common hawk in North America. It was injured in a collision with a car and had a broken radius. A bird's wing is similar to a human arm in layout. The radius is the smaller of the two bones of the "forearm" and is a fairly easy bone to repair. Fortunately, with a bird's more rapid metabolism, as compared to a human's, this bone heals very quickly, usually by just wrapping the injured wing for a week or so. Before long, I was doing some physical therapy on the immature hawk's wing. This was accomplished by repeated stretching and closing the afflicted wing to loosen the ligaments, tendons and muscles. The hawk was placed in a slightly larger enclosure to allow a little more movement.

What we were lacking in our early rehab center was a flight pen for exercise. I came up with a way to exercise the hawk to get it in top flying condition. I attached two leather jesse straps, one to each leg, and a long nylon line called a creance by falconers, to the bird. I then took the hawk out on the soccer/softball/football field in Overton Park where the zoo is located. I gently tossed the hawk in the air to get it to fly and then ran behind it. The bird didn't fly far at first, twenty yards or so, but eventually it flew further and further. Finally, it was flying over one hundred yard and was ready for release.

I chose to release the hawk at Shelby Farms. This area is located in the middle of Shelby County and has several thousand acres of mixed habitat, and is bordered on the south by the Wolf River. It had perfect habitat for a Red-tailed Hawk. Several pairs of them resided there, along with a number of wintering raptors. On the day of release, I went to the bird's enclosure, caught him and placed him in a cardboard apple box. Twenty minutes later, I arrived at Shelby Farms and took the hawk out of the box. It was a beautiful, late fall day, partly cloudy with a mild southerly breeze. I had named the bird Justice, in honor of the inmates incarcerated in the nearby Penal Farm. With one huge heave, I set him free. He flew over two hundred yards and landed on a fence post. He stayed there for about ten minutes, surveying the area to orient himself.

Finally, he launched into a gust of wind and followed the zephyr out of sight. It was a very satisfying experience to see the bird fly away, considering that a few weeks prior, it couldn't fly at all. So, with the release of Justice, came the Memphis Zoo Raptor Rehabilitation Program's first success. There were many more successes and a few failures to follow. By the way, the Audubon Society board did approve to support the program and gave several thousand dollars to the effort.

1978 saw my return to Mt. Magazine. I had not flown there since my crash in '77. I spent a lot of time flying lower mountain sites such as Petit Jean, Lookout Mountain and Raccoon Mountain near Chattanooga. I realized after my crash that I had gotten way ahead of myself. I decided to hone my skills at the other sites before returning to fly "Mag". I also acquired an airspeed indicator and an altimeter, which would help me deal with the higher altitude of Magazine. I was ready to fly there simply because I was a better prepared pilot, skill wise and equipment wise. I chose a warm late fall weekend for my return. Magazine faces south, so whenever it was good to fly there meant warmer southerly breezes, especially in the late fall and early winter.

The trip to Magazine was different than the last time I went. For once, I didn't go with a contingent from Memphis. Accompanying me on this trip was an intern vet student from St. Louis named Mark Caspermeyer. Mark was a student from the University of Missouri and was studying under Zoo Veterinarian, Mike Douglass, an alumnus from the same school. Mark lived temporarily in the Tapp House and was willing to go to Magazine to have something to do. Mark also was a little glad to get out of the Tapp House for a few days, especially since the house had a supernatural resident. More on this apparition later. Mark was enthusiastic about hang gliding, but wasn't interested in taking up

85

the sport. Still, it was good to have him along. He could drive for me and take pictures, and was a fun guy to boot.

We arrived in Havana, Arkansas about five hours after leaving Memphis. The winds looked pretty good, direction-wise and the temperatures in the upper 50's would make the flying more tolerable. As standard practice in hang gliding, I visited the landing field to check conditions and to check in with the landowner, Mrs. Corene Albright. She remembered me from the previous year as the "boy who clipped the tree and tore his lip". I told her that I was ready to go at it again. She said to be careful and that she'll see me when I fly down. I told her that I wasn't going to do any tree trimming this time. She chuckled and said,

"Alright, then".

Mark and I hopped in my car and took the thirty-minute drive to the top. When we arrived, conditions were ideal for my return flight. I was anxious to fly here again, not only to prove to myself I could successfully negotiate the altitude, but simply because I was ready to fly from Magazine. I also had a newer, higher performing glider that was easy to fly and land and got a better glide, too. Of course, it would be outdated in six months. Glider technology was advancing at a rapid pace in 1978. What was hot one season was the next year's training glider. There were, however, a few dead ends and a few glider companies went out of business because of a bad design. The glider I was flying at the time was called a Cirrus 5. It was a good intermediate design that helped me advance safely.

I assembled my glider carefully and checked every bolt, nut and wire several times. I donned my harness, checked my parachute container, tighten my helmet strap and then clipped my harness onto my glider. I checked my airspeed indicator and my altimeter. Finally, I was ready. On this day, there were only a few local pilots in attendance. Most of the regulars were either at some sites in nearby Oklahoma or twenty miles downwind at Mt. Nebo. Mark and one of the locals helped me do a hang check, where I made sure my harness was connected properly and that the glider was put together well. It looked good. I picked up the Cirrus, leveled the nose and began a steady, but purposeful run. I quickly reached takeoff speed and dove the glider slightly for extra airspeed. I made it! I was away from the edge and headed over the shelf called the Headwall. This time, as opposed to a year and half earlier, I did have altitude to spare. I checked my airspeed and slowed down slightly. My altimeter indicated 2,000 feet. I had only lost 100 feet since my launch thirty seconds prior. At this point on my previous Magazine flight, I was close to the trees and losing altitude rapidly in a panicked, terrain-hugging dive. On this flight, I was relaxed and confident.

The view was incredible. After clearing the half-mile Headwall ledge, the mountain dropped away significantly. I remembered to watch for the waterfall that flows off the Headwall. I looked directly below me and there it was! What a beautiful sight to behold. I followed the water as it plunged about seventy-five feet to the waiting pool beneath the cliff. I felt as though I was witnessing a grand natural spectacle. I then changed course slightly to better align with the landing field. I didn't have to think about landing though, since the field was still four miles away. Instead, I looked all around. I was able to look up and down the valley. I noticed that with the sun shining on all the small ponds and lakes, the valley looked like a large thermometer that had been broken with its content of mercury spilled everywhere. I did take note of the sea of trees below me, far enough below that I didn't have to worry about repeating my last landing here. In fact, I looked at my progress and was surprised that I was over the Shoeprint fields, 1500 feet over them! My experience, combined with my new glider and instruments allowed me this comfortable distance.

Within a few minutes, I was over the primary landing field next to Mrs. Albright's house. This field was dubbed the "Arkansas Field", since it looked like the State of Arkansas when viewed from above. The last time I was here, I didn't come close to the altitude needed to see the shape. I still had about 1200 feet to burn, so I decided to fly a little further into the valley and followed the local highway for a mile or so. When I got down to 800 feet, I headed back to the primary field to set up my approach. I arrived back over Mrs. Albright's house with about 500 feet to spare. I did a couple of 360-degree turns to lose some height. I checked the flags and streamers surrounding the LZ (landing zone) and noticed that the wind was blowing from the south. I did one more three-sixty which brought me down to about 200 feet. I then did a standard airplane approach to the field. This consisted of flying downwind for a short distance, and then crosswind for about 70 yards and finally a 90-degree turn directly into the wind. I made this final turn at about 100 feet of altitude and this gave me enough height to glide safely to a soft landing about 200 feet from the house. I did it! I flew safely from Magazine and landed safely where I was supposed to.

I carried my glider to an area near the house. Mrs. Albright came out and offered me a drink of cool well water. She congratulated me and noticed that I didn't have any leaves or branches stuck on my glider. I broke down my glider and by the time I had put it in the bag, Mark had arrived from his drive down from the top. Mark shook my hand and helped me load the glider back on the car. Mark then asked,

"Do you want to go for another?"

I thought for a second, looked back at the mountain studying the terrain from the landing field up to the launch and said,

"Sure, another flight would be fun!"

I did fly again and had another good landing. The sun was setting as I pulled out of Mrs. Albright's driveway on to the main road. I had a triumphant return and some great flights. The glow stayed with me all the way back to Memphis.

Chapter 17

1979

Nineteen-seventy nine brought a few changes; the decline of disco, the Iran hostage crisis, and a new house for Debbie and me. My Father had taken a job with a new company, Home Insurance, and required him to transfer to Jackson, Mississippi. They had to sell their house and offered it to Debbie and me at a price we couldn't afford to refuse. It was only a few miles away from the house we lived in and had one more bedroom and a fenced back yard. Debbie had been working part-time at a local dinner theatre and had a few thousand dollars saved. We used this for a down payment and since Debbie had recently started to work at a bank we had little trouble getting a mortgage loan approved.

Before long, we moved into our new house in west Frayser. For me, this was a great location. The Mississippi River was about a mile and a half away, with plenty of riparian habitat. The Loosahatchie River joined the Mississippi about a mile north of my house. Of course, all of this water and low-lying land brought more than our share of mosquitoes. The City of Memphis had a fogging program designed to get rid of the mosquito problem and it seemed to be pretty effective. I remember as a kid running through the fog behind the control trucks, pretending to be floating among the clouds. Some years later, I found that the fog was actually DDT! People often ask what happened to me. I simply explain…"DDT, man, DDT." After 1972, something different was used, since DDT was banned that year.

The areas near the Mississippi and Loosahatchie Rivers were still very wild. It was not unusual to see wild turkeys, cottonmouths, muskrats, beavers and one of my favorite birds of prey, the Mississippi Kite. The Mississippi Kite is a falcon-like aerobat that spends many hours on the wing. It feeds primarily on flying insects such as cicadas and dragonflies, sometimes on birds such as swifts and swallows, occasionally on frogs and lizards, and even, at times, a bat or two. The river bottomland forest provided the needed habitat for the state Endangered raptor. Many times after work, I explored the area. I spent many hours in this swampy expanse, discovering something new on almost every visit. I even left work, at times, at a normal hour to go to the bottoms.

This year also saw a change in my job status. I was still a keeper in the Bird section. Martin Mahoney, the Assistant Curator of Birds, had decided to give up his position in order to pursue a career in dog training. This was an opportunity for me to try again for the job that I should have had all along. A year earlier, I had blown my chance for the job by getting into an argument with Duane Able, the Assistant Zoo Director. This time, however, I was going to be cool during the interview…I didn't want to mess up my chance.

Cliff mentioned that he wanted me for the position, but the City of Memphis had to open the job to all qualified applicants. Still, I felt I had a pretty good chance to get the job. In mid-April, my interview came up and I felt it went pretty well. Duane didn't hold a grudge from the previous year's debacle. This time, I was pretty calm, and at the end when Mr. Able asked if I had any questions, I said,

"No, not this time!"

Duane emitted a slight laugh of relief and I thanked him for his consideration. Cliff said that I did very well and that the job was essentially mine. They only had a few more interviews to go and then a decision would be made.

By early May, all of the interviews had been conducted. It was decision time and the announcement was officially made in mid-May. Without a whole lot of fanfare, Cliff came to me with a solemn face. My stomach tightened and I held my breath.

"Well John," Cliff sighed and paused, shaking his head he said,

"You…got the job!"

Cliff had presented his best poker face and had me thinking that I had blown it again. He shook my hand and said,

"Finally, we can get on with it".

I guess that he meant that he finally got the person he wanted for the job in the first place. My keeper mates congratulated me upon hearing the news and even my wife was happy with the promotion. At this point, Debbie was becoming a little unhappy with the amount of time I was spending at the zoo. She had even remarked that she was jealous of my job. She stated that she almost wished that I were having an affair! At least she could have been mad at a person and not a job!

The transition went smoothly. Marty was a friend of the zoo Director, Hal Menigar, and he gave Marty a good luck/going away party. I didn't attend, not because I didn't like Marty, but because I was experiencing growing tensions with Menigar. It seems that professional jealousy was beginning to raise its ugly head. The Raptor Rehab program was starting to gain notoriety and with it, more publicity. The public seemed to be fascinated with raptors and all of the local media turned out for the release of a hawk or owl. I became the spokesman for the program and was on TV and in the papers more than the zoo director. I didn't plan for this, it just happened. Slowly though, I was becoming a whipping boy for Menigar. He had ignored me when I was a zookeeper. The Union protected me, even though I wasn't a member. As Assistant Curator, though, I was vulnerable and placed under scrutiny. This over-scrutiny, several years down the line, earned Menigar a visit to the office of the Mayor of Memphis and led me onto a different path.

In 1979, I hunted with a gun for the last time. For a number of years, I looked forward to opening days of squirrel and dove seasons. I usually hunted with Mark Woods or Bobby Berry and we were very safety conscious. We also observed all the hunting laws and regulations. We ate what we shot and did not waste anything. This year, however, I was having second thoughts about killing animals. Remember, I had started a raptor rehab program a year earlier and had seen a number of hawks that had been shot. My ways of thinking were in flux. A keeper in the Primate House, Glenn Rayloff, had invited me to go dove hunting on our off day. We met at the zoo and drove to near the town of Ripley, Tennessee. We found a large, recently cut-over soybean field bordered on the north by a stand of pine trees and on the south by a small pond. Glenn hiked to the north end of the field and I positioned myself near the pond. Between us, we could ambush birds either going to the pond to drink or into the field to feed. We had observed a number of birds entering the field prior to the legal hunting start time of noon. We got ready and waited for noon and the birds.

Twelve o'clock and a few birds made their way into the area. I had a few shots, but missed. So did Glenn. Mourning Doves are very hard to hit, even with a shotgun. I've seen some battle-hardened doves dodge a number of well-aimed shots. A dove passed over me, but I didn't have a shot. It headed straight toward Glenn and he took it down with one shell. Another passed Glenn unharmed. I had a few more shots and so did Glenn, none of them connecting. Suddenly, a pair of birds passed over me and I pulled

93

my shotgun up, led the lead bird the proper amount and fired. The bird fell and I went out to retrieve it. On the way out, its mate had circled back and had landed near its fallen partner. As I got closer, I expected the mate to fly away at my approach, but it didn't. I thought that the fallen bird was dead, but it wasn't. It was still alive, coughing blood from its mortal wound. The mate stood by, half-protecting, half-hoping its other half would fly away with it. It couldn't.

This scene had a sudden and profound effect on me. Seeing the mate's devotion and the dying bird's will to live made me burst into tears! I threw my shotgun down and picked up the injured bird. The stress of this caused the dove to breathe even faster. With each struggled draw of air and bloody exhale, its life ebbed. There I stood, crying, holding the bird until it expired and went limp. Upon this, its mate flew away. I had taken its partner. I was the predator, but didn't need the dove's flesh to survive. It was yet another Life changing moment. A week later, I sold my shotgun to Mark Woods. I have nothing against hunting, and still don't to this day, but it's something I could never do again. I'll never forget the dove and its mate and in the next life, I hope to apologize to them both. This meal of dove was the toughest I ever had to swallow.

Nineteen seventy-nine was also the year I received a national zookeeping award. I didn't know I was nominated so the award was quite a surprise. I was a member of the American Association of Zookeepers, but didn't attend the annual membership meeting. I believe that it was in Portland, Oregon that year. I would have liked to have gone, but there was only funding for two people. The keepers who attended the conference returned with the news. Mary Jo Bunchman found me and told me that I was given a Certificate of Merit by the AAZK, the highest honor given by the organization. A couple of my co-workers had written a description of me and described my daily work routine. I was quite

94

flabbergasted that they had taken time to do this as I didn't think anyone noticed! Well anyway, I received congratulations from the head of the Memphis Park Commission, the Mayors of Memphis and Shelby County, and U.S. Senator Jim Sasser. I received congrats from my fellow zoo workers, with one exception; Zoo Director Hal Menigar. He never said,

"Good job", "Way to go", "Good work", "Your breath stinks", "Go to hell" or anything.

He chose to ignore me. He knew about the award because an article about it in was in the local paper and a clipping was placed on his desk (not by me!). The rift was getting wider and my job just a little tougher.

This year, we also had the first eagle to enter our rehab program. The immature Bald Eagle was found near Jonesboro, Arkansas, and had a slight wing injury. It appeared to have a slight furrow, probably made by a grazing .22 caliber bullet, to its outer left wing. The resulting force caused the bird to hit the ground, but luckily didn't cause a whole lot of injury. The eagle was taken to a local semi-amusement park/zoo in Jonesboro called Funland and Zoo. The people here had him for only a few days before I was called to pick up the eagle for further rehab. Upon returning to the zoo, Dr. Mike Douglass inspected the eagle from beak to tail and only found the wing injury.

We placed him in a rehab enclosure built with money from the Audubon Society. He stayed here for a few days and after this, I started the eagle on the same exercise regiment I had earlier used with Justice, the Red-tailed Hawk. I took the eagle, which I had named "Chief Joseph", in honor of the famous Nez Perce leader, to the soccer field in Overton Park. I gently tossed C.J. into the air, expecting him to only fly a few dozen yards or so. To my surprise, he lurched quickly into the air, and was rapidly nearing the end of the one hundred foot line. Not wanting him to abruptly hit the end

95

of the line, I started running to provide some slack. This gave Joseph more room to fly and we took off together, not unlike a weird kid chasing his broken-string kite. After about one hundred and fifty yards, I was pretty winded and slowed down. This back tension also slowed Chief Joseph enough for him to land, somewhat awkwardly, but safely. A few more sessions with the Chief and I determined that he was ready to go.

It was now late March and most of the migrant eagles had left for the north. I remembered that Reelfoot Lake in northwest Tennessee had some immature Bald eagles that stayed until the end of March. I took Joseph here for release because of this and because of an abundance of fish. He was probably going into his second spring and didn't have any place in particular to be. Young Bald Eagles wander very widely for the first three years of their lives. By the time an eagle is four or five, it begins to get its adult plumage and finds a mate. Here at Reelfoot, the Chief could hang out with birds about his age and at the same time, not have to work hard to find food.

Release day was a little rainy, but not enough to hamper flight. I chose a spot behind the National Guard Armory on the south side of the lake for release. There is a row of cypress trees about 100 yards from the shore, and if Chief Joseph could make it to these trees, he would fare well. As it turns out, there were about three eagles already in the cypress stand. The actual release was uneventful. I pulled Joseph out of the carrier, and with one heave-ho, he was free. He flew flawlessly to the trees and landed near one of the resting birds. He stayed in this tree for about an hour and then flew north into the fog. He was never seen again. Before release, Martha Waldron from Memphis fitted him with an aluminum leg band. To this day, she has not gotten a band return on him. Hopefully, he had a great life and perhaps some of his offspring or some of their offspring still winter at Reelfoot today.

However, the thrill of rehabbing and releasing my first eagle will far and forever outlive Joseph and his offspring.

Chapter 18

Falconry

In '78, I became a licensed falconer. About six months earlier, I had met a man named Dave Vance, a local Master Falconer who had nearly fifty years experience. I had found a letter from Dave on file where he had offered to train a hawk for use in zoo educational programs. I had been interested in learning how to train hawks for quite some time, but didn't know anyone who did it. Dave put his home phone number on the letter so I decided to contact him. Dave was a little curious how I got his number, but he was willing to talk to me about the sport. I bugged him enough that he finally asked me if I wanted to go out with him while he hunted his bird. I quickly accepted the invitation. The following weekend, I met Dave at his home. Dave was a soft-spoken man in his mid-fifties with salt and pepper hair and a slight southern drawl. He invited me in and introduced me to his wife, June. Over coffee he told me a brief history of how he got started in hawking. Dave began hunting with hawks when he was ten years old. For over forty years, he had taught and hunted with a variety of hawks and falcons. At the time, his bird of choice was the Harris' Hawk. The Harris' Hawk is a bird closely related to the Red-tailed Hawk. Its range is from SW Texas to southern California down to South America. It is an intelligent, cooperative species that thrives in seemingly inhospitable arid scrub and desert lands.

Dave had a beautiful representative of the species named Sam. Sam was short for Samantha, but after I got to know her, Sam seemed more appropriate. Dave kept Sam in a mew, or hawk enclosure, in his back yard. He also had a male that he had for breeding purposes. He had two hunting dogs, beagles as a matter of fact, named Dolly and Patty. They were used to hunting with Sam and they seemed to enjoy the experience. Sam also did very well around the dogs and even anticipated their movements when they were pursuing a rabbit. Dolly had been hit by a car a few years earlier which left her partially deaf in one ear. This led to some comical moments when Patty got on the trail of a rabbit. A lot of times, if Dolly wasn't next to Patty when the scent was picked up, Dolly picked up the trail in the opposite direction, much to Dave's dismay! His usual response was,

"Dammit, Dolly, get back here!"

Dave loaded the beagles and Sam into the truck. I hopped in on the passenger side and off we went to catch a rabbit! We didn't have to drive far. About ten minutes away from Dave's house was a wooded/field expanse that was perfect habitat for cottontail rabbits. My job was as a third beagle and brush beater. We pulled off the road and found a spot where it was safe to release the dogs and the hawk. As soon as they were out, Dolly and Patty found the scent of a rabbit. They took off, baying as they went, and this obviously excited Sam. She could hardly wait to get out of the truck. She usually rode on the passenger side of the cab and this allowed easy exit. As soon as Dave opened the door, Sam was away and found a commanding perch in a large oak.

It wasn't long before the dogs had the rabbit in sight. I could see Sam as she watched the dogs in their pursuit. Sam flew to a smaller tree that was closer to the dogs and was directly in the path to intercept the rabbit. The Cottontail likes to circle back close to where it was disturbed and Sam knew this. Dave hollered,

"Get ready to watch, John. This'll probably happen quicker than you think!"

As I watched Sam she flew to another tree that was closer to the approaching rabbit. She landed and then immediately dove out of the tree at about an 80-degree angle. I saw a flash of the rabbit and the twisting, gyrating pursuit flight of Sam. Dave was right indeed! The action was rapid and over as quickly as it had began. Sam missed! Dave said that she probably caught a rabbit about 40% of the time. We hunted a little longer that day, but Sam didn't have any more opportunities of the cottontail variety. She did, however, catch a mouse and engulfed it on the spot. She was finished for the day. I was impressed with Sam and the experience.

I went out hunting with Dave several more times over the next month or so. Sam did catch several rabbits. Dolly continued to go in the opposite direction when Patty found a rabbit trail. I began serious study of technical aspects of falconry, including information that was included on the Federal Falconry Exam. Tennessee had decided to make falconry a legal sport, and I wanted to become a legal, licensed falconer. Dave offered to sponsor me as an Apprentice Falconer, the beginning level of falconry. The Apprentice Falconer can either keep an American Kestrel or Red-tailed Hawk. After two years at this level, I would be eligible to be a General Falconer where I could keep two birds of several different species. Dave loaned me several books that helped me with information I needed for the Falconry exam. At the time, there were about twenty people in Tennessee practicing falconry. Everybody had to take the exam and had to score at least 80% correct. The test was pretty straight forward, but a few of the multiple-choice answers were correct for the same question. I made an 82. I barely passed. Dave didn't ace the test. The multiple choice test also threw him, too. I believe that Dave scored a 92. After the test, we discussed the problem questions with our Tennessee Wildlife Resources agent and he agreed that several of the questions had several correct answers. Unfortunately, he could not do anything to change the situation, but promised that our input would definitely be considered on future tests. I had passed the falconry exam. All I needed was to have my facilities inspected. I already had a bird.

Chapter 19

Charger

The Bird was named "Charger". Charger was a year old female Red-tailed Hawk that came to our rehab program via a high school student. It seems that this student had brought the bird to school after capturing it in his backyard. He looked out his back window one morning and saw a hawk sitting in a tree. The student got a mouse from somewhere; I don't know if his house was infested, or he had a pet mouse he "*did in*", or perhaps he kept snakes and the mouse was to be food for the serpents. For whatever reason, he threw the mouse in the back yard, the hawk came down and pounced on it. The fellow threw a cardboard box over the bird and took her to school. Upon examination, the bird had some leather "anklets" on her legs. She had been someone's falconry bird. A teacher at the school called me about the bird. I drove to Southhaven High School and met the teacher and the student. I extracted the hawk from the box. She was a fairly large female and was in good feather condition; the former owner had taken good care of her. With the hawk out of the box, a large crowd of students assembled. I did an impromptu show with the bird and ended it with emphasis not to shoot birds of prey. This school was in a semi-rural area and I figured that many of the students probably hunted. Before I left, the teacher, Mrs. Griffin, asked me if I had any birds I could bring back to the school. I had a few birds and told her I could return in a week or so. The student that found the hawk asked if I would name it after their high school mascot, the Charger (a horse). I said that I would.

Upon my return to the zoo, Dr. Douglass did a thorough exam of the hawk. He noticed that she was a little thin, but other than that, she was in good shape. She was placed in a rehab enclosure and was given a healthy dose of food, which she rapidly engulfed. Meanwhile, I called Dave to see if he knew of anyone that had lost a bird. After a few days of checking around, he called to report that no one in the area had lost the bird. He theorized that she was either kept illegally and was lost or she had been lost by a falconer further north and had instinctively migrated south. Dave suggested that I keep and train her as my first falconry bird. At the time, it was still legal to use a rehab bird in falconry. Later when I became a General Falconer, I sent several rehab birds to my Apprentices. This got a bird in the hands of the falconer fairly quickly and also gave the bird a second chance. All of the rehab birds were first year Red-tailed Hawks. Had a human not found the injured bird it would have died. Getting some additional hunting experience helped the young birds when they were again released. Also, no healthy young hawks were removed from the wild. Now, an Apprentice Falconer *has* to live trap an immature bird, thus removing a healthy bird.

Charger turned out to be a quick study. Dave coached me through the various ins and outs of weighing and dropping a bird's weight. Usually, one drops a bird about 15% of its wild-caught weight. Some birds, however, may be a little thin in the wild, especially a bird in its first year. Dave taught me how to gauge a bird's relative weight and health by feeling its keel or breastbone. Look at a chicken breast in the grocery store and you'll notice that it is divided by line in the middle. If a bird is healthy and relatively fat, then there won't be a whole lot of flesh on either side of the breastbone. A bird that is thin will have very little flesh on either side. To determine a hawk's relative weight, take the keel between the index finger and thumb. If the breastbone isn't protruding, then

103

the bird has a good amount of weight. If it is very pronounced, then the bird is thin. Ideally, a bird at its flying weight is somewhere in between. Also, a hawk ready to hunt and fly has a definite posture called "yarak". The bird perches upright with its chest feathers slightly ruffled and wings partially opened and slightly drooped. I quickly learned how to apply all these measurements and observations to Charger. I weighed her everyday and noted her behaviors and keel depth. I was also able to apply all these procedures to raptor rehabilitation.

One thing I did with Charger was to "man" her every day. I carried her around on my gloved hand and exposed her to a variety of sights and sounds. I usually tried to spend at least an hour a day with her. Charger was fairly comfortable around humans from the beginning. Dave believed that she was a bird taken from the wild before she was able to fly. This type of bird in falconry is called a "brancher". At this stage, the young bird has already imprinted on its parents, but does not have any flying skills developed. This is of great advantage to the falconer in that the bird is not set in its ways and is fairly easy to train. Obviously, the person who had lost Charger had spent a lot of time with her. She was calm and very well mannered at first. She did, however, start the annoying habit of screaming when her weight began to drop. This screaming is something a young hawk will do to its parents to get them to feed it. A human imprint will do this frequently when its weight is down. It was somewhat pronounced with Charger. Although she wasn't an imprint, she did start to vocalize like one. The more her weight dropped, the more she began to scream.

One of the more difficult things to do, at first, is to get a hawk to eat off the glove. A hawk has an inherent mistrust of humans. To take food from a human goes against the bird's nature. Charger was no exception. I steadily dropped her weight to the point where she was interested in the morsel of beef I had for her. After I

104

weighed her and before I lifted her from the scale, I placed the meat on my glove. Almost as soon as she stepped on the glove, she was interested in the meat. She rapidly consumed the morsel and was looking for more. This was literally a big step. Her hunger overpowered her fear of me. She was not totally trusting as yet, but at least she was accepting food from a foreign source, instead of catching it herself.

Next in order was to step onto the glove for food. If she ate off the glove, which she did, then stepping to the glove followed. This was pretty uneventful, as she was hungry. From the time I put her back on her perch, she had already turned back around to look for my glove. I concealed the glove behind my back and placed a piece of meat between the thumb and index finger. I brought the gauntlet forward and she immediately looked for food. I held the glove a short distance from her feet and then showed her the tidbit. No sooner did I reveal the morsel that she stepped on the glove. Obviously she had remembered this from her previous training. I returned her to the T-perch and decided to try to get her to hop about six inches to the glove. Once again, a rapid response. She knew all this stuff; I was the one learning here! By the end of the session, she was flying about twelve feet across the room. I called Dave and excitedly told him the news of the day. Dave wasn't too surprised and commented that Red-tailed Hawks have excellent memories. Dave suggested that I now fly her on a creance or line. This was to take place outside. So the next day I went to the local hardware store and bought 100 feet of nylon rope. Looking back, the rope was well strong enough for the task. It probably had one thousand pound breaking strength, more than enough to hold a three pound Redtail (in fact, I later used it as a tow rope to get a stuck car from the mud!).

I did all my required zoo work and readied Charger for her new session. I had the portable previously mentioned T-perch, which, in reality, was a stand for a hay conveyor. This worked nicely for working Charger on the creance. I set up the perch in a small opening between the Tapp House and the Petting Zoo and rolled out the 100 feet of line. I weighed Charger, got the appropriate amount of food, and put it in a pouch on my belt. I placed the hawk on the stand and tied the end of the 100-foot line to the ball-bearing swivel that was attached to Charger's jesse straps. I then tied the loose end of the rope to my belt just in case she tried to fly before I was ready. I walked about 15 yards from the perch, placed a piece of food on my glove, and blew my whistle to get Charger's attention. All along, I had blown my police-type whistle every time Charger ate a piece of food. This was to get her to Pavlovianly associate the whistle with food. It worked very well, for when I blew the whistle this time, she instantly left the perch and was on the glove. This was old routine for her, but for me, it was a supreme thrill! I returned her to the perch and moved out twenty yards, This time, when I raised the glove and before I hit the whistle, Charger was off and on my hand. The next time, I went thirty yards. Same result. I was rapidly running out of line. She was doing much better than I had expected! Once again, the "teacher" was the student.

It wasn't long before Charger was flying 100 feet. I had made a lure for her out of an Electrolux vacuum cleaner bag and a rabbit skin I got from the local leather store. It had a rawhide thong in the middle to which I tied a piece of meat. The lure is used as a backup mechanism in case the bird won't respond to the food on the falconer's glove. Also, it can be used as a device to exercise a bird, in the case of falcons. Lure flying a falcon is an art within itself. I got about 50 feet away from her and turned my back to hide the lure. I had a nice piece of stew beef on it and when I turned, I swung the lure and dropped it on the ground. Almost simultaneously, Charger launched from the perch and hit the lure before it came to a complete stop! She attacked the lure as if it were alive and tore most of the rabbit fur off of it. The next day, I did the same procedure with her and the same results. This time she tore off what remained of the rabbit fur until nothing remained. The lure was literally a canvas vacuum cleaner bag with a rawhide thong. This didn't stop her from going after the lure with everything she had. She hit the lure with the same abandon as she did when it had fur. She was ready for her first free flight.

Flying a bird free for the first time can be compared to a first date. If it is done correctly, there is nothing to worry about and the bird will keep coming back. However, if done incorrectly, the bird will bolt and will keep going; rather like a few of my first dates. The big day came and I took her out to the soccer field in the park. I undid her leash and hopped her to the top of the soccer goal. She calmly sat up there, vocalizing as she always did, unaware that she was free. I kept my eyes on her as I backed to about fifty yards away. She was anxiously watching me, expecting me to raise my glove at any moment. Finally, I readied a piece of meat, placed the whistle in my mouth and gave a short blast. At the same time I raised my glove. With a quick leap she was away from the goal and on towards my glove. My heart was beating so loud that I heard it in my ears. All of my fears of her flying off were unfounded; she landed feather-soft on the glove and ate the tidbit. I couldn't believe it! To her it was old news. To me an extreme rush of endorphins cascaded through my body from my ears to my little toes. Free flying Charger was easier than I thought. I flew her a few more times, increasing the distance for every flight. Piece of cake! She eventually flew one hundred yards, and to make things easier, she flew back to the top of the soccer goal to await the next run. Several days of this and free flying was routine, until one pleasant fall afternoon about a week later.

At this point, Charger was flying well over two to three hundred yards. The soccer field had a large sweetgum tree about two hundred yards from the north goal. I had brought her over from the zoo several times and after checking the field for anything strange or unusual, I untied her leash and let her fly ahead of me to the tree. She usually waited until I got within 100 feet before she was ready to fly to my glove. On this particular afternoon, however, I didn't see the man jogging with his dog. When I went to release Charger, I noticed that her flight path looked a little different. Instead of her usual vector towards the sweetgum, she had a different path in mind. She flew with marked determination as if she were after something. I quickly scanned the area in front of her and was overcome with horror. Ahead of me by some two hundred yards was a man jogging with a tiny dog, a daschund. As it turned out Charger was making a beeline towards the little canine. Jogging with a daschund was cruel enough; its little legs churning for all they were worth, but cruelty today wore brown and white feathers and had an appetite for some flop-eared rabbit. I saw the scene playing out before me, wishing I could somehow change the channel to some cartoons. Charger was closing on the wiener and I did my best to deter the attack. I was running, yelling and waving my arms but it was too late, sound doesn't travel quickly enough in situations like these.

Charger changed course to intercept the flappy–headed grass sweeper. Meanwhile, I ran as fast as my lawsuit-panic-induced legs could carry me. Charger grabbed the dog but missed any vital parts. The jogger grabbed Charger by her wing, flipped her in the air and the momentum carried her to a perch and a regal pose on a garbage can. She had her wings partially spread as if saying,

"Yeah, I caught a weird-looking rabbit!"

The man was somewhat surprised, enraged and confused and after saying some terrible things about my mother and myself, calmed a bit. The dog wasn't really hurt; it had a scratch on its muzzle, nothing compared to what it could have had; a trip to Oscar Meyer heaven. I offered to pay any veterinary bills and the man said that everything was forgiven.

"Besides", he concluded, "It isn't everyday that your dog gets attacked by a hawk!"

I agreed, not realizing how commonplace this was to become.

After the Daschund incident, I decided to fly Charger in more remote locales. Where I lived in western Frayser there was some good rabbit habitat; woods with blackberry and honeysuckle tangles and a few overgrown fields. All this was less than half a mile from my house. I got her accustomed to riding on a perch in the back of my car so transporting her was not a problem. I got off work at 4:00 p.m. so there was still enough daylight for our forays. One of the objectives was to get her to follow me as I walked along a tree line or crossed a field. She learned to do this quickly and when I crossed a field, she usually let me get about halfway across before she flew. She usually flew right next to me and picked out a tree in direct line with my path. On one of these field-crossing trips, she spied a rabbit before she landed in the tree. She immediately gave pursuit and chased it until it zigged and zagged into a heavy thicket. No doubt this was an experienced rabbit. Charger was in a small cottonwood tree when I got to her. She was peering into the mass of vines where she had last seen the bunny. I went into the thorn-infested mess in attempts to dislodge the rabbit to no avail. It was staying put and probably had a series of escape paths in the vegetation. Charger watched me with great interest as I extracted myself pulling vines first off my arms and then my legs. She continued to look for the rabbit, but it was long gone. Later, I did scare up a mouse that she promptly pounced on, dispatched and ate in one seamless motion. This day was over.

I tried to get Charger out several times a week, weather permitting. On one of our outings near my house, she encountered another canine of the shrunken variety. We were crossing a field that usually had a number of rabbits, several we had jumped a few days earlier. When we got about halfway across, Charger and I both spotted a "rabbit" that I thought was feeding out in the open. Charger, who was normally vocal, suddenly went quiet as she watched little mammal. I undid her leash and cast her off in the direction of the unsuspecting lagomorph. I watched her fly low to the ground in attempts to hide her approach. I started looking in the area around the rabbit and noticed that there were two young boys who were out there playing with matches. One child had a furry-looking hat. I also noticed that the rabbit that Charger was closing on was actually a Jack Russell terrier that was probably one of the boys' pet. I initially thought that she was going after the kid's hat, so I started running towards the boys. I was screaming and waving my arms, trying to warn the boy of his impending doom and my soon-to-be lawsuit. Both boys stood up and had a look of stark terror on their faces. Imagine a hawk with a four-foot wingspan and a screaming, half-crazed looking fellow running behind her! As far as they knew I was probably yelling,

"Go get 'em!"

The pair ran and dove into some nearby tall grass. Right before Charger got to their location, she did a wingover and hit the "rabbit" on the ground. The next thing I heard was "Errr, errr, errr", the agonizing yelps from the little terrier. I shouted,

"Not another dog!"

Sure enough, when I arrived on the scene, Charger had the little canine clamped by the muzzle. Luckily she had missed his eyes and basically had only a hold of its fur. The dog had a slight scrape on its nose. It was yelping and back peddling for all its worth and Charger, who was clearly in command of the situation, was dragging forward the terrified terrier. I separated the pair, checked the dog over, and except for the scratch, it was unharmed. I held Charger's jesse straps tightly as I let the pooch go and it ran, without looking back, all the way to its home. Meanwhile, I tried to find the boys. With Charger on my glove I went into the tall grass calling for the kids…

"Hey y'all come on out…I need to talk to you about your dog".

They didn't materialize and may have gone out the back way during my exam of the dog. They were probably thinking,

"He's caught Sparky and we're next!"

I never saw the kids, but what a tale they had for their, I'm sure, disbelieving parents.

Another time, in the same area, Charger flew over a small hill and for a few minutes, I lost sight of her. I heard the barking of a dog nearby, so I ran towards the source of the sound. Sure enough, there was Charger in a tree overlooking a backyard that contained a Sheltie. I rapidly deployed the Electrolux lure and brought her down and away from potential trouble.

In the meantime, Charger had gone after a few rabbits and was close a few times. She also caught and ate a few more mice, lizards and toads. The most interesting thing she pursued was a Woodcock. This odd looking bird is a member of the Sandpiper family and is mostly active at night. It lives in wet woodlands and eats mostly worms. It has a long beak that is slightly hinged on the end. It listens for a potential worm meal, probes it beak in a likely spot and if a worm is located, the Woodcock can open the tip of its beak enough to grab the worm for extraction. The Woodcock, when flushed, usually rises straight up for a few seconds and then switches to fast horizontal flight. Charger and I were in a wet woodland one day looking for "swamp rabbits". Suddenly, a Woodcock took off from nearly under my feet and begin its slow climb out. This attracted Charger's attention and she launched from the oak tree in which she was perched. She was immediately on the Woodcock's tail, but when it went into horizontal mode, it quickly left Charger in its vortices. She knew she was beaten and only gave chase for about 40 yards. She was pretty smart in that respect.

Once, at the zoo, I tried to get her to catch a pigeon. One of the keepers in the petting zoo had caught this bird in a grain bin and asked me if I wanted it as food for Charger. I said no thank you because Rock Doves are carriers for a fungal infection known as frounce. This fungus grows in the raptor's mouth, eventually causing death by suffocation. I did, however ask that he hold the bird for a hunting exercise. I went and got Charger from her enclosure, quickly readied her and brought her to the petting zoo. A very small field was located between the petting zoo and the aquarium and here is where I met Don Melton. Don had the pigeon and let it flap its wings to draw Charger's attention. As soon as she saw this, she was ready. I held her tightly and then told Don to let it go. The pigeon took off with Charger right behind for the first twenty or so yards, but soon it pulled away and Charger slowed and landed in a nearby tree. She knew that pursuit was futile. Charger knew when she had a chance at catching something.

Charger went after her second "swamp" rabbit not soon after the terrier incident. We were about a mile north of the area near the Loosahatchic River. We were in yet another vine/briar thicket near the river when suddenly a "swamper" burst out from near my feet. Swamp rabbits are slightly larger than cottontails and supposedly have webbing between their toes. It is probably just a race of the Eastern cottontail. In its panic, the rabbit veered into the relatively open area under the riparian canopy. Charger anticipated this and was well on her way to nailing the bunny. As she was closing, the rabbit neared a honeysuckle thicket and in a final act of desperation, flung its cartwheeling body into the middle of all the vines. This tactic worked! Charger was so baffled by this that she landed in a nearby tree, very perplexed! She looked stunned and amazed. It took me about a minute to get her to come down to my glove. She kept looking into the honeysuckle, but the rabbit never did appear. I went over and kicked around in the vines to no avail. I finally gave up on it and left the area. As we were walking away, Charger kept looking back towards the vines. No doubt, in Charger's world, this rabbit had just become a legend.

The final chapter to the dog stories occurred a few days after the tumbling Swamp rabbit. We had just crossed an overgrown field with Charger selecting a tree that was overgrown with honeysuckle (one may see why this introduced vine is considered a pest). By the time I reached her location, Charger was intently staring below into the mass. Suddenly, she dove from her limb into the greenery. Almost as quickly I heard a large dog barking. I yelled out,

"Don't shoot (the hawk), don't shoot!"

As I stumbled and clawed my way through the vines, I saw a hunter holding his Springer Spaniel by the collar. Charger, meanwhile, had landed on a sapling and had it bent to the ground. She had her wings spread defiantly as if she was saying..."Yep, no doubt about it, that's a dog!" The spaniel had a slight scrape on its muzzle. I quickly got Charger under control, gave the fellow my phone number in case of veterinary bills and got the hell out of Topeka. The hunter said that he almost shot her, but heard the ringing bell on her leg. Luckily, she lived to catch her first rabbit.

Charger got her first rabbit in a field in the southeast part of Shelby County, where Memphis is located. A Memphis falconer, Lawrence Bolieck, took Charger and me to an area loaded with rabbits. It was a good rabbit year and the population was at a four year high. Cottontail populations rise and fall over a four to five

113

year cycle. After the peak, the population nosedives with only a few rabbits to carry on the species. Luckily and famously, rabbits reproduce rather quickly and the population starts to recover within a few years. This year in this location, the rabbits were abundant.

We first took out Lawrence's Red-tail, Misty. Misty was an intelligent, seasoned hunter and worked well with Larry's beagles. We started beating the brush to scare up any rabbits, and before long, one exploded from the nearby grass. The beagles were on its trail and Misty, upon hearing the baying hounds, positioned herself in an oak tree by a small stream. As previously mentioned, a Cottontail tends to circle once it is flushed and Misty was ready to intercept. It was a pure pleasure watching this bird. She listened to and watched the beagles as they drove the rabbit towards her. Suddenly she leaned forward on the limb and then went into a power dive. The rabbit leapt across the stream and made what was to be its last flight. It all seemed to occur in slow motion; Misty caught the rabbit in mid-air and mid-stream. The force of her dive coupled with the rabbit's leap propelled the two to the stream's other side and the bunny's instant death. Misty grabbed the rabbit in the head and the force of landing snapped its neck. I yelled to Lawrence to come and retrieve Misty and her prey. Larry offered Misty a piece of chicken in return for the rabbit. As he put one foot on the bunny, he held his chicken-loaded fist above Misty's head. She jumped up to the glove and left the rabbit on the ground. In this way, Lawrence and Misty could hunt again later. Now it was Charger's turn.

Larry put both of his beagles back in his truck. Charger's reputation had preceded her. I got her off the perch in my car and on to my glove. I then followed Larry to another part of the field. He said that he had seen several rabbits in this area just a few days earlier. I casted Charger off, or threw her in the air in non-falconry terms, and she located a large red oak tree for her command location. She flew to the tree and selected a large limb for her hunting perch. We caught up with her and began beating around all of the likely rabbit hideouts in the vicinity. I almost stepped on a mass of gray-brown fur and off went the Cottontail. Charger had been looking in the opposite direction, but caught sight of the rabbit after it was about twenty yards from me. She launched from the limb with diving, determined flaps. She closed the space quickly and in a few seconds was on the rabbit. She grabbed it by the head and the bunny emitted a piercing scream of fear. When I got to her, most of the struggle was over, but the rabbit was still alive. I finished its life, not something I really wanted to do, but my ultimate goal was to get Charger back into the wild. So, I had to swallow hard and do the job. I didn't take the rabbit from her, but rather let her eat part of it. A Cottontail can sustain a Red-tailed hawk for several days. I wanted her to catch a rabbit or two to gain an edge in survival that she might not have trying to live on mice and insects.

In about ten minutes she had eaten a full crop's worth of meat. A bird's crop is a temporary food pouch and this allows a hawk to carry its meal with it. Afterwards, she was ready for a nap, or at least I was. It was a bittersweet moment for me. I was happy she caught a rabbit, but sad that I had to ultimately kill the poor thing. At this point, I was having second thoughts about hunting and killing. Dispatching this rabbit brought up some strong emotional turmoil. Still, Charger needed to do this and I had to provide her the opportunity. I did want to ultimately release her. Lawrence came over and congratulated Charger and me. It had been a long trail of brush-beating and near misses that brought us to this day.

Charger did eventually catch another rabbit and, of course, several more mice and toads. It was now close to the beginning of Spring and near to the time to put her up for the molt. But, I felt Charger deserved to be free. She had proven to be a capable hunter and was in good feather condition. But, I didn't want to release her in west Tennessee; too many people, too many dogs. I made the decision to release her at Lookout Mountain near Chattanooga at the place where we launched our hang gliders. The area was not as populated as the place where I lived. There were plenty of large fields, perfect for mice and rabbits. I planned a trip in March of '80 and got a leg band put on Charger before release. The bander, Martha Waldron, selected the proper size and recorded the number. The band had instruction for anyone who found either the band or bird to "Avise Bird Band, Washington, DC". I don't know why the Feds didn't put a "d" in avise. Perhaps budget cutbacks? Maybe someone figured they could save $50,000 if they didn't use a "d". Anyway, off to Chattanooga I went. Charger was fattened before the trip to give her several days of fat reserves in case she had difficulty finding food. I arrived early Saturday morning and found a motel for the rest of the late night/early morning.

Saturday morning dawned clear and cool. A cold front had just passed through and winds were out of the northwest at 10-15 m.p.h. These were perfect soaring conditions for Lookout Mountain! I was anxious to fly, but had one thing to do before I went skyward. It was time for Charger to receive her freedom, for the second time. The first time was probably accidental and she did not have all the skills she needed to survive. This time, I felt that she was better prepared and was ready to have a real chance at surviving in the wild. I drove up to the launch and there were about twenty hang gliders in the air. Several of my friends greeted me and asked if I were going to fly. I told them I had something special to do first and put on my falconer's glove. Charger was in a sky kennel, like the ones used by airlines to ship dogs and cats. She was fairly quiet and I reached in and grabbed both legs, just above the feet. She squealed and chirped in protest, but quieted down as soon as she saw the cliff and mountain's edge. A number of spectators were watching the gliders fly and focused their attention on Charger and me. Several people asked, some with anger in their voices, what I was doing with the hawk.

I replied, "Returning her freedom!"

This shut them all up.

In between glider launches, I stepped up to the edge of the launch pad, and on the count of three, tossed her skyward. She held her wings in until she reached the apex of the momentum from the toss. She then unfurled and began soaring the smooth, cool air. The assembled cheered. Time almost ceased as I stood in wonder and watched her work the invisible currents. I knew what it was like to do what she was doing. But (insert sound of an LP record being scratched), Charger made a huge tactical error. She turned downwind and flew into what is known as the rotor. This is an area directly behind a sharp cliff that produced a turbulent roll of wind. Charger hit this and resembled a dishtowel in a clothes dryer. For a few seconds there, I thought that a year's worth of work with Charger was literally going to come crashing down in failure. She did about three half rolls/tumbles until she flew out of the rotor and out of sight over the back of the mountain. It was a bittersweet moment. She was free, but it was hard to see her go. I later launched and soared for a while. I looked for Charger, but she was nowhere to be found. She was probably in a tree getting her bearings.

One month later, I was back at Lookout getting ready to enjoy some fabulous spring air. A pilot came up to me and said,

"Hey, you're the guy that released the hawk last month!"

I said, "Yeah" and that her name was Charger.

He said that he was on launch when I released her and that he got a pretty good look at her. He continued by saying that just a week ago, he flew with a hawk that looked just like Charger. He said that the bird had a band on it leg and flew pretty close to him.

117

He was pretty sure it was her. I hoped that it was. To this day, I've never heard anything more about her. I don't know of any band returned or number sent into the Banding Lab. Who knows, maybe she stayed around there and eventually found a mate. Perhaps, some thirty years later, some of the Red-tails that I occasionally fly with at Lookout are some of her grandchildren. Hopefully, she didn't end up in someone else's backyard or worse yet, at the local kennel. Godspeed to you Charger and all of your kin!

Chapter 20

The Tapp House Ghost

In one of the earlier chapters, I mentioned a veterinary student named Mark Caspermeyer. He was an intern from the University of Missouri and had come to stay for about six weeks. The Zoo officials decided to put him up in one of the rooms of the Reserve Birdhouse, also known as the Tapp House. When I was introduced to Mark and found out where he was going to stay, I half-jokingly said,

"Watch out for the Tapp House ghost!"

He laughed and sheepishly asked,

"What ghost!?!"

I said,

"Oh, it's probably nothing, maybe nothing more than my over-active imagination".

I was trying to downplay it all. He inquired,

"Is there something really here?"

I then had to justify my jovial concerns. It all started in November of 1977, when I was a keeper in the Bird Section. I usually got to work an hour or two before anyone else and had my entire cage cleaning completed by the time the food was delivered. We did most of the food preparation in the kitchen of the Tapp House. Almost without exception, I was alone while getting the food ready. It usually took me about twenty minutes to make the individual pans of food. One morning, I had the distinct feeling that someone was behind me watching as I worked. I turned, expecting to see one of my co-workers, but there was be no one there, at least, in the physical sense.

This went on for several weeks with the same results; no one there. I didn't think too much about it until the day I was the late keeper assigned to lock the birdhouse. I was in the living room of the Tapp House burning time by reading a magazine. Suddenly, the door to the incubator room, in the middle of the house, slammed shut! I went back to investigate, expecting to see either a guard or the back door opened by a gust of wind. I saw and found neither and experienced a strange cold feeling.

"Hello, is there anybody here?!?" I nervously inquired.

No answer. I went and checked the back door and it was dead bolted shut with the chain attached to its holder. No windows were opened either. It was a cold day and there was no reason to have the windows opened. I then opened the door to the incubator room, with one eye closed from the fear of what I might see. To my relief and then my concern…zip, nada, nothing but a room full of dormant incubators and the lingering cold presence. I looked in the bathroom across the hall, no one there. I decided to go lock the Birdhouse early that day. This situation was a little too spooky to hang around for another ten minutes.

The next day, I arrived a little later than my usual hour early time. I cleaned one section of the birdhouse and went up to the Tapp House to prepare food when a few of the other keepers arrived. The first person in was Buster Bradshaw. Buster was a curly-headed, cheerful fellow and he inquired why I wasn't ready to take my first break and why I wasn't ready to make the birds' afternoon food (implying that I was usually way early). I explained to Buster what had happened the previous day. He quipped in his Mississippi drawl,

"Aw, it was probably just the win' or some logical explunation".

"No Buster, I checked all of the possible angles for answers, but came up with none." I replied.

To this, Buster mockingly replied,

"Whoooooooo!," his voice rising in a ghoulish tone while he wriggled his fingers near his head.

To that I said, "You can make fun of me if you want, but I know something happened here that has no physical explanation".

Buster saw that I was serious and this was unusual, since Buster and I usually joked around with each other. I told a few more of the keepers, too, and the looks were the same as if they were saying,

"John, you've been working a little too hard and not getting enough sleep!"

The next morning, I decided to try to blow off the incident and got to work at my usual time. Again, the presence was there while I prepared the morning food. I looked over my shoulder several times, half expecting to see something or someone and mostly hoping that I wouldn't. I probably made morning food in record time and went down to feed the birds in my care at the birdhouse. Nothing more took place until a few weeks later.

One morning, I went to work at my usual time on to find Buster Bradshaw in the employee lounge waiting for me.

"Hello Buster, you're here early", I exclaimed.

"John, I need ta tell you sumthin. Yesturdee, I wuz tha late keeper and I wuz in the Tapp House waitin' to lock the Birdhouse. I wuz readin' a magazine, not Playbowie as you might think, an' suddenly the door to tha inkabaiter room slammed!"

I nodded in a knowing way. Buster continued,

"I thought you wuz playin' a trick on me and I jokinly went back there saying, aw right, come on out John! But nuthin'! Tha back door wuz locked, tha windas wuz locked and I thought, damn, this is spooky an' I'm gettin' outa here!"

"So, the door slammed while you were there?" I asked.

"Yeah, I made funna ya, but sumthin' definitely happened yesturdee. I'm sorry for not believin' ya".

"Well, I think that there is something supernatural taking place here, but I'm not sure what", I added.

"I wunner if sum'one died in here?" Buster mused. I continued,

"Yeah, I was thinking about that possibility, too! I know that none of the Tapps have died. Possibly it could be someone before the Tapp family lived here".

The next day, I talked to Henry Carter. Henry was a frail little man with his head bigger than the rest of his body. He had been at the zoo since the late 1950's and he knew its history. I asked him if anyone had died in the Tapp House and he said,

"Oh yeah, Mrs. Gray killed herself in the back bedroom of the house. It was a real mess! I had to go up there and clean her brains off the wall!"

Hmmm, pretty interesting! I asked Henry if anyone had ever seen anything in the house.

"You mean a ghost?!? Oh, one day all them Tapp kids came pouring outta the house saying they saw a ghost, but I think their imaginations were in high gear. I don't believe in that kinda stuff."

Maybe there was something to all those feelings and door slammings after all. I did a little more investigation into Mrs. Gray's death. It seems that Mrs. Gray had a degenerative spinal disorder that was causing her extreme pain. On the night of her death, a big zoo party was in swing. Mrs. Gray was despondent that she couldn't attend the party. Mr. Gray, her husband, who was also the Zoo Director, had come to check on her and found her dead with gun in hand. Interestingly enough, only a few months after her death, Mr. Gray married the zoo secretary. They apparently were having an affair and now Mrs. Gray was conveniently out of the way. Something didn't jibe here.

Over the next several months things started happening to other people. One of the oddest things to happen was when a number of young Wood Ducklings were moved from one room to another. Every year, we received a number of wild Wood Ducklings from the surrounding neighborhoods. We had about twenty or so in a rearing pen in one of the converted bedrooms. We also had a similar pen in the adjacent room, but it was empty. I was working with Tuli Ross that day and she had prepared a tray of food for the ducklings.

"John, will you take this pan of food to the Wood Ducks?" she asked.

So I did, the only thing was that the ducks were not in the pen.

"Tuli, where are the little Woodies?" I inquired.

"Right there in the pen in front of you, you goofball!" she said mockingly.

"This pen?!?" I pointed straight ahead to the empty pen.

"Yeah, that pen!" she replied, almost sternly.

"There aren't any Woodies here",

I said and with this Tuli replied,

"There has to be, I counted them all this morning!"

With this, she came from the kitchen into the room. With a little shock, Tuli began looking around the room, saying…

"They have to be here, they were here this morning!"

Young Wood Ducks can jump fairly well, so there was the possibly that they had all jumped out of the pen. We both searched the room, to no avail. I happened to glance into the other room that had a similar pen and there were the Wood Ducklings!

"Hey Tuli, look! Here are the ducklings," I exclaimed.

"Alright John, that was real funny! You had me going there for a few minutes".

123

I responded "Tuli, I didn't put them there!"

"Yeah, right!" she said, looking a little puzzled.

"Well, if you didn't put them in the pen, who did?"

That was the question of the day. Somehow, all of the Wood Ducks were in that pen. Tuli and I were the only keepers working in the area that day.

"Maybe, it was Mrs. Gray who moved the ducks", I dryly and seriously responded.

Tuli shot back, "You're kidding, right?"

"Halfway" I continued, "but do you have an explanation other than one of us having a brain fade?"

We were at a loss.

On two different occasions, something or somebody held me and then a co-worker in the bathroom. I had gone into the Tapp House bathroom to do the usual thing one does in the bathroom. After completion and the required hand washing, I went to go out and after unlocking the door and turning the knob, I felt someone on the other side holding the door. It felt as though someone had his or her foot near the bottom of the door and a stiff arm in the middle. I tried several times to force the door open, but couldn't. I started laughing and said,

"Okay Tuli, you can let me out now!"

Still, there was resistance on the other side of the door. I then commented,

"Okay, I'll just stay in here the rest of the day and if anyone needs me, you know where I am".

I tried the door one more time. This time, it opened very easily. I ran out and around the corner, intent on catching Tuli, but she wasn't there. I looked in several of the rooms, but she was not to be found.

"Come on out!" I exclaimed.

Still, no Tuli. I finally went out the front door and there I saw her. She was walking from the direction of the concession stand with a cup of iced Coke in her hand. There was no way she could have been holding the door to the bathroom!

"Hey, what's up, you look a little worried!" Tuli quipped.

"Well, someone was holding the door to the bathroom closed and I naturally assumed it was you. Obviously, it wasn't!" I nervously replied.

We both went and checked the door several times, with both Tuli and I checking if we could get the door to stick. We couldn't and in fact, it opened easily every time. Tuli was still skeptical of what might have been taking place. I didn't care what she thought; something was definitely amiss.

About a month later, Barbara Larson, another bird keeper, came up to me and asked,

"John, were you holding the door to the bathroom this morning?"

"The Tapp House bathroom?" I inquired.

"Yes, the Tapp House bathroom. Please tell me you were holding the door shut!"

Barbara was obviously a little nervous.

"No, Barbara, I didn't hold you in the bathroom, but the same thing happened to me a month ago. I thought Tuli was playing a trick on me, but she had been at the concession stand".

Barbara continued,

"Yeah, I was talking to you while I was trying to open the door, you're such a prankster, and finally I was able to open the door and you were not there! I tried to get the door to stick shut, but it opened up as pretty as you please."

"Well, we obviously have a ghost who likes to play tricks!" I added.

Barbara had become a believer!

There were times that I felt the spirit's presence suddenly appear. It almost felt like a door opening and the spirit entered. One summer day, I was sitting in the living room of the Tapp House. I had a fan blowing at my back and one blowing from my left out of one of the rooms. I felt a very distinct, cold cell of air pass from my right to the left! It felt as though someone had walked past me! I immediately got goosebumps and felt the hair on my neck and arms stand on end. I began to get the feeling that she was trying to tell me something.

Earlier I mentioned Mark Caspermeyer, the vet student who stayed in the Tapp House for a while. Since the incubator room was air-conditioned, he decided to set up his bed here. I jokingly told him to watch out for the Tapp House ghost. We nervously chuckled, but soon after he started living there, things began to happen. He had just gone to bed one night, around 11 p.m. He then heard the sound of someone walking down the hall. He said that it almost sounded like someone in house shoes! He waited for the person to pass and quickly opened his door, expecting to see me! Nothing and no one!

"Alright, John, I know it's you, come on out!" Mark exclaimed.

He looked around the house, hoping to see a guard or someone living. All the doors were locked with the safety chains across them! He got a little spooked and had trouble going back to sleep that night. The next night, at approximately the same time, 11:00 p.m., the same thing happened again! Mark searched the house to no avail. For a little while, Mark stayed at my house. He eventually met a girl and started staying at the Tapp House again. He still heard the footsteps and used them to get closer to his girlfriend.

Perhaps the most chilling event occurred in 1980. This year, we had a young Chilean Flamingo hatch in one of our incubators. This required us to hand raise it. It was named Clifford, in honor of

Cliff Ross, the Bird Curator. For a while it had to be fed every two hours. Then it only began to feed when certain people fed it; Beth McLain and me. If Clifford didn't eat at his 4 o'clock feeding, either Beth or I had to go in later to feed him. On some of those late feedings, I felt the presence of Mrs. Gray. The thing I dreaded to do the most was to open the front door, reach in and flip on the light switch. I was always afraid that she would touch my hand when I did this. Sometimes, I felt her presence as soon as I entered the house. I simply said out loud,

"I know you're here, I just don't want to see you. If I see you, I'll probably have a heart attack and there will be two of us here!"

Sometimes, I didn't feel a thing. The times I did feel her, I got a strong mental message that she did not kill herself and that she was murdered. Of course, this may have just been speculation on my part.

One night, as soon as I went in the house, she was there. The feeling usually followed me for a short time and was gone. This time, however, it stayed with me the entire time I prepared the food and took it back to the room where Clifford was. This was also the same room in which Mrs. Gray was found dead. As I fed the flamingo, the feeling of her presence got stronger and stronger. It felt as though a living person was standing next to me. This feeling was almost electric and I got a little spooked. We had a piece of butcher paper taped on the window. This was so something outside the house wouldn't scare the bird. Suddenly, the paper pulled away from the window in a big curl and landed right next to my feet! That was it for my feeding attempt!

"You're not eating tonight",

I told Clifford as I left the room, the house and the zoo post haste. I went home and had a beer!

In 1983, The Tapp House burned. The cause of the fire was due to poor wiring. All of the birds inside, including a talking crow named Jacque, were killed. They were either killed directly by the fire or from smoke inhalation. I went through the still-smoking rubble along with several other keepers.

"I hope this frees you", I said out loud.

Tuli asked, "Who were you talking to?"

"Mrs. Gray", I replied.

Tuli looked at me, this time, with an almost acknowledging nod. Still, she never truly believed that there was a spirit there. A few nights later, Jim Mulhern, one of the night guards, saw a women-like figure amongst the rubble. As soon as he came in view, the figure darted into a clump of privet hedge. He thought the figure was a student from the college across the street from the zoo. Part of the initiation process of one of the fraternities was to go into the zoo and bring back something of proof that one was there.

"Okay, come on out and you won't be in any trouble", Mulhern assured the "student".

Jim had a clear view into the hedge, since it was backlit by a streetlight. The hedge shook for a few seconds and stopped. Mulhern approached the bush and to his astonishment, no one was there! He quickly walked completely around the hedge, shining his light all around the area. Nothing! He searched all around the area. No one was there! A few weeks later, the remains of the house were bulldozed and grass seeds were sown. Perhaps Mrs. Gray had some peace.

After the Tapp House was leveled, odd things started to happen in the Aquarium. The zoo's aquarium was the only place where a separate admission was charged. The .25 cents per person went into an animal purchase fund. Even on the coldest days, when hardly anybody visited the zoo, a cashier had to be posted in the aquarium. One by one, the cashiers began coming to me. They all had the same troubled look. Three cashiers came to me with the exact story. It seems that the turnstile by the cash register turned on its own, and not just one or two rotations! It turned a number of times, as if a number of people were passing through at once. Obviously, this unnerved the cashiers and one lady said that she got up, went outside and had a smoke to calm her nerves.

Keepers in the aquarium said that they would come into the building and noticed that all of the air was turned off to the tanks on one side of the building. This happened for about a week. They also reported sounds of a heavy object hitting the floor in the back, only to find everything in place when they investigated. Another time, the keepers heard someone in the employee restroom and it sounded as though someone was washing their hands. After a quick head count, they realized that it wasn't one of them. Finally, the "person" stopped moving around in the bathroom. One of the bravely elected keepers opened the door to find nothing! There was a small vent window at the top of the bathroom, but it was too small for anyone to exit from the room.

One more incident occurred in the Aquarium. One day, several keepers and the Assistant Curator of Reptiles, Walter Douglas, were having lunch in the service area of the Aquarium. Walter was standing, talking to two of the keepers, Jean Evans and Barbara Larson. Barbara and Jean said that Walter turned to look behind him, as if he were looking for something. Walter then turned back around with a look of surprise and shock.

"What's wrong, Walter?" Barbara asked. "I thought somebody behind me grabbed my arm!"

Obviously, no one was there and this greatly troubled Walter. He later recounted the incident.

"John, it felt as though someone had grabbed my arm, like this", Walter demonstrated by grasping my arm on the bicep.

"When I looked around and no one was there, it scared me!"

Walter continued, "If I could have turned white, I'm sure I would have!"

Walter is an African-American man, so his comment really emphasized his point. This spirit had a physical aspect to it.

Perhaps, one of the most compelling physical encounters occurred about a year after I had left the zoo. I had returned for one of my many visits and as soon as I came through the gate, the Guard, Jim Mulhern, met me.

"John, boy have I been waiting to talk to you!"

Jim had a bit of concern in his voice.

"What's up?" I asked.

"Do you have time for a cup of coffee", Jim queried.

"Yeah, I always have time for coffee", I responded.

We went to the main concession stand, got our coffee and found a table. Jim started,

"John, I had the strangest thing happen to me a few weeks ago. I was doing my rounds of the east end of the zoo. I went to check the waterfowl lot to make sure all the birds were safe."

A fence surrounded the waterfowl lot. On top of the fence was an electric cable that was energized at night. This was there to keep raccoons from entering the waterfowl exhibit. Before the use of the electric cable, raccoons had killed a number of incubating birds, including swans, geese and flamingos. The exhibit had an L-shaped walkway with a gazebo in the middle. On each end of the walkway was a gate that was closed at night and each closed gate completed the electric circuit. The guard turned on the electricity at the beginning of the shift and the waterfowl keeper turned off the current in the morning. The cable was very effective and no birds were lost after its installation. A side note: a figure, a woman dressed in blue had been seen by the waterfowl lot and reported by several guards over several years. All of the guards were unable to

130

explain this apparition that vanished after it was spotted. Mulhern continued,

"I had just turned off the electricity and began walking down the east walkway. Suddenly, I felt someone grab my right shoulder and began to pull me off balance and off my feet. As I was falling backwards, I pulled my nightstick to counter the intruder and swung it, expecting to make contact. I only met air! There was no one there! I quickly got to my feet and shined my light, looking for my assailant. I searched all of the bushes and only saw ducks and geese. I can't explain this at all, but I was definitely being pulled off my feet by something!"

Jim had a serious look in his eyes.

"Man, that's incredible! I guess there's something to the Lady in Blue thing, huh?!?" I exclaimed.

"If it was her, she's pretty strong!" Jim chuckled.

We both shook our heads and finished our coffee. In all of this, we knew we had experienced something supernatural. There were no physical explanations for any of the events that happened at the zoo. All of the people to whom these things happened, including me, became believers in something beyond our physical realm. Now, most of the people these events happened to have either left the zoo or have retired, but odd things and sightings continue to happen at the zoo. It sad to think that Mrs. Gray is still uneasy, perhaps still looking for an answer. I hope maybe one day she will find her eternal peace.

Chapter 21

1980-The Year of Indecision

We were driving each other crazy. My wife had had enough of my zoo job. I was spending a lot of time at work; partially because I loved my job, partially because I did not want to spend as much time at home. Debbie had become jealous of my work and even proclaimed that she almost wished that I were having an affair with a woman. At least she could be mad at a person. In turn, she complained a lot about my time at work. I didn't know what to do. I tried to spend more time with her, but half of it was spent arguing. This, in turn, made me not want to spend as much time with her. Our life together was becoming like a basset hound chasing its tail. Meanwhile, we had been trying to get Debbie pregnant. She had wanted a child for several years and I figured a baby would make her happy. Maybe, too, she could focus her attention on the child and less so on me. This may have been selfish on my part. I was beginning to realize that I perhaps had gotten married too soon. After a few months of mulling things over, I made a decision.

One January day, I decided to leave Debbie. I was very unhappy and I needed to get away from her before I lost my sanity. I had spoken to my co-worker Buster Bradshaw, about moving in with him, at least on a temporary basis. Buster was recently divorced and was very agreeable with my query about living quarters. Throughout the day, I rehearsed what I wanted to say to Debbie. I went over and over the possible scenarios in my head. She had gone to the doctor to see why her back was bothering her.

I had gotten home about thirty minutes before she did. About five o'clock, Debbie pulled her silver Chevette into the carport. Filled with dread, I awaited her entrance through the door. I had never broken up with someone before today. I was always on the one who heard, "We need to talk!" Debbie turned the knob and walked through the door. Before I could say, "We need to talk", Debbie said,

"Hey, you know I went to the doctor today, and guess what? I'm pregnant!"

I didn't have much to say other than,

"That's great!"

The rest of our conversation was a blur. I was completely stunned! What a turn of events! I had prepared myself for exiting my marriage and beginning a new life and now I was contemplating my future with a new human life and my same wife! I was stuck and couldn't figure a way out of my situation. I decided to stay with Debbie. After all, it was going to be my child, too, and I wasn't going to duck my responsibilities as a father. Maybe, too, this pregnancy would shift Debbie's attention from me to the new life inside her. Something had to change besides Debbie's girth. The next day, I told Buster that I had decided to stay with Debbie because she was pregnant.

"Bummer man, I mean, good deal, I think", was Buster's reply.

"My thoughts exactly, my friend", I said with resignation in my voice.

"Really, I hope it works out for ya, but the room's still there if ya need it".

Buster's words of consolation did little to coat my confused state. Instead of celebrating a new life, I felt like someone had died; me!

Over the next few months, little had changed, except for Debbra, of course. I spent just as much time at work, maybe even more so. Debbie was excited about the coming child and started preparing the nest for the arrival. However, instead of her attention being focused away from me, she seemed to step up her verbal attacks. My home situation continued to decline and it was getting harder to stay there. The time was near to do something about it.

I talked to Buster Bradshaw to see if he if he still had a room available. He did and I only had to convince myself that leaving Debbie was the right thing to do. I mean, after all, she was pregnant and how could I leave someone, especially my wife, in this condition? However, I was very miserable and staying for more verbal abuse was not in my best interest. I was starting to feel very trapped, not unlike a fox caught in a leg-hold. I was close to chewing off my leg to get away from the situation. I weighed all the possible scenarios; certainly divorce was a great possibility with abandonment as the main charge against me. Ridicule, from my family and friends was a concern. Finances would be a challenge, since I would have to pay rent at Buster's and my share of the bills with Debbie. The hardest thing would be living with my conscience. I knew it was wrong to leave, but, at the same time, it was wrong for me to stay. My mental health couldn't take much more. This was one of the most agonizing decisions of my young adult life. I was twenty-four years old. I knew there was more to life than this. I needed to be happy again, no matter what it took to achieve this lofty goal. Later in the day at work, I found Buster and told him I would take the room. I got home from work and packed my essential belongings. Waiting for Debbie to get home seemed to last an eternity!

Debbie arrived from work and I rose to meet her as she came through the door. She was now six months pregnant and was really starting to show. Apparently, I had a worried look on my face.

"What's wrong with you!" Debbie asked.

"I, um, am, ah, leaving you, Debbie!"

I couldn't believe I had said those words.

"Yeah, sure, you're kidding, right?!"

"No, I'm not, I can't handle it here anymore! I've got to get out before I go crazy," I sadly replied.

Debbie, with anger and disbelief said,

"You go crazy?! I'm the one who's pregnant here, carrying your baby and spending time by myself while you're at that stupid zoo! I should be the one who's crazy, not you! Fine, go ahead and leave and I'll get you for abandonment!"

She didn't think I was serious and didn't believe me until I picked up my suitcase and opened the carport door. Before exiting, I turned and looked at her and said,

"I'll be at Buster's".

The last thing I saw as I shut the door was Debbie crying and running towards the bedroom. I had either just made one big step towards freedom or one huge mistake. I walked out to my Vega, threw my suitcase in and drove to Buster's house. I was overwhelmed with guilt and a strange sense of relief. As I turned onto Buster's street, I broke into uncontrollable, guttural sobbing. Freedom felt very sad!

My first night at Buster's was hard for me. Debbie called several times all the while crying and begging me to come home. I explained that I couldn't come home at the time. I was wrestling with my conscience and my emotions. I felt I had done the wrong thing, and halfway thought about going back to Debbie. But, I wanted to try living on my own for a while. I had not lived on my own, ever. I went from living with my parents to being married. I needed to clear my mind and being without the tension and conflict would help. The next day, when Debbie was at work, I went and got more of my belongings. It was hard to go home, especially thinking that I might not be living here again. I got what I needed and left before anyone saw me. I almost felt like a stranger. I guess I was trying to emotionally detach myself from the situation. I got my stuff and drove back to Buster's house. On the way, I stopped and got a six-pack of Miller. I wasn't one for drinking a lot. Over the next six months, that was going to change!

The next week, Debbie's tone changed from sorrow and disbelief to anger. Apparently, she had called my parents and told them what was happening. One night, soon afterwards, I got an angry, reaming phone call from my parents. I guess I spent an hour listening to how shocked they were and how bad I was for leaving Debbie and how spoiled I was and always wanted my way. I was feeling like a real sh*t. But, they didn't know about the browbeatings that I had endured long before Debbie became pregnant. They didn't understand what it was like to listen to someone ridicule you, nearly every day, for what you believed. Only after I finally got to tell my side of the story, did their attitudes change. They had a little clearer idea what was going on with me. I told them that I didn't know how long I was going to be away from home. But, for my sanity and peace of mind, this is what I had to do. I also told them that I was going to keep up my financial obligations to Debbie. I reassured them that I would be there for the baby, even though I might not be there for Debbie. I told them that I was going to be okay and that I was sorry for my timing in this situation.

"Well, we're sorry we jumped to conclusions, Son!" my Father replied.

My Mother added,

"We're here for both of you, but please consider going back home!"

"I have to sort everything out right now and I couldn't do this at home with her", I reassured. They ended their conversation with,

"We love you!"

I knew that they did. If only I were as sure of my feelings for Debbie.

Moving out was the best and worst thing that could have happened to me. I still had a lot of guilty feelings, but I also felt very free. Living at Buster's at first was a lot of fun. We nightly consumed quite a number of de-inhibiting liquids. In fact, I drank more in the first week than I had in the previous year. I eventually moved from Buster's house in Frayser, which was about 25 minutes away from work. I relocated to a house about five blocks from the zoo with two co-workers, Dan MacDoogal and Frank Eck. Dan was the Assistant Curator of Mammals, but was a reptile man who took a promotion. Frank was a soft-spoken Mammal Keeper who worked in the Petting Zoo. They had a spare room that they rented me for $100 a month. The house was eventually dubbed "Williford House". It was on Williford Street in Mid-town Memphis. The location was perfect. It was close to work and close to Overton Square where a lot of restaurants, bars and shops were located. I frequented many of these establishments after work. Also being close to work, I saved money on gas and allowed me to spend more time at work if I wanted.

For the next several months, I saw several women and hung out with some of the Zoo's best partiers. I had been spending a lot of time with several people from work. We'd usually go hit a bar after work and would find a place with some live music. This group also became soccer fans as Memphis had a team in the North American Soccer League. The team was named the Rogues and its mascot was a rogue elephant. It was only right that a crew from the zoo should lend its support. The promotional office of the Rogues had several gimmick or promotion nights to draw fans. The Zoo Crews' favorite was 25-cent beer night. The joke for me was I could get drunk for fifty cents! Well, not quite, but by 75 cents, I was feeling pretty good. I also really enjoyed soccer and looked forward to the games.

One Saturday night rolled around and I found my way to Richard Weeks' house. Richard was the Curator of Education. His house was an old two story Victorian style home that was common to Midtown Memphis. The house used to be white, but was now rather grayish due to the peeling paint and the exposed wood. I knocked on the partially opened door and was greeted with a chorus of,

"Come in! We're all upstairs".

I wound my way up the staircase and entered what was sure to be the kitchen. Upon entry, I was surprised to see that there were roaches, hundreds of them! Roaches were on the wall, the ceiling, the floor, the table, the couch, everywhere! It was the Orkin man's dream! I didn't want to stop walking for fear of becoming roach food or at least an exit vehicle. I had a six pack of beer in my hand and Richard, said,

"There's room in the fridge for your brews".

I opened the fridge door and once again, roaches. Damn! I have nothing personal against roaches but I believe what we had here was a fully blown infestation! I almost expected to see a bunch of roaches on the couch with the TV remote watching their favorite show. I pulled one of the beers from the plastic ring, set the remainder in the fridge and said to the roaches,

"If you can figure out how to open 'em, you can have 'em!"

I thought I heard one say,

"Alright, but shut the door! You're letting out all of the air conditioning!"

Everyone was out on the porch, no doubt to get away from the insects. I found my way out to the porch and leaned against the door stoop. I still had to watch the entomology exhibit that was going on inside the house. Richard noticed my fascination with the roaches.

"Yeah, I have a few extra critters running around the place!"

At that point, everyone burst out laughing…"a few!" someone exclaimed,

"Try a few THOUSAND!"

At that point, I noticed that a huge, seven-legged, fifty-cent-piece size roach near my feet. Right then, Richard said,

"Cheech!"

It seems that he had named this one Cheech after the famous comedian. He said that Cheech came out when everyone was smoking weed and someone always blew marijuana smoke on him. Conveniently, someone was smoking a number and sure enough, blew the roach a "shotgun". Cheech stood there for a number of minutes and then slowly walked towards the kitchen. No doubt he had the munchies and was looking for something to eat. Looking back, it was funny and ironic; a stoned roach!

For the next few months, the partying continued. September saw the beginnings of autumn. I continued to drop by to give my wife support money, but I had no intentions to get back with her. She was in the final phase of her pregnancy and was anxious to give birth. During this time, I had a dream that told me that I would have a daughter who will be born on my mother's birthday, September 12th. It was also Debbie's birthday, too. The dream even gave a precise time; 3:30 in the afternoon. I was curious to see if this came true.

September 12th, I got a call from Debbie's friend, Jackie Johnson. She said that Debbie had gone into labor and was at Baptist Hospital. I took the rest of the day off and went down to the waiting room. I had gotten there on time; it was 2:30. Debbie's parents were there and after a few awkward moments, they warmed up to me. Mr. Davis said that they were glad I was there and I apologized for the situation. They both understood since they had recently gotten back together after being divorced for several years. An hour or so had passed, but still no word of a birth.

It was now a little after 4:30, still nothing. About ten minutes later, a nurse came to the waiting room and asked for the people who were here with Debbie Stokes. We all waved our hands and I said that I was her husband. She said that Debbie had given birth about ten minutes ago, at 4:30, to a healthy baby girl. My first thought was "Well, the prediction missed by one hour". But wait a minute, it was 4:30 Daylight Savings Time. So it was 3:30 after all. The nurse then stated that she'd be ready for viewing in about 20 minutes. Mr. and Mrs. Davis congratulated and hugged me and I thanked them and Jackie for their help.

I said, "Her name, I guess, is Lendi Marie. That's the name Debbie had chosen if we had a girl."

Everybody looked at me and nodded. In about thirty minutes the nurse told us we could go down to the viewing area to see the newborns. We got down there and they had about twenty babies lined up, buffet style. I tried to guess which one was Lendi, only to wildly miss; I chose an African-American boy to be Lendi. Mr. Davis saw her first and said,

"Here's the Stokes baby".

I went down to the window. There she was. Not really too different looking than the rest; pinkish, wrinkly, rather non-descript. It was hard to believe that I had a daughter, but there she was. I had seen some baby primates at the zoo and marveled how much they looked like humans. As I looked at Lendi, I marveled how much she looked like a little orangutan! Despite that, I began to realize that the baby in front of me was my daughter. It almost didn't seem real. I wasn't really ready to have a child, but there was no going back either. I didn't seem responsible enough to be a father, but it was a job description that I had better get used to.

Still, having a child wasn't enough to want to go back home. After all, I had gotten used to the freedom I had. But then again, I was now a father. Thus began my period of real internal turmoil and guilt.

I waited for another hour and the nurse came down and said that they were getting ready to take the Stokes baby to her mother. We all shuffled to the elevator that took us to Debbie's room. I felt a little awkward, since I was the dick who left his pregnant wife. When we got to the room, Lendi was already with Debbie. Debbie was aglow with her new motherhood, and now she was beaming with our newborn daughter at her side. She looked at me with a half glare, half sigh of relief and said,

"Here's your daughter."

I moved up for a closer look. It was still hard to believe that I was now a father and that I had a daughter. I stayed a few minutes longer and soon left. The tension between Debbie and me was pretty high and I didn't want to stay around too much more than I had to. Perhaps I felt guilty and didn't want to discuss our situation. Even though Lendi had arrived, I wasn't ready to return to Debbie.

Now that she was here, I tried to see Lendi as often as I could. I was still very painful to go see her. Debbie would ask me when I was finally going to settle down and come home. I still wasn't ready to do that. I still had too much "freedom" to explore. Still, guilt continued to nag me. On one of my visits, I had the opportunity to take Lendi outside in the moonlight. I had seen something on the TV miniseries "Roots" that I wanted to do with Lendi. Kunta Kente's father took him out into the full-moonlight when he was a small infant. He held him up to the heavens and presented him to the Universe. I did the same with Lendi and presented her to my departed ancestors and the Universe. I brought her back inside and Debbie wanted to know what I was doing.

I said, "Just showing her the moon".

"Do you think she got anything out of that?" Debbie queried.

"Well, it was just a pretty night and I wanted her to see the moon".

I knew she wouldn't understand. It was a special moment though, and when Lendi was older and understood what I did, she thought it pretty special, too!

Chapter 22

1980 Part 2-Osprey Hacking

In 1980, the Memphis Zoo participated in an Osprey hacking project. The Tennessee Wildlife Resources Agency was interested in restoring several species of raptors in the State including the Bald Eagle, Osprey, Peregrine Falcon and Mississippi Kite. Hacking is where a young bird of prey is placed in an artificial nest in suitable habitat and is fed without human contact. The bird is usually a month away from flight. The idea behind hacking is: the area where a raptor makes its first flight, will be the area or region it returns to nest as an adult. In this way, hacking can restore populations that have been extirpated from an area. In 1980, the Osprey was still listed as an Endangered Species in Tennessee. On the whole, the Osprey was slowly recovering from DDT pesticide poisoning. DDT was banned in '72, but it took a number of years of affected populations to rebound. There were very few nesting pairs of Ospreys in Tennessee in 1980. I agreed to place a young pair on a hack tower about 15 minutes from the zoo. The location was Kilowatt Lake, an oxbow of the Wolf River that runs along the northern perimeter of Memphis. The area was still fairly wild and the lake was deep enough to support a number of species of fish that the Osprey could utilize. Kilowatt Lake also was deep enough to support high horsepower "cigarette" boat races. These races were held sporadically and didn't affect the Osprey program. However, one factor did; the temperature!

The summer of 1980 has gone into the books as one of the hottest summers in Memphis' history. In August, there were 21 days of 100 degree plus temperatures in Memphis. Unfortunately for the young Ospreys, this record heat occurred at the worst time. In early August, two young Ospreys (also known as the Fish Hawk) were taken from their nest in the Chesapeake Bay area of Virginia and transferred to the Kilowatt location. They were about four weeks old at the time. Ospreys sometimes produce four young per year, so removing these two did not have a significant impact on the local population. Besides, the Chesapeake population was well on its way to recovery and could tolerate removal of a few of its young. Tennessee had about twenty-four of the Virginia Ospreys relocated to 12 hack towers across the state. West Tennessee had two towers, one at Kilowatt in Memphis and one at Reelfoot Lake about 100 miles to the north. Reelfoot had several pairs of Ospreys that were nesting; the additional two birds would be welcome additions. There were no Ospreys nesting in the Memphis area, but many were spotted every spring and fall on migration. There were a number of potential nesting areas, but there were no birds left to occupy these places. Hacking was the best way to bring back the Osprey in the region.

The two Kilowatt birds arrived via David Ward, an agent from the Tennessee Wildlife Resources Agency and were placed in the lake side tower. This tower was only about twenty feet high and was built by topping an Eastern Sycamore tree. A wooden 6'x6' platform was built on top of the topped tree and on this platform was constructed a nest of sticks and grasses. I was concerned that the platform was not enclosed like many of the hacking stations I had used. I was worried that a Great Horned Owl could attack and eat the parent-less birds. I was also worried that the young would prematurely jump from the tower and get lost on the small peninsula where the tower was or drown in the nearby lake. My second fears were soon fulfilled.

144

I named the six-week old birds Ben and Lula after some local big time birders, Ben and Lula Coffey. Ben and Lula, the humans, were very active in the Mid-South bird watching scene and had accumulated a wealth of bird knowledge. Ben was also a bird bander and had discovered where Chimney Swifts were migrating in the fall. I thought it only appropriate to honor Ben and Lula by naming these first pioneer Ospreys after them. Both of the young Ospreys looked fine, initially, but I noticed when we took Ben out of his transport carrier that his left wing drooped. I got the wildlife officer to hold the bird while I gently felt the wing. I felt the unmistakable crunching of broken bones as I felt the ulna and radius area of Ben's wing. Both felt broken. Sometimes only one of the two bones is broken, so the unbroken bone acts as support for the broken one. All one needs to do is wrap the wing for a few weeks until it heals. Unfortunately, these breaks felt very bad. The agent said that this Osprey had jumped from the nest when they went to get him, so the break probably occurred when it landed.

We went ahead and put Lula on the platform and gave her a herring to eat. I felt very bad leaving her here by herself, especially since the tower did not have protective sides or a top. It was starting to get late, probably about half an hour before sunset, and the mosquitoes were looking for some blood to drain. I drove back to the Zoo and wrapped Ben's wing to prevent further injury. He whistled defiantly as I applied the stretchy, self-sticking bandage called Vet Wrap. Now the wing couldn't be damaged any further, so I felt a little better about leaving Ben overnight. I also gave him a herring and he eagerly devoured it. I did have concerns for Lula. With no protective sides and the temperatures forecasted to be 100 degrees, I really worried that she may not be at the tower in the morning.

The next day, I got up earlier than normal and went to the hack site at daybreak. I had grabbed a couple of fish from the zoo the night before and had kept them in my fridge. Thank Sir Francis Tupper and his wonderful storage containers! Ever mindful that I was in Cottonmouth habitat, I walked carefully through the low vegetation towards the tower, especially since it was still a little dark. As I got within visual range, my heart began to race. I could not see Lula! Did a Great Horned Owl get her or had she jumped from the tower? These questions quickly went through my mind. But, just as soon as I was about to switch to panic mode, Lula popped her head over the edge of the platform and began to whistle in a very excited tone. She was alone in an unfamiliar setting, so I couldn't blame her for her distress.

"Don't worry girl, I'll be back in a little while with your breakfast!"

Yeah, I spoke to her as if she understood English…

"What is it Lassie?!? Is Timmy in the well again?" Well then, let's leave him in there a little while to teach his little dumb a$s a lesson!"

We talk to animals to, I guess, placate ourselves. I noticed that Lula was panting slightly. At 5:30 in the morning, it was nearly eighty degrees. The tower had a couple of 1"x8" boards to provide shade and these were looking woefully small. I fed her two large herring via a long handled pool skimmer. It was rather like playing lacrosse, except with fish. On the first attempt, both fish fell out of the basket before I could get them up in the tower. The second attempt resulted in the herring morphing into flying fish as I had too much momentum and catapulted the fish into the brush below the tower. After searching for five minutes in the still low morning light, I found both fish, which were "breaded" with leaf litter. No problem, I'd just wash them off in the lake. I wandered to the shore and nearly stepped on a water snake. I don't know who was more frightened, the snake or me! I'm not afraid of snakes at all, but early in the morning in an area known to have cottonmouths,

146

anything slithering one might tread upon could be a water moccasin!

With the fish rinsed, almost with my urine, I returned to the tower for one more try. I reloaded the basket and this time, I slowly raised the basket to hold the fish in place once I got closer to the platform, I increased my swing and presto! Two fish on the platform ("Do you wants some chips with your fish, Miss?"). As soon as the fish landed, Lula pounced on one and started eating. Satisfied with what I saw, I headed to the Zoo.

I went back to check Lula on my first break at 10 a.m. She was still on the platform and was panting a little heavier than the first time. It was close to ninety degrees. She was taking interest in her surrounding and was watching a muskrat swim in the lake below her platform. At least she was still on the platform. I went back to the zoo and checked Ben. He was eating well and Dr. Douglass set aside some time to examine his wing. The first obvious thing we did was to get an x-ray of the wing. The radiograph showed that both the ulna and radius were broken near the wrist joint. This was bad for two reasons. The first was that both bones were broken, so there was no "good" bone to support the broken one. The second reason this was bad was because a break near the joint is particularly hard to set and heal. Mike decided to pin the ulna, since it was larger, and hoped that the radius would align itself once the ulna was stabilized. No sooner was the decision made, we prepared Ben for surgery. Dr. Douglass gassed the Osprey with Halothane to make it drowsy. Once it was sleeping, he intubated the bird by placing an expandable plastic tube into the glottis. This was done to aid the bird in respiration and to insure that the proper amount anesthesia was flowing into the lungs. The glottis is an opening of the expanded trachea that terminates at the base of the tongue. With the tongue extended, a bird can breathe while swallowing large chunks of food. A

147

mammal would surely choke to death if it tried to eat the same portions.

Next, he removed the feathers on the area of the wing where the incision was to occur. Mike checked Ben to make sure he was truly "out", and then proceeded to make an inch wide cut near the wrist. When he was able to actually see the bones, Mike remarked that it was broken worst than the x-rays showed. Still, he continued with his plan to put a stainless steel "pin" into the hollow wing bone. The whole procedure took about thirty minutes. Near the end, Mike turned off the halothane and gave Ben pure oxygen to awaken him.

"Don't get your hopes up on this one", Mike prophetically proclaimed.

He wasn't too sure if the bones would even heal properly; even less certain that the bird would ever fly.

"Well, if nothing else, we could use him as an educational bird", I answered in an optimistic way.

Mike responded, "The biggest thing I am afraid of is a bone infection".

Ben began to slowly wake in my arms, so I placed him in one of the inside holding enclosures in the hospital. I was rather bummed. Here was a bird that had never flown in its life and probably never would. Still, I was determined to give him the best possible chance.

Meanwhile, the temperature continued to climb. The forecast was for highs in the upper 90's to low 100's. It is not unusual in Memphis for the temps to be in this range at this time of the year. But the forecast for the next week didn't indicate that it was to get any cooler. This posed a serious problem for the remaining Osprey. The tower didn't have a whole lot of shade. Over the next several days I checked Lula about four times a day. Even at the first check at around 6:30 a.m., she was already panting. The temperatures were already in the low nineties at this time of the day. To give her additional fluid, I took a large syringe and filled the fish with water. This made the sunfish look like puffers. By about the fifth day, Lula came up with her own solution to the heat.

I had checked on her on my way into work at 6:30 and by the time I had returned to feed her at 11 a.m., she was gone! I first thought that she was resting low in the platform, so I catapulted the fish into the nest. I didn't see her stand or whistle, which she usually did. Halfway out of curiosity, and halfway out of fear, I climbed to the platform. She wasn't there! I immediately scanned the ground below for signs of her, but didn't see anything. My first thought was that perhaps a Red-tailed Hawk had gotten her, but there was no sign of a struggle and any blood or feathers. I climbed down from the tree and began to search in a radius around the nest. I began to gradually search further and further from the nest when something told me to look out in the water. Sure enough, there she was floating as if it were the normal thing for an Osprey to do. I made my way to the shore directly in front of her and she swam or more actually, rowed to shore with her wings. She whistled angrily in protest as I grabbed her and made my way back to the platform. It was very awkward to climb the tree while holding her feet and body, but I somehow got her back on the platform. She shook herself to remove some of the water from her plumage and then pounced on one of the sunfish water balloons I had for her food. I was soon to realize that this was to become her daily routine. By 12 p.m., it was already 100 degrees. The heat was tough on man and bird.

Lula pretty well had her routine down in that she was on the nest in the morning and by noon she was doing her best Ester Williams impersonation. This apparently worked to cool her for the rest of the day, because she was on the platform when I checked her in the afternoon and evening. The heat continued, too.

149

It was now going into its second week of 100+ degrees. One day, the temperature had reached 109 degrees! Lula seemed to be unfettered by it all. This day, however, her routine had changed. I came to check her around eleven and she wasn't in her usual places, either in the water or along the shore. I checked and rechecked the vegetation along the shore and found nothing. Suddenly, I heard her distinctive whistle across from the tower in a small cove. I had first thought that she had jumped and swam across to the other side, but as soon as that idea was formulated, I was proven very wrong.

I saw a large bird take off from a small tree across the way. At first I thought that it was a Red-tailed Hawk that had come to attack her. The bird began flying towards my general direction and started a distinctive Osprey whistle. It was Lula. She had fledged! She gracefully landed on top of the hack tower and peered over the edge at me. She whistled again and I was so happy to see this that I almost cried (not a sissy whimper, but one of those "almost cries" when your favorite team win a championship or when you slip off the pedals while riding a bike). It was a proud moment, one I wasn't sure she would make it to. She had been at the tower a little over ten days and she was now flying. My job now was to continue providing food until I knew she was catching her own fish. At least now I knew she was not going to be in the water. She could also seek shade in some of the taller trees. I returned to the zoo, feeling pretty good. It was 105 in the shade!

Meanwhile, Ben's wing was healing, but the x-rays didn't look quite right. The breaks were starting to calcify but the bones were looking a little thinner than they should. Mike wasn't too happy with what he saw. He added a calcium supplement powder to the fish. Ben always ate his fish and the supplement probably would not change his eating habits. I really felt bad for this bird. He was trying so hard, but it seems that life had dealt him a bad

150

hand. He just happened to be in the wrong nest at the wrong time. I guess in the end, the "next place" has a great reward for those of us human, animal or otherwise, that didn't get to experience a good life here. I think of some poor animal stuck in a research lab or at a subpar zoo or someone that has suffered a life of extreme poverty and never had a good moment in his or her life. I hope and believe that there is something much greater than here. This belief has helped me in my life, but it is still hard not to feel empathy for a creature in Ben's situation. I hoped, at least, to make his life useful.

I saw Lula for about a week or so more after she fledged. She came back to the platform for food and several times, when I arrived, she flushed from the nest. Towards the last few days, I did see her attempt to catch fish several times. I did, on one occasion, see her catch a small fish that she ate "on the wing". It was now near the end of August. The heat wave had finally broken after 21 days of 100 degrees plus temperatures. One day, after a frontal passage, the sky was very blue and full of cumulus clouds. This was the last day that I saw Lula. I heard her whistle from up above me. She was riding a small thermal and seemed to be immersed in sheer delight. Seeing her wheel in the rising air made me want to join her. I knew what she was feeling! She took the thermal up until she was about five hundred feet and then she went into a long glide. She ended her flight by landing in a tree across the lake. She whistled in my general direction. I had put some food on the platform for what would be the last time. The passing cold front had triggered her desire to migrate.

The next day, Lula was gone. I scanned the lake from a number of locations, but she was nowhere in sight. I went back in the afternoon and then the evening. Once again, Lula was nowhere to be found. I did this for a few more days and had the same results. Nature had provided her with an internal map, with its way points programmed from genetic memory. If she successfully made the migration south, then her destination was South America. There she would remain for about a year and one half until she sexually matured. At this point, she would return to the area where she took her first flight-Kilowatt Lake. The Spring of '82 would determine if we were both successful in our quests; mine to restore Osprey nesting and Lula's for survival.

Ben, meanwhile, had continued to fight. He was tame enough to sit on my glove, so he would have made a great educational assistant. Sadly, it was not meant to be. His wing bones, instead of thickening and getting stronger were actually getting thinner. Something was very wrong. About a month after arriving in Tennessee, Ben died. He had developed a bone infection at the site of the break. Despite Dr. Douglass' attempts to help him, Ben's health continued to erode. One morning in early September, a week or so after his sister had left, I found Ben dead in his enclosure. It was a sad moment, but strangely too, one of relief. He would have never been a wild bird, never to soar the mighty thermals or battle an eagle to retain his hard-earned catch. So death was a merciful end to his short life. His family's genetic material would have to be carried on by one of his remaining siblings, perhaps Lula.

Chapter 23

"Return Home or suffer the consequences!"

It was now 1981. My daughter was four months old. I saw her
when I could, but really didn't get to spend a whole lot of time
with her. She was too young for her mother to trust her with me. In
other words, her mother didn't trust her away from her side, with
the exception of being cared for by her Grandmother Janice. I still
wasn't ready to return home, but I really wanted to bond with
Lendi more. It pained me to leave her when I got the chance to see
her. She was my flesh and blood and even though I wasn't thrilled
that her mother was pregnant with her, I was very happy she was
now with us. I always felt guilty when I left, wishing I had more to
give her.

I guess that guilt was really starting to get to me. I wasn't
sleeping well and I started feeling like what I described as "third
person, twice removed". I was sleep depraved and had trouble
remembering things, such as people's names; people I had worked
with for years. When I was at work and would see one of my co-
workers coming, I had to repeat that person's name in my mind
until I said "Hello" to that person. I felt a little drunk and at times,
felt very nervous. I was beginning to lose myself. I finally decided
that if I were going to be myself again, that I would have to start
acting like my normal self.

Lendi, was growing quickly. She was more aware of the world
around her. On one of my visit with her, I took her outside. The
day was fairly warm, as it can be in February in Memphis. The
birds were active and there was a Mockingbird singing nearby on a

153

lamppost. The song attracted Lendi's attention as she tried to locate the source of the melody. She cooed in delight during her outdoor experience. Later that evening, after returning home from my visit with Lendi, I got a message from my inner "Voice" which I had recently become aware. This time the directive was clear; return home to Lendi and Debbie or suffer the consequences. I know it probably sounds crazy, but this wasn't like Son of Sam listening to a German Shepherd directing him to kill people. This "Voice" seems to be a guide. It is always in the plural tense as in "We" and has given me choice in my actions. It has warned me of danger and in one case was very clear.

I was getting ready to pull into an intersection after the light turned green on my side. All of a sudden the Voice said,

"Watch out for the blue car!"

I immediately slowed down and a blue car coming from my left ran the red light and whizzed in front of me barely missing my vehicle. "Oh, that blue car!"

Another time, I was driving down a winding road that was slick from rain. Everything seemed fine, when suddenly the Voice said,

"Slow down for three seconds!"

I slowed down as I counted to three. Nothing happened then, but about a mile down the way, where the road took a sharp turn to the left, an out of control car, probably with bald tires, was in my lane. I saw the driver's eyes, full of fear, as she regained control and back into her lane. She had barely missed hitting me and had I been there three seconds earlier, I might have been involved in a head-on collision! So, the Voice has offered me some sage advice over the years and I have paid attention!

It was now telling me to return home or "suffer the consequences." I didn't know what this exactly meant, but I made plans for my return. On one of my visits with Lendi in March, I got up the nerve to ask Debbie if I could come back home.

"What did you say?!? Debbie asked in disbelief.

"Can I come home?" I replied.

"I don't know if I should let you, considering how you hurt me and left us alone here!" Debbie scolded.

"I know I have hurt you and I am very sorry, but I want a second chance to make this work. I can understand that you are skeptical, but I would like to try to make this work."

I didn't know what else to say. The main reason I wanted to go back is because the Voice suggested that I do just that. I didn't have romantic feelings for Debbie like I should have, but I did love my daughter, so it was worth the trade. Debbie reluctantly agreed to let me return home. I was very apprehensive about doing so because, as far as I could see, Debbie was still Debbie, sarcasm and all. All the reasons I bailed out the first time were still there. Still, "suffer the consequences" kept replaying in my head. I guess I didn't want to find out what that meant.

By mid-March, I had moved back in with Debbie and Lendi. At first, it was awkward and I think Lendi was a little confused. We quickly settled into being a family. Lendi accepted me as her father and I even got her to say her first word. She didn't say "Momma" or "Dada", but "bird", much to Debbie's dismay. Lendi was six months old now and was starting to crawl a lot. It was fun to watch her scoot along the carpet, reminding me much of a terrapin or tortoise. She would see something she wanted to investigate and away she went. It was really nice to be around her. My life was getting back to what most people term "normal".

We took a trip to Chattanooga for a little hang gliding and to see some of Debbie's relatives. Debbie's Aunt and Uncle had not seen our new daughter and they were the closest relatives to Debbie's father. Lendi seemed to enjoy the adventure. We stayed in a motel where she was fascinated with everything. I took a flight off Raccoon Mountain and Lendi watched birds and flying humans. This was a good bonding time for us. We got to know each other a little better and this early time together proved invaluable in later years.

Lendi was now walking more and I took her outside more to show her a little bit of the natural world. She noticed the honeybees that were flying and gathering pollen among the clover flowers. I plucked a flower to show her and she held it close to her face for a closer look. The resident Mockingbird was singing and the song caught Lendi's attention. She was amused by the different songs and sounds the bird made and even emitted a little chuckle. We were having a good time until Debbie came out and demanded that I take Lendi out of the grass (fearing that she might get some type of disease). I assured her that she wasn't going to get a life threatening condition from being in the grass. Lendi wasn't allergic to grass or flower pollen. The worst thing she possibly could have gotten were chiggers. I relented and brought Lendi back in the house. I am sure I was thinking "What did I come back for?" The answer was there looking up at me.

I hung around for another eight months or so and it was apparent that Debbie and I were not going to make it. I tried and we had some good moments, but my love for Debbie wasn't there. It wasn't fair to her, nor was it fair to me. The reason the Voice told me to go back or suffer the consequences was now clear to me; to establish a bond with Lendi. This has paid off as the years have gone by. For several years, Debbie continued to snipe at me by telling Lendi things that she said I said to her. When I picked up Lendi for a visit, she would frequently say something that her mother told her about me or something I said in the past. Lendi would then say,

"Is that true, did you say that?"

I would tell her "No" or "She twisted the statement around". Lendi would say,

"I didn't think you would say that! I just wanted to hear it from you."

Debbie and I mutually agreed to a divorce and we separated for good in March of 1982. Our marriage was dissolved in May. It was a classic case of getting married too young. I did get a wonderful daughter out of it, though! One of my former roommates from Williford House, George Heinrich, and I got a two bedroom, two bath townhouse in Frayser. George was my roommate for a number of months and eventually found a new girlfriend and moved in with her. He did leave me a wonderful present in the form of his cat named Denver. Denver and I became fast buddies and when George asked if I wanted her (due to the fact his new girl was allergic to cat dander), I gladly said "Yes!" Lendi and Denver also became friends as well. Denver played with Lendi and was very tolerant of being awkwardly held by a two year old child.

Relationship-wise, this was a period of down time. I dated a few women after my divorce, but nothing serious came about until later in the year. I needed the break anyway. It gave me time to clear my head and focus on other things. My sister Mary needed a place to stay and moved in later in the Fall. We got along well and she helped with half of the bills. Life was good!

I looked back on the previous year. I had really stepped out of my normal character and had "sown my oats". It probably wasn't the best time to leave, but it was something I had to do. Now, over thirty years later, I am astonished that I even did what I did. I am, however, in an odd way, grateful for the experience and thankful I didn't accidently kill someone or myself.

Chapter 24

Satch

In April of 1981, I was contacted by a Federal Wildlife Undercover Agent named Joe Forrester. He wanted to know how much room I had at the Zoo to hold some confiscated raptors. He said that he was working on a sting to try to shut down an illegal bird selling operation. It seems that an individual was locating all of the hawk and owl nests in the area where he lived. When the time was right he climbed to the nests and removed the young. He then sold the young birds, which was and is very illegal. Licensed raptor breeders can sell birds to licensed falconers now, but what he was doing wasn't close to legal. In fact, Joe said the man had done this so much that he was actually affecting the local raptor populations. Several people had called, expressing concern about the fellow's underhanded activity. Since raptors are considered migratory birds, this case went from being a State legal case to a Federal one. This Agent had been in contact with the suspect and had arranged to buy what birds the guy could get in a few week period. Joe thought he may have up to thirty birds that might need to be held for evidence.

Meanwhile, I began to modify what enclosures I had to handle that potential number of young raptors. Fortunately, late spring was not too busy as far as rehab went and we only had a few Screech Owls that we were raising for release. A week or so went by and Joe called to let me know that he may be getting close to acquiring some birds. Joe had the perfect look and demeanor to be an undercover agent. He could put on a Red Man ball cap and some overalls and talk NASCAR or he could don a tuxedo and a martini glass and do a James Bond act that could fool high society. No one knew the real Joe until it was too late.

Before too long, Joe called and said that he had a young Red-tailed Hawk, roughly four weeks old, that he had just acquired and needed to bring it to the zoo. I met Joe early the next morning and he had the bird in a dog carrier. He said that the bird was in the fellow's possession for several weeks and by all accounts was a human imprint. He said he was going back to get a few more birds and that he was pretty close to nailing the man. I took the young hawk and put him in an enclosure that had once been an old restroom that we had modified to hold birds. The youngster was about half grown but his feet and tarsi were already adult–sized. A young raptor's feet and legs grow faster than the rest of its body, so appearance-wise, a hawk at this age looks rather cartoonish with a still smallish body and monster-sized feet.

This young Red-tail had beautiful blue eyes, something somewhat unusual for a hawk of this species. Most young Red-tailed Hawks have yellow-white irises. All that aside, I placed the young bird in one of the old parrot enclosures and placed several dead mice in there for him to eat. It wasn't long before he discovered them and ate them quickly enough that it looked as though he had swallowed a tennis ball with his now bulging crop. Throughout the day, I checked on the bird and gave him a few more mice to eat. He was at the age where he was growing rapidly and required a lot of food. At a certain stage of development, young hawks and owls eat almost twice the amount of food as the adult parents do. For some species of owls, particularly Great Horned Owls, this means hunting nearly round the clock, making for some nearly exhausted adults. I had food available, but I wanted to supplement the mice with some other natural food.

My drive to work took about 25 minutes to complete. Along one stretch of the route flowed the Wolf River and an oxbow lake named Kilowatt, the same lake where I hacked Lula. Near the road were a lot of English Sparrows that were feeding on waste grain that was blown off transport trucks. This meant a lot of sparrows and odds were that many would be hit by vehicles. Sure enough, I started scanning for birds that were recently departed and I usually averaged two to three a day. I always checked to see if any cars were coming so I wouldn't get caught in the act of picking up the road kills. One morning, I spotted the ultimate road-killed prize; an Eastern Cottontail Rabbit. I pulled on to the shoulder and quickly glanced up and down the road to see if anyone was coming. There was a car about half a mile behind me, but I figured I could do a quick snatch and run. The rabbit looked pretty clean as I grabbed it by the back legs. I ran rapidly back to my still running car, jumped in, and put it in drive, all while holding the rabbit with my left arm. As I pulled on to the road, I noticed that the rabbit smelled pretty bad. The impact had torn a hole in the abdominal cavity and some of the intestinal juices were leaking.

Without thinking and not aware of where the previously one-half mile rearward vehicle was, I flung the leaking lagomorph out the window. As it cart wheeled into the blue, the car that was behind me was now right beside me. As the driver passed, he was surprised by the flying rabbit sailing past his passenger side. He snapped his head around to look back at the rabbit and then quickly looked back at me, as if he wanted an explanation. I didn't make eye contact with him. I just stared straight ahead until he was far past me. I did see him look in his rear view mirror several times. He probably thought I was snacking on the rabbit and threw my leftovers out the window. It was a good thing that he wasn't a second earlier or I may have thrown the rabbit onto his windshield and caused the poor guy to crash. I would have had a tough time

160

explaining that one to the cops! I might have had to come up with something more bizarre than the truth. Needless to say, the fellow in the car had a story for work that day.

Joe called me after a few days to tell me that there wouldn't be any more birds coming my way. It seems that someone had tipped the fellow that Joe was an undercover agent and did not supply any additional birds. Joe said that it didn't matter. He had enough evidence from previous activity to bust the guy and closed his operation down for good. In a conversation with Joe I asked,

"What was the most unusual wildlife case you've had?"

He said," By far, the case that really sticks out is that of Berry Thorne".

"Berry Thorne, who is that?" I queried.

"Berry Thorne is the character name of this fellow who worked for a famous country singer's dude ranch. I had gotten a very reliable tip that ole Berry had shot and killed a Bald Eagle. I decided to go out to Berry's house to check out matters for myself. I pulled into his driveway and I was stunned to see an adult Bald Eagle's head and feet tacked to his garage wall. Also on display were the wings and feet of a Red-shouldered Hawk and a Red-tailed Hawk. I thought that this guy was either arrogant or stupid or a combination of both. They sometimes go hand in hand".

Joe continued, "I knocked on Berry's front door and this fellow opened the door, looking very much like a character straight out of the Hee Haw TV show. I introduced myself and told him that I understood that he had shot and killed a Bald Eagle. He looked at me as if I were speaking a foreign language! I began to think that this guy was going to give me a hard time. I pointed to his garage wall and said that the head and feet of the bird were those of a Bald Eagle. What I wanted to know was where the rest of the bird's body. I asked him did he sell the body parts, bury them or what?" Joe then said Berry surprised him with his answer.

161

"We et 'em", Berry said without hesitation.

"Say that again", Joe responded.

He continued, "I thought the guy was pulling my leg, like the old joke about a guy that ate a Bald Eagle...What did it taste like? Somewhere between Peregrine Falcon and Spotted Owl. He said Berry's wife brought out a calendar and pointed to a picture of a Bald Eagle and said,

"It looked like this bird here".

"I thought these people were trying to fool me so I asked about the Red-shouldered Hawk and Red-tailed Hawk and as I pointed at their wings, Ole Berry replied without blinking an eye,

"We et them, too!"

"Berry's wife proceeded to tell me how she made dressing to go along with the roasted eagle".

"What was going on with Berry... was he a poacher and was selling the parts?" I asked.

"No. The more I talked to Berry and his wife, the more I realized that these people were literally ignorant about what they did. As amazing as it sounds, Berry didn't know it was illegal to kill an eagle. He was just killing those birds for food!"

I queried Joe further, "What did you do in that situation, I mean legally?"

Joe said, "Since Berry was truly ignorant about the laws, so much that he ate a Bald Eagle, I recommended that he be put on probation for a year and I told him not to shoot any more eagles, hawks or owls and to my knowledge, he hasn't done it any more".

To me, Ben Franklin probably would have found this ironic, since the eagle cooking occurred around Thanksgiving and Ben wanted the turkey to be our National Bird.

A few weeks went by and Joe called and said that the case was wrapped and the guy had pleaded guilty. He said that if I wanted to use the hawk for education, that he had no problem leaving the bird with me. I told Joe that I could use him and that it was good to have him at this age, since it made training a little easier. So, I now had a young Red-tailed Hawk for education. He was nearly fully grown now and was "hard-penned", a falconry term meaning that all of the feathers were now grown and hardened. The hawk needed a name. A night or two after Joe said I could have the bird, I watched a made for TV movie called *"Don't Look Back, the Story of Satchel Paige"*. Satchel Paige was one of the first African-Americans in National League Baseball and he had to be aggressive to survive in the league. I thought that "Satchel" would be an excellent name for this young fellow and the name stuck. I started calling him "Satch" for short.

I had gotten Satch at a good point in his development. In another week he was ready to be put into training. I moved him into a converted enclosure, but had to tether him to a bow perch. This perch type allowed him to be securely fastened without the fear of entanglement. I got his initial weight, nearly three and one-half pounds and essentially didn't weigh him for the next five years.

I trained him the old fashion falconry way via observation of his behavior and posture. He was a quick study. He first started eating off my glove. This was a good sign of trust and made the next phase fairly easy. I put him on a T-perch to see if I could get him to step to my glove. I had been cutting his food back some to get him a little hungrier. He didn't hesitate to step to my glove for food. Each time he ate a piece of food, I blew a whistle to get him to associate the whistle with food. Animal trainers now call that whistle a "bridge". In falconry, it is important to use a whistle in a situation like this, since sometimes, in heavy brush, the falconer and the bird can become visually separated. To jump ahead, I was free-flying Satch at the Zoo and lost sight of him. I thought that he was in one direction, so I blew my whistle and held my glove up with a piece of food in the direction where I thought he was. He came and landed on my glove from completely the opposite direction. The whistle training had paid dividends in that circumstance.

Satch learned quickly. He rapidly progressed to the free flight stage and the last thing I needed to do, was train him to fly to the lure. Satch's lure was made of the previous canvas Electrolux vacuum cleaner bag, but this time it had rabbit fur more closely sewn to it than in previous attempts. I had a rawhide thong in the middle of the lure so I could tie a good piece of food to it. It was essential to have the lure garnished with a piece of meat that would be a good reward for him when On this day's session, one of the first things I did after having Satch fly to me a few times was to try to get him to attack the lure. I had it hidden in the back of my falconry vest and had a swivel at the head of the lure. I had about twenty feet on nylon parachute cord tied to it with a loop for a handle. I put Satch on the perch and walked about twenty yards away. I slowly reached into my vest, found the handle on the cord and in one motion flung the lure out in front of me, all the while blowing my whistle. The lure landed meat side up. Satch looked at it briefly and then launched off the perch. He struck the lure squarely in the middle and squeezed it several times to "kill" it. He found the meat and when he took his first bite, I blew my whistle. Each time he took a bite, I blew my whistle until the food was gone. I then tried to get him to jump from the lure, back to my glove. I held my tidbitted glove up to try to get Satch to hop up to it, but he insisted on hanging onto the lure. He mantled over the lure, where he spread his wings to hide the lure from view. This was a good thing, since he was treating the lure as if it were alive. I was finally able to get him to release the lure by stepping on the parachute cord near the top of the lure and then offered Satch a large enticement. This had been a good session!

The next day, I was able to get Satch to fly well over one hundred feet and he quickly responded to the lure. He was ready to be free flown. I decided to wait until the following day to insure that he was hungry enough without hesitating. I took him out to the small field next to the aquarium, set up the T-perch, and placed Satch on it. I actually had some help from a young fellow named Mike Beckson. Mike was the son of the Curator of the Reptiles and Aquarium, Chuck Beckson. Mike had been helping some with Satch and today he held Satch's leather straps until I got far enough away. I signaled to Mike that I was ready and he released the jesses and stepped back from the perch. Satch stood there, looking around as he had been in our previous sessions. I had the lure ready in case things went south. I put a piece of mouse on my glove between my thumb and forefinger, held it aloft and blew my whistle. I also said a little prayer that Satch wouldn't fly off. Satch leapt from the perch without hesitating and flew the 100 feet to my glove without problem. I got Mike to put a piece of food on the T-perch and as I walked back toward the perch with him, Satch saw the food and flew to the reward. I turned and ran back past the hundred foot mark and turned, blowing my whistle as I did. Satch responded and flew right to my glove. Mike once again put a treat on the perch, Satch saw it and flew back from fifty feet away. Nice job!

The last order of business was to fly him to the lure. From nearly fifty yards distance, Satch attacked the stuffed canvas bag with much gusto and hopped nicely back to my glove. You would have thought that he had been doing this for years. My anxiety about flying him free was gone. He had passed the test with, excuse the pun, flying colors!

Satch gradually flew father and soon, I had him flying out of the trees. On one of our training sessions, I noticed an immature female Red-tailed Hawk in a tree about ¼ mile away. I had seen

165

her a few days before in Overton Park and she probably discovered the smorgasbord that was the Memphis Zoo's rodent, English Sparrow and Starling populations. I didn't think too much about her presence and took Satch down to the Aquarium field. When I hopped Satch to the perch, I did hear the female "Kee-yar" in response. I thought maybe she was saying "Hello" in Red-tail language. Turns out, it was a threat call. I flew Satch to me one time and as I was walking him back to the perch, he began gyrating his head wildly, as if he was watching something very intently. Above us was a Carolina Chickadee that was fussing due to Satch's presence. I looked up and said to Satch,

"Certainly, you are not afraid of that Chickadee, are you?"

He wasn't! The next thing I knew, there was a very audible "whoosh" followed by Satch doing his best to dive off my glove. Accompanying all of this was a brown and white blur of feathers as the female Red-tailed Hawk tried to rout Satch out of her territory. She didn't make contact with either Satch or me, but she had so much momentum from her high speed past that she was able to travel another 50 yards to land on top of a telephone pole. Satch was very shaken and not surprisingly, didn't want to fly any more. I took him back to his enclosure, but before I put him up, he looked back at the hawk and gave a "kee-yar" of his own defiance. The female hung around for a few more days, and eventually moved on, perhaps to find a territory she could call her own. For months afterwards, Satch looked for her. From that day on when he saw another Red-tailed Hawk, he would scream.

I flew Satch more often and took him into Overton Park around the soccer and softball field. I made sure that there were no dogs around as I didn't want any encounters like I had with Charger a few years earlier. He was great at following me and was quick to respond whenever I blew the whistle. I eventually started doing some flying demonstrations with him at the zoo. I did all of

166

the "Satch stuff" well after I had all of my work completed and was available for any supervisor duties as needed. Still, my activities had not gone un-noticed by Zoo Director Menigar. He called me into his office one day, as he fairly often did to chew me out for something for which other people got praise. He always seemed to do this when my direct supervisor, Cliff, was off duty. This time he seemed to be friendly.

"You wanted to see me Hal?" I asked, not knowing what to expect.

"Yeah John, I have noticed that you have been flying that hawk in the afternoon around the zoo".

I answered,

"Yeah, Satch has been doing great and the public really seems to like it and plus, I get to educate them about the importance of predators!"

I, for some reason, expected Menigar to say something like,

"That's great, keep it up" or "that's pretty neat and we have gotten some phone calls from people who said it enhanced their experience at the Zoo".

No, that was not what I heard. What was I thinking?

Menigar continued, "It seems you have been taking a lot of extra time doing this. Time you could be using to improve the Bird Section or work on your Quarterly Report which is now past due!"

I countered with, "I already had my report turned in two weeks ago and that I have all of my work done and am available for anything else anyone in my section needs. I always come into work 1-2 hours early to get my work done."

"You've got to stop doing that. Our insurance doesn't cover you when you are not on the clock", Hal snapped in reply.

"Well, I am not really on the clock since I am on salary and get paid for 40 hours regardless of how many extra hours I put in each day" I said this in a matter-of-fact way.

He didn't like this Spock-like response.

"You are no longer to fly that bird when you are here on Zoo time and if I see you, you'll be written up!"

"I thought part of our job and mission was to educate the public" was my reply.

He retorted, "That's the Education Department's job, not yours!"

I wasn't going to go down without a fight..."I thought it was in my job description, as well"…

Menigar replied, his jaw clenched to suppress his rage,

"End of discussion! I'll be watching you…like a hawk! You can go now!"

I turned and walked out of Menigar's office, in an act of defiance I flew another type of bird, my middle finger. Of course, I had my back to him when I did this so he wouldn't see me. One of the zoo's secretaries saw this and started laughing. Menigar bolted out of his office, looking around to see if I had done something else. The secretary didn't say a word and I gave Menigar a friendly wave as I left the office.

Menigar was off on the weekends, so I still did my Satch training, but limited it to the side of the zoo where a whole lot of people wouldn't see me. I also did the bulk of the training after 4 o'clock, since this was when I was officially off work. I didn't have to worry about other supervisors telling on me. Several of them had trouble with Menigar, too. There were two other guys in my "Whipping Boys" club, John Sowell, Grounds Supervisor, and Chuck Beckson, Curator of Reptiles and Aquarium. We joked with each other that "your turn" is coming up soon.

Satch had been doing great flying outside and had been responsive in several situations. I had gotten a call to do a program in Booneville, Mississippi for an outdoor education event at Northeast Junior College. I was to fly Satch for the attendees several times for this event. No problem, except there was a problem...rain! Satch had never flown inside; not even in a classroom situation. All of the presenters that stayed were asked to move into the basketball arena. This area easily seated 2-3000 people and there were probably 2000 people inside this day. I was second to do my demo with Satch.

The first presenter got a good round of applause when he finished and this may have spooked Satch. Anyway, I had a Screech Owl and an American Kestrel, both couldn't fly, so I walked them around the best I could. Afterwards, I set up the T-perch in the middle of the gym and went and got Satch. I talked about him for a minute or so and then flew him to the perch. He did well with this and everyone applauded. I had his perch under on goal and backpedaled until I was about under the opposite hoop. I blew my whistle for Satch to come. He instantly launched and started flying to me. I locked eyes with him as he flew towards me and for a split second, I saw him glance upwards. He had picked his landing spot and it wasn't my glove. He landed squarely on top of the backboard. At that point, everyone in the gym, it seems, either laughed or cheered. I thought, "No problem!"

Well, I was wrong. Big problem! Satch was a little confused by all of the noise. I walked to half court, stuck up my glove and blew my whistle. He looked at me and for a second, I thought he was going to come down for the food. There was silence in the gym as the mini-drama unfolded. I added more food to my glove and held it aloft, blowing my whistle as I raised my arm. Nothing. This went on for another few minutes as the crowd became restless. I knew there were more presenters behind me. I pulled out the lure and swung it over my head and then dropped it to the floor. He was mildly amused by all of this and was starting to get comfortable. He even pulled one foot up and watched as I swung the lure like a drunken cowboy swinging a lariat. I knew he wasn't

169

going to fly to me. Fortunately, the college had a tall ladder used for servicing the non-retractable backboards. One of the maintenance guys rolled it out as I heard a wave of laughter sweep across the gym. Boy, if I only had a trap door I could have disappeared for a quick exit from this embarrassing situation. I got the ladder under Satch's goal and soon as I was near enough, he jumped to the glove. The place erupted into cheers. I got Satch, my lure, waved to the crowd and left the gym. Satch did get better about flying in the great indoors.

Since Satch was raised by a human, he was a human imprint. When he matured at around three years old, he began to exhibit nesting behavior. Satch viewed me as his mate and expected me to help with the nest building chores. As soon as we got an enclosure where I could "free loft" him (or let him loose in his enclosure), I constructed a nest platform to hold sticks and grasses. Usually around late January, I'd bring Satch materials for the nest. I'd place some sticks and grasses in the nest platform and some on the floor of his enclosure. I placed the sticks where I thought they should go and Satch would usually move them. This nesting behavior usually lasted several months during which Satch became very territorial. My fellow co-workers had to be careful when entering his enclosure. He continued this annual nesting cycle throughout the years. My last nesting year with him was 2002. At that point, he was 22 years old.

One of the most unusual things I ever did with a bird happened with Satch. I was in an opera with him! No, we didn't have to sing in Italian, but I did have to do a small amount of acting. I was passed a note from the zoo's secretary that the Director of Opera Memphis had called and was looking for a stuffed falcon to use in the opening scene in an upcoming opera. I called the Director and explained to her that we didn't have a stuffed bird for them to use, but I'd be glad to train the actor (or in this case the person was called a "Super") to work with Satch. She was excited about the possibility about having a live bird in the opera. The opera was a comic opera written by Mozart. The Memphis Opera's version of *"The Abduction from the Seraglio"* was not in Italian, but in English.

A few days later the Director called back and said that no one was interested in handling a live bird. She asked if I were interested in the part of the falconer with Satch playing the role of the falcon. I asked when the performance was going to take place and she told me the date. I quickly checked my calendar and told her I was open on the date of the opera. She said that it was wonderful that they would have a live bird in their production. She also informed me of the upcoming rehearsals and when I needed to be there.

The first few rehearsals, I didn't bring Satch. I merely learned what I needed to do and where to go in the opening processional. Everyone seemed to be genuinely interested that there was going to be a live bird in the production. I met the main performers and my other "supers" or extras. I was to walk across the stage with Satch on my glove, talk to the Pasha or the opera's narrator and then exit. The opera was set in ancient Turkey and I basically just mumbled to the Pasha that,

"The bird caught two heads of game today."

He uttered something back like "Very good!"

We rehearsed this several times and the man playing the Pasha had a sense of humor. I'd say my lines and he'd reply something like,

"Does it taste like chicken?"

I'd laugh and say, "That's what I heard!"

He'd give a hearty laugh! This seemed like it was going to be fun.

The Director informed me that it was time to bring Satch to the rehearsals. We were getting close to the Opera's opening and were rehearsing every night. I brought Satch and everyone in the cast came over and looked at him. Several people wanted to pet him, but I told them he didn't like to be touched. They all marveled at his beauty and most of them commented that they had never seen a hawk up close before now. Our first run though went well as did all of the others that night. The next night was the same.

However, the final two rehearsals were in full dress and makeup. Since I was a Turkish falconer, my costume consisted of a very heavy Turkish robe. This robe was more like wearing a heavy carpet. It was pretty stinky and probably had never been dry cleaned. My "hat" looked like someone had taken a cone of cotton candy and stuck it on my head. The makeup person had me in pale pancake with heavy black eyebrows and black mustache. I looked like Groucho Marx in drag! After I had all of this applied for the first time, I went and picked up Satch from his perch and he didn't quite know what to think or who I was. He had his hackles up and even did a "Kee-yar!" scream in protest. I started talking to him and he gradually began to recognize me. I am sure he was thinking, "What the hell!?!" He gradually settled down and accepted my bizarre appearance.

Two of the supers were Turkish body builders. They were like any typical body builders except they were blue! Apparently the blue body dye was supposed to accent the fellows' physiques. Satch had never seen a blue human before and come to think of it, neither had I. In the regular rehearsals, these guys were in their street clothes, but tonight, like everyone else, they appeared like they would in the opera. Satch was very leery of the Blue Guys and every time they would get close, he screamed! In our dress first run-through with Satch, the Blue Boys were behind us in the processional and Satch didn't like them near, so he "Kee-yarred!"

Everyone laughed, but this wouldn't work in the real show. We all re-blocked and went through the opening scene again. Same result; Satch screamed!

I got with the Director and we came up with a different approach, literally, to the problem. The change to the blocking had Satch and me a couple of people behind the body builders and this worked just fine. The body builder split off stage left and we proceeded stage right to the Pasha. I adjusted Satch on my glove and he flapped his wings to adjust his balance, The Director saw this and asked if I could get him to do this each time. I said yes and we included this in our part. We had one more run through and we were finished with our part of the rehearsal. I put Satch back on his travel perch and I then removed my entire costume. I was in a hurry to get Satch back to the zoo and then home, so I left my makeup as it was.

The zoo was about five miles from downtown Memphis and my route took me down Poplar, one of the busiest roads out of downtown. I had Satch on a traveling perch behind me in my two-door Cavalier. At a traffic light, a policeman pulled up beside me on my left and he glanced over and noticed Satch on the perch behind me. I looked over at the cop and nodded a "Hello". I had forgotten that I still had the makeup on and I couldn't help but notice that the cop kept looking at Satch and then me. I didn't look back at the policeman. I just stared straight ahead and drove carefully down the road. At the next traffic light, the policeman pulled up alongside me again. He kept staring over at me and in my peripheral vision, I could see he was on his radio. I don't know what he was thinking, but Overton Park, where the Zoo was located, was populated with a collection of some strange people at night. He was probably thinking I was headed to the park and he was right. The next light had me turning left into the park. I'm sure

173

the cop wasn't surprised! I drove into the Zoo, put Satch away and went home and took off my makeup.

The next night was the real thing, the real opera. I had to work that day and a lot of my co-workers told me to "break a leg". At the end of the day, I loaded Satch in my car and went to the convention center where the opera was to be presented. I went backstage and put Satch on his traveling perch in a secluded area. I got into my costume and waited for the makeup person to apply my Groucho Marx face. The Director called the cast together and went over the entire opera blocking. All of the people in the opening scene went over our entrance, including me minus Satch. We were ready and all we had to do now was to wait for the curtain to rise. I was a little nervous, but I was looking forward to the opera's start. Soon, I heard the doors open to the audience and people began filing in and taking their seats. Wow, this is actually about to happen! Before long, I heard "15 minutes". Then "10 minutes" and "5 minutes" and at this point, I went and got Satch on my glove and waited. Finally, we all heard "Places Everyone!" I could hear my heart beating in my ears. Satch was craning his head around as he witnessed this assembling spectacle. I got into position behind the veiled dancers.

"Alright, here we go. Have fun!" were the Director's words.

The orchestra started the opening song as the curtain began to rise. As soon as the curtain was fully raised, we started our processional; "The Abduction" was underway! Satch and I moved through stage right and over to the Pasha. I made Satch move his wings and I heard people in the audience applaud. I said to the Pasha,

"The hawk caught two head of game, my Master"

He replied something like, "Well, zippy-do-da. That's great!"

I didn't know it, but before I exited, Satch took a slice (shat, dump, dookie) onto the stage. I proceeded offstage. I put Satch on

174

his perch and took off part of my costume. I walked to the stage wing to watch part of the opera. Suddenly, I heard the audience roar with laughter. Two of the Supers came off stage and I asked them what happened. One of the guys said that their scene was to run over to the Pasha to deliver a message. The fellow in front slipped in Satch's mess and fell with the guy behind him tripping over the first guy. Both almost went into the Orchestra Pit! The audience apparently thought it was part of the opera and laughed accordingly. I apologize to the guys and said I'd try to watch Satch's activity for the next performance.

The next performance went well. Satch didn't leave any unexpected deposits and audience members clapped when I adjusted his balance as he flapped and moved his wings. It was a simple thing, but yielded a great response. I went offstage and put Satch on his perch. The Director came over to me and commended us on our performance as she exclaimed,

"That was excellent! Bravo and thank you and your feathered friend Satch for helping us make this a great production!"

I nodded an acknowledgement and simply said,

"Thank you, it was fun!"

With this, she shook my hand and went on to watch the show from the wing. It WAS fun and something I'll never forget. I removed my costume and makeup, put on my street clothes and got Satch and back to the Zoo we went.

In 2009, Satch escaped from captivity. He still lived at the American Eagle Foundation at Dollywood where I used to work. He was put outside on a perch to get some sunshine and fresh air and broke his leash. He flew away to parts unknown. I wasn't informed of his escape until nearly a month after the fact. If I would have known the day of the event, I would have gone to try to find him. More than likely, he probably became tangled in a tree where he died or perhaps a Great Horned Owl captured him. He

175

was never seen again. He was twenty eight years old, but at least he spent his last day(s) in the wild. To this day, I miss him! We had many adventures and shared a lot of time, trips and miles together. There will never be another like him. To my old friend Satch I say,

"Kee-yar!!!"

Chapter 25

Hitchhiking up Walden Ridge

On one of my annual trips to Chattanooga, I decided to go to fly the hang gliding site known as Whitwell. This 1600 ft. AGL (above ground level) launch is located above the town of Whitwell, Tennessee. Whitwell is in the beautiful Sequatchie Valley. Some have compared this 80 mile long valley to some in Europe. It is a great place to fly hang gliders cross country, since there are numerous landing fields and friendly locals. I was about to meet one very colorful local denizen.

I went to the landing zone (LZ) to see if anyone needed a ride to the top. A few fellows from Florida were in the field and said that if I gave them a ride up, then they could leave a car at the LZ. After we all flew, they would give me a ride back to retrieve my car. Good deal! We loaded their gliders onto my Chevy Chevette and piled harnesses and helmets into the hatch and up the mountain we went. After 15 minutes up the winding, steep two lane road, we arrived at the launch. There we met Greg DeWenter from Ohio. He was set up and ready to fly, but decided to wait until we were ready to fly. The winds were perfect, blowing straight in from SE at 12-15 m.p.h. We quickly assembled our gliders and one by one launched into the soarable air. I flew for about an hour and noticed that the Florida pilots had headed out to land. Greg and I flew for another thirty minutes or so and landed. I noticed that the Florida pilots were not around and Greg commented that as well.

I said, "Maybe they went to the store and will be back in a few minutes".

We disassembled our gliders for transport. After 30 minutes had passed, we figured the Florida pilots had left us stranded in the landing field. Greg and I mulled over our possibilities of how we were going to make back to the top. His car was up there, too. We hoped that someone would come along that was going up to launch. It didn't happen. We decided to hitchhike. We took our harnesses, instruments and helmets along to let people know that we were hang glider pilots and not a couple of guys that might kill somebody. We walked for about a mile to the part of the road that started to get steep. We were passed by a number of people until a guy in a souped up Ford Pinto stopped and said,

"Where you boys headed?"

I said "We are going to the hang glider launch," and he replied,

"I can't give you a ride all the way there, but I can give you a ride to the top of the hill".

"That'll be great!"

Greg climbed in the back of the little Ford car and I got in the passenger seat. The guy explained that he had dropped a V-8 in the Pinto and it had tremendous acceleration. I felt we were now strapped into a rocket sled. He was yammering away about the car and all I could do hold was on in semi-terror as we shot our way up the narrow mountain road. To add to this, there were huge coal trucks barreling down the mountain and they were taking more than their side of the road. I'm sure my eyes were as big as a Bush Baby's as the huge trucks and the small car barely missed each other. Meanwhile, Greg was trying his best to not to spew all over the back seat. We finally made to the top road and the fellow said that he was sorry that he couldn't take us to the launch, but he was already late for work. We thanked him for getting us this far and for not getting us killed in the process.

We still had about two miles to go, but at least we were on top and headed for our cars. Several vehicles passed us by and we had walked for about ½ mile. We were about to give up getting a ride when around the bend came a truck. This was no ordinary truck. It was the color of Bondo, primer and rust. The passenger door was missing and so was the right side of the truck bed. I said to Greg,

"I'll bet you this is our ride!"

"How do you figure that?" Greg asked.

"I dunno, I just have a feeling".

Sure enough, the truck slowed down and the driver pulled up and said,

"Where you bowies go-win?"

"We are going to the hang gliding launch!" I cautiously replied.

"Well, git in!"

In the truck, was the driver, who was sandy blonde-haired fellow, slim build, missing several teeth, and a thick Southern drawl. Next to him was a stereotypical fourteen year old or so Southern boy. He had red-hair, freckles and overalls. He looked like a character straight out of Huck Finn. The driver looked at us and said,

"Where you bowies from?" Greg couldn't understand him, so I had to translate. Once he knew the question, he stated,

"Dayton, Ohio". The driver then looked at me...

"Memphis". He got really excited and said,

"Memphis! Do you know where Collierville is?!?" I nodded,

"Yeah, it is on the outskirts of Memphis".

Before I could get another word out he continued enthusiastically,

"I go to Collierville every year and I get some of the finest wiiii-innne you ever tasted".

The teenager kid said, "I drink wiiiinne, too!"

Obviously, Slim and Huck Finn liked the Collierville wine. The driver noticed the instruments I had in my hand. He asked, nodding towards my variometer,

"What's that, some kinda weapon?'

"No, it measures the rate you go up or down on a glider," I replied.

"How fast we goin' in the truck?" Slim asked.

"It can't tell me that, just the rate of climb and descent".

Before long, we were back at the launch site. We hopped out and I thanked him and offered him 10 dollars for the ride.

"I don't want yer money, I'm just glad to hep", Slim said.

He walked towards the edge of the launch ramp and said,

"Who-wee, you fellas got bigger balls than me to jump offa here, that's for shure!"

"Well, you have to work your way up to flying off something like this." I replied.

Slim continued, "You bowies smoke marijuana?"

I thought he was asking if we had any of the herbal remedy with us. Greg shook his head to say "No" and I said,

"I used to, but not anymore."

Slim then said," Well, up here, you don't need no marijuana! Down there (pointing down below launch) grows the 'Sang plant. You dig the sang plant up, chomp on the root and who-wee, you as high as a kite and lookin' for a woman!"

Greg asked "What is he talking about when he says Sang plant?"

I started mumbling, "Sang…Sang…Sang…Ginseng!"

Ole Slim harvested and sold ginseng root. He motioned for us to come over to his truck.

"I wanna show y'all my prized possessions".

He held up a big prospector pan and a large manual drill. He explained that he would go into the abandoned coal mines in the area with his large drill or "screw" as he called it, and dug out coal. After he got a truckload of it, and I had no idea how he kept the coal in the back of his truck since it was missing the right side, he would take it down and sell it. He probably didn't make a whole lot of money doing this or selling ginseng, but he seemed to be genuinely happy. I told him good luck and thank him again for the ride. As I got into my car, he said,

"Maybe I'll see you over in Memphis next year when I go to get my wiii-iinc in Collierville!"

I said, "Maybe so!"

In an odd sort of way, I hoped to see him there as well. It goes to show you, you don't need to have a lot of money to be happy. Slim seemed to be rich in ways that money couldn't buy! Greg and I looked and each other. I said,

"Well, that was an adventure!" He nodded in agreement and added,

"One I don't care to repeat".

He said it all with that statement. We then got into our cars, drove to the landing field, loaded our gliders and headed home. In some ways, my life was enriched with that hitch hiking adventure.

Chapter 26

Kalopin

In late October and early November, the migrating Bald Eagles begin to arrive at Reelfoot Lake in Northwest Tennessee. This year, 1982, I got a call from Wendell Crews, an official with the U.S. Fish and Wildlife Service who was stationed at Reelfoot Lake. He explained that a Tennessee Highway Patrolman had found an adult Bald Eagle that had apparently hit a power line. It was next to Highway 22. The Trooper had brought the bird to Wendell and he believed that the eagle probably had a broken wing. He said that if the Zoo could take it that they would have someone bring the bird to me. I told him that I would be waiting and that we would have things ready to go to check the bird. After about two hours, the agent from the USF&WS arrived at the zoo with the bird in a cardboard box with air holes. The agent accompanied the eagle to the vet hospital. I had some handling gloves ready and donned them before I opened the box. I slowly pulled back the flaps, peered in to locate the bird's feet and head. Kathy, the Vet Tech had a towel ready to wrap the eagle once I got it out of the box.

The eagle was fairly alert as I slowly slipped my gloved hands into the box and grabbed her feet. As I pulled the eagle out of the box, Kathy placed the towel over her head to keep her calm. The eagle was fairly large with an estimated seven foot wingspan. Dr. Douglass was out of town, so our back up Veterinarian, Dr. Eugene McGehee, Jr. was called and was standing ready in the hospital. After we got the eagle stabilized, Dr. McGehee did a total check of the bird's eyes, mouth, feet and wings. The right wing was sound, but the left wing, when extended had the all too familiar crunching sound of a broken bone. To me, it felt like the humerus was broken and the way the wing was drooping, it seemed like a bad break. We went ahead and had gas anesthesia ready that we administered via a cone mask. The eagle slowly went to sleep, which made it easy to do her x-ray. While she was out, we weighed her; 10 pounds, a little light by not too much. We got the bird ready, donned our lead aprons and fired the shot. We took two views to give a better idea of the break. Kathy took the x-ray cassette and put it into a machine for development. Within five minutes, we had the film. The break was about half way down the humerus and was a fairly clean. It was one of those fractures that wouldn't heal just using bandage wraps. Surgery was needed to pin the wing.

Dr. McGehee made a quick decision to operate and since the bird was already out, it made it easier to prep her for surgery. My main job in all of this, besides holding the bird, was to monitor the eagle's breathing and her relative alertness. If she started moving, the Halothane gas was adjusted to take her back to more of a steady state of sleep. Dr. McGehee studied the x-rays and opened a "pin pack" to select the proper sized pin to match the inside diameter of the humerus. He held several pins up to the life-sized x-rays and finally decided on what he deemed the proper size. The first step to inserting a pin is to make an incision in the skin at the top of the humerus as an entry point for the pin. Then the pin is placed into a pin setting device, which looks very much like a hand drill, complete with a chuck to accommodate various sizes of pins. Everything was ready.

Dr. McGehee made an incision on the wing joint above the humerus. He loaded the pin into the holder and slowly inserted the pin into the bone. He aligned the pin down the bone the best he could. He was able to feel and visualize the pin as he moved the wing to and fro to guide it through the broken bone. After guiding the pin in the bone, Dr. McGehee was satisfied with the placement. He took a pair of bolt cutters and clipped the pin to where it was flush with the shoulder. He then closed the end of the pin into the eagle's skin with a couple of sutures. Before the wing was wrapped, another x-ray was taken to look at the pin alignment. It looked good. The wing was then wrapped with a stretchy bandage that only sticks to itself and not the eagle's feathers. The wing was then wrapped to the bird's body to stabilize the whole affair.

I held the eagle for about fifteen minutes after surgery. She was still very groggy and I wanted to make sure she was going to be okay. We had one of the smaller hospital enclosures set up for her. In there was a small perch and a blanket to cushion the eagle once she fully awoke. After fifteen minutes, the eagle suddenly went from groggy to "where the heck am I and why the heck are you holding me attitude". She quickly moved her feet in order to free them and then tried to bite my chin. Luckily, I was ready for this so she did no harm. I placed her in the cage and let her feet go on the blanket. She leapt from my hands. She was a little unsteady at first, especially since her left wing was bandaged, but got her balance. She looked around the small cage to get her bearings. We slowly left the room and left her there in the quiet. We put two large herring for her to eat, hoping she would eat overnight.

The next day, I arrived early to check the eagle. I didn't know what to expect as I slowly peeked around the corner. She saw me with her sharp eyes and vocalized a warning call that sounded somewhere between a shriek and a pig's grunt. I checked to see if the herring were still there, but they were not. She had eaten and that was a minor victory in itself. Sometimes getting a wild bird to eat can be difficult, but she didn't seem to have a problem. I went to the zoo commissary and got a few more herring. I went back to the hospital and slowly opened her enclosure to put in the first. To my surprise, she was very calm, only protesting a little. Apparently, she was hungry and eyed the herring with much interest. I laid the fish down and withdrew from the cage. I left the room and hid around the corner. I heard her move in the enclosure and then heard the unmistakable sound of an eagle dismantling a fish. Her appetite was not suppressed by her injury, bandages, or captivity. Later that day, I gave her four more herring and by the next morning, they were gone. Meanwhile, I had readied an enclosure outside with lowered perches. The cage was 8'x 12'x 7' high. It had plywood sides and a wire top. It also had a gravel floor. I had included a small water tub so the eagle could drink, but not so deep she could drown. The following morning, I moved her to the enclosure. She hopped and flapped her free wing to keep her balance and seemed to be happier in the larger space.

The eagle needed a name. I decided to name her after the lake where she was found, Reelfoot, except I decided to give her the Native American name for the lake, Kalopin. The name comes from the legend of Reelfoot Lake. Prince Kalopin of the Chickasaws had developed an insane crush on a woman of another related tribe, the Choctaws. She was already bequeathed for marriage, but this didn't stop Ole Kalopin. He got his name from the fact he had been born with a deformed foot or a club foot. In the Chickasaw language, Kalopin means *"Walks with a reeling motion"*. The object of his affection apparently didn't find his deformity very attractive and spurned his advances. This didn't stop him, though. Despite everybody's warning, including threats of retaliation from the Great Spirit, Kalopin led a raiding party to what is now south central Mississippi. In the middle of the night, he stole away the Choctaw maiden and eventually made it back to his home in present day NW Tennessee, near the Mississippi River.

Sure enough, the Big Guy brought his wrath upon Kalopin, his people and the unfortunate Choctaw captive, and whipped up one heck of an earthquake. This occurred during the winter of 1811-12 and the initial tremor measured an estimated 8.5 on the Richter Scale. Chimneys were toppled in Atlanta, some 400 miles away and bells rang in Boston, about 900 miles from the epicenter. Numerous quakes and aftershocks, which originated from the New Madrid Fault, occurred for nearly one month. The force of the first quake was strong enough to cause the Mississippi River to flow backwards and during this, Kalopin et al were forever lost. The New Madrid Fault is still very active and the Reelfoot Lake region experiences a hundred or more minor quakes each year. The lesson in all this; Don't steal another guy's woman!

Kalopin adapted well to the new enclosure and even made use of her lowered perches. She ate well and was doing fine. However, I checked her one morning after she had been there for several days, and she had removed all of her bandages. She stood on one of her perches with her injured wing drooping noticeably. Luckily, Dr. Mike Douglass had returned from his trip and when he arrived at work, I brought him up to speed on the eagle. He suggested that we re-wrap Kalopin's wing so I got my gloves and went in and caught her. I noticed that her wing pivoted un-naturally at the break site so I carefully gathered her wing in a manner not to cause any damage. The wing felt as though something was wrong with the pin. I noticed something shiny on the floor of her enclosure. It was the pin! She had somehow managed to remove the pin as well as the bandages. As soon as Dr. Douglass examined the wing, he ordered an x-ray. He was concerned that there was more damage to the bone. We readied Kalopin and ourselves for an x-ray.

After the film was developed, the picture showed that there was no further damage. There also was some healing. The diameter of the pin may have been too small, but it didn't help the situation that she had gotten off her bandages. We were lucky her wing was not damaged considering that it had been free for an unknown number of hours. Since Dr. Douglass had to do morning rounds at the zoo, we re-wrapped the eagle's wing and put her in a smaller enclosure. Doc said that he needed to replace the pin and scheduled surgery after lunch.

Kalopin was readied for a second surgery in less than two weeks. It was pretty much the same procedure as the initial operation. This time, Dr. Douglass used a pin with a slightly larger diameter than the first. It fit more snugly and was slightly longer than the first. The surgery went well and after she recovered from the anesthesia, I put her in a smaller hospital enclosure until she had her wits about her. The next morning, after checking her wing, I put her back in her outside cage. The next three weeks were uneventful. She didn't remove her bandages and continued to eat well. Dr. Douglass decided it was time to have another look at her wing. We took the eagle into the hospital and did an x-ray. Doc looked at the film which showed excellent calcification of the bone. Mike put the bird under, removed the pin and closed the extraction site. He left the bandages off and stretched Kalopin's wing a few times. After her anesthesia had worn off, I put her back in her outside pen.

She didn't know quite how to react once she was released on the ground. Her wing drooped a little, but this was normal for a bird that hadn't really moved her wing in weeks. She hopped up to a low perch and flapped her mending wing a little. Dr. Douglass said that we would have to do some physical rehab on the wing in the form of daily stretching, extending and distending the limb, to loosen the muscles, tendons and ligaments. For about a week, I caught her twice a day, morning and afternoon for her stretching sessions. I was starting to see progress. By the end of the week, she was no longer drooping her wing. When she flapped both of her wings, she was getting more extension. She was now ready for her next phase of rehab.

The next step was to get Kalopin out and force/encourage her to fly. This involved putting some long, traditional style jeeses on her legs and then tying a long creance or line made from nylon parachute cord. I had 100 feet of line from when I trained Satch and I figured this to be about the right length since I would be running behind her. I tied the line to slits in her jesses using a bowline hitch. This was easy to tie and would not easily work loose, even if the line experienced a lot of tension. The next step in all of this was to take her out to the soccer field in Overton Park, toss her into the air and run behind her, just like I did a few years earlier with Chief Joseph. I got my friend and co-worker Mark Woods to help me. Mark and I alternated the handling and tossing of Kalopin. In these first attempts, I volunteered to be the runner. While I waited ready with the line, I felt like I was in a track meet in the hundred yard dash waiting for the starter's pistol. Our first attempts and throws were fairly gentle and without a lot of force. We just wanted her to use her wing to catch her balance and perhaps stretch her muscles. We did some manual wing extensions in these early sessions to warm her up.

The first day, we tossed her about five times. The first time she flew about ten feet, most just flapping to arrest her descent. When she landed, I held the line tight while Mark grabbed her feet and legs and gathered her wings and body in close to his chest. By the fifth "flight", she had gone about ten yards and was drooping her wing. We decided that she had had enough for one day. The next day's session was even better. On the first toss, she went ten yards. We did about ten tosses that day and by the last one, she had flown about 30 yards. I actually had to run a little on the last one.

These exercise sessions also drew a crowd. Think about it, you don't often see two guys throwing a Bald Eagle on a string into the air and chasing after it. Soon, Kalopin's exercise sessions became an afternoon event. After a week of these, Kalopin was flying better, more than 50 yards. We also had sometimes 20-30 spectators watching us exercise her. People actually started calling the zoo to see if we were going to exercise the eagle on a particular day. I was concerned that Menigar would get wind of this and stop me from exercising the bird. Strangely, he didn't say anything to me! Kalopin even made the local paper and one of the local network TV news did a story on her as well. I was again concerned that this would be a red flag to Menigar, but nothing was said.

After a couple of months, Kalopin was flying over 100 yards. On one windy day, she flew over 100 yards one way, turned and flew another fifty yards in the opposite direction. She also gained over thirty feet of altitude. As I was running along behind and below her, I had to figure out a way to bring her down without causing her to crash to the ground. I always kept a coil of about twenty extra feet of line to release once she got close to landing. This allowed her to get her feet below her as she flared to land. I gathered a couple of extra coils of line as I ran. I felt that as I started to slow down to bring her down, I could release the extra line as she got close to the ground. She was starting to fly towards a line of trees and I didn't want her to land in any tree, even a relatively small one. As I started to slow down, Kalopin began to lose altitude at a rapid rate. She had also turned slightly downwind. She looked as though she was going to hit the ground pretty hard, so at the last possible moment, I released all the extra line. The end of the creance was tied to my waist, so I wasn't worried about losing the line. To my surprise and great relief she landed without any problem. She had a look in her eyes like, "Damn, I almost made my getaway!"

It was now the end of March and Kalopin was ready to go back to Reelfoot. I contacted officials from the refuge to let them

189

know the good news. I said I could bring her for release the next day. The fellow I talked to told me to "hold that thought" because he wanted to discuss this with some of the other refuge people. He told me he would call me back the next day with a decision. I was a little stunned by the conversation. This eagle was ready to go and they didn't seem like they wanted her released. The next day, I eagerly took the call from the refuge manager. They had decided that they wanted me to hold on to the eagle until the next fall. They felt that since she was an adult and all of the other adults had left the lake for their home territories, she would be at a great disadvantage. Since she was out of the wild for nearly five months, her mate had possibly found a replacement and that she would be displaced from her nesting area. I understood the logic, but didn't agree with the decision. I felt that despite this that at least, she would be back in the wild. I reluctantly told the refuge people okay.

I was very disappointed and frustrated. This eagle was ready to go and I couldn't release her. I was tempted to release her anyway, but with all the publicity that had surrounded this bird, I couldn't go against the decision of the refuge management. It was a sad situation. Kalopin was all dressed up and had no place to fly.

I passed on the news to Dr. Douglass and Director Menigar. Both seemed to be disappointed as well. I told them I wanted to keep working with Kalopin to keep her in shape. Surprisingly again, I met no resistance from Menigar. The biggest limiting factor with my exercise method was warm weather. By the middle of May, it had become too warm to fly her with any consistency. I was afraid to stress her too much. Also, the exercise field was now dedicated to people playing soccer and softball. Her hospital enclosure was not large enough for her to keep up her flight conditioning. I had to find an alternative.

We had a pair of Bald Eagles on display at the zoo. Geronimo was the male, Quachita, the female, but they didn't seem to be a "pair" of birds. They hadn't really made much of an attempt at nesting. With eagles, as it is with many animals, there has to be a little chemistry for the birds to mate. In captivity, if the female doesn't like the male, she will frequently attack him. These birds were basically indifferent to each other. Their enclosure was a fairly large exhibit that was built in the 1930s. It had been renovated a few times. I helped convert it from a walk through aviary back into an Eagle Exhibit. It had a couple of trees; one was a large dead sweet gum tree that we had brought in as a nest tree. There was plenty of room for Kalopin to get some exercise. I ran the idea past Cliff, my boss and Bird Curator and he told me to "Go for it!"

I didn't know how the introduction of Kalopin to the aviary would go. Since Geronimo and Quachita weren't really a pair, I thought everything would be okay. I took her from her hospital enclosure and placed her in the aviary at the edge near one of the doors. She walked around and hopped onto a small log. Both Geronimo and Quachita spotted her and vocalized for a few moments. I got out of the enclosure and moved some distance away. Geronimo soon flew to a small tree above Kalopin and looked at her. Quachita observed from the dead sweet gum. There was no aggression. I watched for another thirty minutes and everything went well. Kalopin went into the shallow stream and took a bath. She also ate a fish. At the end of the day, Kalopin had made her way up into one of the smaller trees in the aviary and the other two birds pretty much ignored her.

Several weeks went by and Kalopin had settled in to life in the aviary. She had made her way up to the large sweet gum and was observed flying from the sweetgum to the smaller trees on many occasions. She was getting some exercise and the fact that she was making her way up to the largest tree showed me that she was getting in better flying shape. Good, it was all going to work out for Kalopin. Come Fall, and cooler weather, I could remove her from the exhibit, return her to a smaller enclosure and resume her exercise sessions.

Well, life has a way of shaking things up. I got a call one morning on my day off. It was Mark Woods and he informed me that Kalopin and Ouachita had been fighting and that I needed to get over to the zoo to do something about the situation. I quickly dressed and went to the zoo. As soon as I got to the front of the zoo, I heard the warning screams and threat calls from the direction of the eagle exhibit. I rapidly walked towards the enclosure and was met by Mark. He already had a net and some gloves there in case we needed to remove one of the birds. What Mark saw earlier was Kalopin and Ouachita locked together. Now, Kalopin was on one side of the exhibit and Ouachita was in the larger pool. We put on our long handling gloves and went in to check the combatants. Each bird earlier had appeared to have their feet and talons locked into each other's legs and chests. Ouachita hopped out of the pool and we quickly caught her. She was wet but unharmed. Fortunately, neither bird had found any vital spots. We caught both birds and checked each one for wounds. There were not any to really worry about. However, Kalopin had four of her primary or main flight feathers, broken. I could repair those through a process called imping, but my main concern was that she, Ouachita, and possibly Geronimo would be involved in more fights. We were lucky this time and I reluctantly decided to remove Kalopin from the aviary. In hindsight, I should have removed Quachita from the exhibit to give Kalopin a chance to continue her exercise.

I felt sorry for Ouachita. She had been in the breeding program at the USF&WS facility in Patuxent, Maryland. This facility had large breeding pens that had welded wire tops and

192

sides. This protected the birds from predators such as raccoons, but was terrible for the birds if they flew into the wire. I have seen a number of birds from the Patuxent facility that had head and beak damage. Ouachita was one such bird. Her head had a flattened look to it and she was literally bald in some spots. The skin above her left eye was drawn tighter than her right eye. She wasn't a pretty bird and I felt if I put her in a smaller enclosure, she would do further damage to her head. She and Geronimo had been paired together and didn't produce young. They were surplused from the breeding project and sent to the Little Rock Zoo. They were there for several years and the zoo decided to renovate the enclosure. I had visited the Little Rock Zoo in 1979 and met the bird keeper in charge of the birds of prey exhibit. She told me that they were going to get rid of all of the raptors in the exhibit to make way for a tropical bird exhibit. With that information, I was able to go back to the Memphis Zoo and convince Cliff to turn the walk through aviary back into a birds of prey display, for which was what it was originally built. We got Geronimo and Ouachita later in 1979. Geronimo and Ouachita had been great exhibit birds, so I didn't want to spoil this peaceful situation.

Kalopin spent the summer of 1983 in the hospital enclosure where we housed her after her pin was removed. I tried to exercise her one cool morning in June, but it was still too hot. She panted a lot and didn't really fly very far. It was just too stressful to exercise her this way. I would have to wait for the weather to cool down in autumn. It finally got cool enough in October to resume her training. She was, as expected, very out of shape. We stretched her wing several times before we tossed her. Her first flight only went for about ten yards. The next day, she did not go too much farther. A month went by, and she was only flying about 50 yards. She didn't seem to be responding as well to the exercise. The pressure was now on to get her in shape for release this winter. She was being fed more of a local fish diet, and this seemed to have strengthened her. By late December, she was up to about 100 yards. Still, this wasn't the same bird that was ready to go back the previous March. I don't know if she had hurt her wing somehow. The scrap with Ouachita didn't seem to hurt her wing at all. Maybe it was the long layoff.

Menigar was now starting to question me about the bird. He began to grow weary of the press this bird had generated. There were even some rumors around town that I had been cruel to Kalopin. One of my fellow Curators, Houston Winbigler, had taken a call from a citizen who had heard that I had somehow hurt the eagle and had been cruel to her. He quickly defended me and said that I had done nothing but good for the eagle. He was mad that someone would even think that way. I thanked him for my defense. Human nature can be pretty strange. It seems that the public was losing patience with me, too.

I took Kalopin out every day that I could for the next month. She still wasn't flying the way I had hoped. I don't know if she was tiring of the system or for some unknown reason physically wasn't up to the rigors of flying. Then came a small bombshell. At one of our senior staff meetings, Menigar asked me for a progress report on Kalopin. He said that a lot of people had been calling about her, wanting to know how she was doing and when she might possibly be released. I thought, stupidly, that Menigar was truly interested in her plight and progress. I told him what I knew and he said,

"I have got a release date for you." I was somewhat puzzled and he continued,

"You're are either going to release that bird on the Zoo's annual eagle watching trip to Reelfoot Lake or you are going to tell the press and everybody that you have failed in her rehabilitation and we will send the bird to another facility!"

194

The Zoo's annual trip, which I had been leading for three years was only three weeks away.

"I'm not sure if she will be ready by that time or not. I want to see her flying a little farther…"

Menigar cut me off…

"Well, either release her at Reelfoot in three weeks or send her away! I am tired of dealing with this bird! End of discussion!"

Everybody at the meeting looked at me with the expression like "I can't believe he just told you that!" I had been given an ultimatum!

For the next three weeks, Kalopin was exercised every day, even if it was raining, we took her to the soccer field. We could get her to fly about 100 yards, but no more. It was as if she said after 100 yards, "That's it, I'm not flying anymore!" A few times, with a little coaxing, we were able to get her to take off from the ground into the wind. Usually on these flights, she would fly 20-30 yards and land. So, I knew she had the capability to launch off the ground. The day before the Reelfoot trip, Mark Woods and I managed to get her to fly about 90 yards in a strong breeze, but after that distance, she landed on her own free will. Mark asked me,

"Are you going to let her go tomorrow?"

I said,

"What option do I have? It's either try her tomorrow or send her away. We have put too much time in this bird to not give her a chance!"

Mark agreed. Menigar wanted me to inform him of my decision after we exercised her. After we trudged back into the zoo and put Kalopin in her enclosure, I went to Menigar's door and knocked. He looked up and said,

"Have you made a decision? What's it going to be, release or failure?"

I told him that I was going to take her to Reelfoot.

He said,

"Well I'll call the media to let them know. What time are you leaving the zoo and where are you going to release her?"

I told him that the bus leaves the zoo's front parking lot at 4:00 a.m. and that Kalopin will be released at a boat ramp just south of Airpark Inn on the northwest side of the lake. Any media personnel are welcomed to follow the bus or meet us at the ramp area.

"I am planning to go on the trip as well." Menigar announced. "Some friends of mine, my wife, and I will follow the bus to the lake".

"Alright", was all I could respond, but in reality I was thinking, "That's just great! The last person in the world I wanted there would have a front row view".

I called the Refuge to let them know of my plans and they even offered to have a boat standing by in case we needed it. We were to leave at 4:00 a.m. to catch the eagles as they left their roosts. There was a lot of feeding activity from sunrise to about 8:00 a.m. Since Reelfoot was two hours from Memphis, the early departure time would get us there at sunrise.

The next morning, I got to the zoo at 3:15 a.m. I had set aside a sky kennel and a large net and handling gloves so I could quickly grab Kalopin and have her in my car. I, too, was to follow the bus to the release spot. I had a hatchback car, so I had plenty of room for the kennel. It didn't take much to catch Kalopin. She was asleep, so I just walked up to her, grabbed her feet and gathered her wings and placed her in the carrier. I drove slowly through the zoo and out to the parking lot. The bus was there and people were already loading. I went aboard and talked to a number of people who were going on our tour. A few asked about Kalopin and I told them that I thought she was ready to go. By 4:00 a.m., the bus pulled out of the Zoo's parking lot and up Highway 51 we went.

We arrived at Reelfoot Lake State Park a little after 6:00 a.m. The sun was just starting to rise and several eagles were flying around, searching for food. I pulled into the lead before we got to the boat ramp and led the bus and the caravan to the small parking area. I chose this spot for release because it had a row of cypress trees about 100 yards from the shore. This stand of trees would offer Kalopin a target to fly towards and plenty of low limbs for her to choose for a landing. This area also had plenty of fish and was frequented by a lot of waterfowl, another food source. Once she settled in, she had a good place to find food.

Quite a crowd had gathered. I noticed that two of the three network affiliate TV stations from Memphis had sent a crew to cover the release. The local Memphis paper had sent a reporter as well. Personnel from the Tennessee Wildlife Resources Agency were there with a boat, just in case we needed it. There were also a number of other people who had not come with our group. They had apparently followed Kalopin's story. It had the feel of a special event and it was. It is not every day you get to see an eagle released and Kalopin had become a celebrity. This is not the way I wanted to send her back to freedom. If something didn't go as planned, it would be in front of a few hundred people. Still, I wasn't given much of a choice; try to release her today or send her away and admit failure. Open up the flaps to the big top tent and let the circus begin!

Everyone had filed off the bus, the spectators got their cameras ready, the wildlife officers got the boat fired up and the television crews readied their equipment. I was very nervous and it didn't help to see my nemesis, Menigar, wandering around the scene like a NASCAR fan waiting for a crash. We locked eyes for a second and he had a small smirk on his face. I tried to ignore him

197

and focus on the immediate task. I went to the back of my car and opened the hatch. I heard cameras clicking as a spun the kennel around and put on my gloves. Wanda Elder, one of the raptor rehab volunteers and trip co-leader, was there to help me with Kalopin. As I extracted the eagle from the kennel, Wanda helped me gather her wings. She also helped me put on a transmitter. The cameras clicked and whirred with everything we did. I did a short interview with the media, basically saying that I hoped that she would fly to the tree line and get her bearings to where she was and later fly away. I mentioned we had a boat standing by in case things didn't go as planned.

The moment of truth was upon me. The stage was set; lights, camera, action! I didn't rehearse my lines or check my look, but I did say a quick prayer asking that this release would go well. I took Kalopin within ten yards from the water's edge and readied her for release. I switched my grip on her feet, turned her on her stomach, and held her wings, just as we had done when we exercised her on the soccer field. I told the crowd that the release/launch would be on the count of three.

"Here we go…one, two, three!"

I shoved Kalopin into the air with a combination of a shot put/javelin throw. I aimed her slightly up as well. She poured into the air with several strong flaps and at first, dipped down low over the water. I thought she was going to hit the water, but managed to stay airborne. Behind me, I could hear the crowd cheering and applauding. My focus, however, was on Kalopin as she was now flying about two feet above the water heading for the cypress trees. It seemed like time had slowed a bit and she continued to churn the air...50 yards…70 yards… and at about 100 yards away, near the trees, she landed in the water! All I could mutter was,

"Oh sh*t!" as the crowd emitted a group "Awwaaaaahhh!"

This had now turned from a release to a rescue, from a dream to a nightmare! I ran to my car and grabbed the large fishing net and hopped into the waiting jon boat. I could see Kalopin floating and flapping as she was trying to swim towards the tree line. A Bald Eagle can float quite well and can swim with it wings. We quickly covered the 100 or so yards. I slipped the net over her head and then her body as I hoisted her out of the cold water. I grabbed both feet and extracted the soaked and shivering eagle from the net. I heard a small cheer from the crowd. Not exactly the kind of cheer I wanted at the moment. We headed back to shore and I soon faced one of the most embarrassing moments of my life. This far exceeded the time when Satch wouldn't come down from the basketball goal. This was my personal Hindenburg crash, flames and all. The home team missed the field goal at the last second which would have won the game. Shanked it to the right! There are many more metaphors I could say, but I was now stuck in the moment. The crowd and cameras gathered at our landing point. If there was ever a good time for a second Great Reelfoot Earthquake, it would have been now. Something that would swallow me up so I wouldn't have to face the truth. Reality sometimes sucks!

One of the first things asked was what went wrong. The only thing I could figure at was that she still thought she was on the creance and flew her usual 100 yards. The question then was what was the immediate plan for her? Would we try again to release her? If so, when? Paul Brown, from the T.W.R.A. pulled me aside and said that I had a place to stay if we wanted to let Kalopin dry off for another try later or on Sunday. This sounded great and I relayed this to the crowd and press. I was able to save face a little with this, but it wasn't about me, it was about giving Kalopin another chance. Wanda offered to continue leading the tour. She had been a number of times and knew where to take the group. I gladly said yes to her offer and this would allow me to focus on Kalopin. Afterwards, Menigar walked up to me. His eyes were bloodshot and he acted like he was high. He had a slight smile and simply stated the obvious and muttered,

"That didn't go very well!"

No sh*t! Thanks in part to your ultimatum, you as$wart! These inside words that didn't pass my lips, but if someone deserved a free punch in the face, it was Menigar! He added,

"I'll see you at the zoo on Monday".

With this, ZigZag walked back to his car, got in and drove off; I am sure celebrating my fine, public humiliation.

With camera still rolling and clicking, I put the disheveled Kalopin back in the kennel. A lot of people wished her well and hope that things would work out better later. I thanked everyone gathered for their support and patience. I just wanted to get this over with and regroup. I followed Paul to the Agency's headquarters on the south side of the lake. Here I was able to put Kalopin in a moderately heated room to allow her to gradually dry. Several hours passed and I checked Kalopin. She still wasn't totally dry and it was getting late in the day. I made the decision to try her the next morning and at a different location. I was able to stay in the headquarters overnight.

The next morning, we took the eagle to Kirby's Pocket. This section of the lake was on the opposite side from where we tried to release her on Saturday. This was also a boat launching ramp, so the wildlife guys had their boat in the water. This time, there was no press, no crowds and only a few puzzled fishermen. I decided to place Kalopin on the ground, this time about 30 yards from the water's edge. There were plenty of cypress trees, stumps and snags available for landing. The wind was blowing from the direction of the water, so Kalopin could launch into the wind. Once I placed her on the ground, I backed away about thirty yards. Kalopin sat there, just looking around. I'm sure she was trying to get her bearings again and continued to sit for several minutes. I didn't want to force her to fly, but I didn't think she realized that she was free. I started walking towards her in hope she would take off in the direction of the lake. She hopped a little and then I began a full speed run, waving my arms and yelling trying to scare her into the air. She took off and flew down the slight slope of the boat ramp. She made it about fifty yards and splashed into the water again. This time, it looked as though she favored her left wing. Once again, we fished her out of the lake. This isn't how I expected this second attempt to go! Something was wrong and I couldn't force her to do this again. As I put her back in the kennel, I had to accept the fact that she was not going back to the wild. Defeat was hard to swallow.

I drove back to Memphis and put Kalopin back in her hospital enclosure. I called members of the press and updated them on Kalopin's second attempt. I called Wanda and then Mark to let them know what had occurred. The next day, I stopped by Menigar's office to let him know that Kalopin didn't fly away, again. He simply said,

"Well, that's too bad!"

I expected him to tell me to start looking for a place to send her. But nothing. He had gotten what he wanted; my humiliation in a nice publicity package. He couldn't have scripted it better. Dr. Douglass did an exam of her and found nothing that should have kept her from flying properly. Kalopin remained in the hospital enclosure through the end of the summer. Geronimo and Ouachita didn't nest that spring either.

Later in the fall, we were able to incorporate Kalopin back into the eagle exhibit. Everything went a lot more smoothly this time. There was little aggression between Kalopin and Ouachita. But, it wasn't breeding season either. A few years later, Ouachita

201

was temporarily released at Reelfoot. Since she wasn't making it as a breeding bird and Kalopin and Geronimo had paired, we decided to see if she could be hacked back into the wild. There were a few cases were some long term captive eagles were returned to the wild by hacking them out as if they were young eagles. This made sense. The bird was free to discover the new area and if it had trouble hunting or finding food, it could return to the hack station. I ran the idea past Bob Hatcher who was the Head Non-game and Endangered Species Coordinator for the Tennessee Wildlife Resources Agency. Bob was in charge of all the eagle release projects in the State of Tennessee. Through his guidance, breeding pairs were restored across the state. Bob thought that Ouachita was a good candidate for this hacking release and arrangements were made to send Ouachita to Reelfoot during the summer releases. I was working at another facility by that time and I was there when Ouachita was hacked. She adjusted well to the hacking enclosure and after two weeks, was released. She was spotted a number of times in the area and it seemed that she was going to make the transition.

However, a problem developed. Since she had been in captivity for a long time, she had no real fear of humans. The TWRA fellows who delivered the fish to the hack site said that whenever they got close to the road by the hack station, she would appear and started flying alongside their vehicle. When they stopped, she landed nearby expecting food, so they fed her. The type of truck they drove was similar to the truck we used to deliver food throughout the zoo. She associated the zoo truck with food. She had now done the same with this truck. This wasn't a problem for the short term, but the hacking season was nearly finished and soon the guys would no longer be delivering fish to the station. They feared that she might wander away from the area and either get injured by someone or hurt a person. She was recaptured by a wildlife officer.

Reelfoot Lake State Park was in the process of finishing an eagle display near the R.C. Donaldson Museum. The timing couldn't have been better. Ouachita was sent back to the Zoo for a short period and eventually went on display at Reelfoot. She lived several more years in captivity and was in the company of a number of other eagles. One morning, she was found dead. No sign of injury or foul play. She didn't have the best life, but at least she was comfortable and had a rare chance to return to the wild, even for a short time.

Kalopin and Geronimo had made some attempts at nesting and I even found an egg, albeit broken, in their enclosure. After I left the zoo, another nesting structure was erected, but they never produced any offspring. Up to ten years after leaving the Memphis Zoo, I could go up to the eagle exhibit to see Kalopin and Geronimo. She always recognized me and would give an alert call when she spotted me. She had not forgotten me. I mean, how could she?! We had spent a lot of time together. I wish I had been successful in returning her to the wild, but sometimes, things are not to be. A few years back, I got a call from Knox Martin who had taken over the Raptor Rehab Project at the Zoo after I had left. At this point, Kalopin had been in captivity for over twenty years. He had some bad news. He informed me that Kalopin was found dead in her enclosure that morning. He said that nothing was conclusive of why she had died and a necropsy didn't reveal anything. Perhaps she died of old age. We never really knew how old she was since she came to us as an adult. Upon arrival, she could have been five years old or fifteen. Still the news saddened me, but then I realized that death had given Kalopin something I couldn't; freedom!

Chapter 27

Osceola

During Kalopin's recovery time at the zoo, we got in another Bald Eagle. On January 20, 1983, I got a call from a wildlife officer in eastern Arkansas. He said that he had an immature Bald Eagle that was found near Lepanto, Arkansas. He told me that a couple of rabbit hunters were hunting near Spear Lake and were crossing a field where they spotted this eagle on the ground. They noticed as they walked towards it, that it began to run but could not get into the air. It was favoring its left wing and essentially dragged it as it attempted to become airborne. The guys chased down the eagle and surrounded it. To control the eagle, one fellow took off his jacket and tossed it over the bird. This covered the young eagle's head and allowed the hunters to get control of the bird's powerful feet. They kept the bird wrapped in the jacket and went to the nearest phone. They contacted an Arkansas Game and Fish Wildlife Officer to let him know of the injured eagle. The officer contacted me, arranged for transfer from the hunters and eventually met me an hour or so later near Osceola, Arkansas.

Wanda Elder went with me and we met the officer at a gas station just off Interstate 55. The officer had the dark-headed eagle in a burlap bag, which may not sound like the best way to transport the injured bird, but in this case, it worked out well. It kept the broken wing immobile and kept the feet at bay.

"The wing's pretty bad!" the wildlife officer said as we did the initial check.

Wanda helped me extract the eagle from the bag. The bird was fairly small which indicated that this was a male. We noticed that he had feather lice, a sign that he wasn't doing as well as he should. Wanda gathered his feet and put him in position to check his left wing. He had a smell to him that indicated that his injury was old. The left wing was definitely loose. As I manipulated the wing, I felt bone grinding against bone. I also noticed a fair amount of dried blood on his feathers. Curiously, he had dried blood on his beak and feet. I emitted a "hmmm" as I looked at this. The officer piped in,

"Oh yeah, the rabbit hunters said that the bird was apparently feeding on a dead 'possum at the point where they first saw him."

Perhaps, this opossum had sensed the possibility of a meal and tried to attack the injured bird. In this case, the 'possum's plan had a fatal flaw. I wrapped the wing with a figure 8 wrap and put a wrap of the stretchy bandage around his body to immobilize the wing. We put him back in the burlap bag, since it helped keep his wings and feet together. His head stuck out of the top of the bag and he seemed to be content. Wanda gathered the eagle and held him in her arms. I helped her into the passenger seat and closed the door. With traffic, we were about an hour from the zoo.

"Yuck!" Wanda exclaimed.

"What, what's wrong?" I asked.

"I've got lice climbing up my arms!"

I said" Don't worry, they are host specific and only eat feathers on birds and totally harmless to human".

"Yeah, that's easy for you to say since their not crawling on your neck and face!" Wanda exclaimed with much fervor.

When we got back to the zoo and drove directly to the hospital. Dr. Douglass instructed us to bring the eagle into the exam room. Wanda and I extracted the bird from the burlap bag. While Wanda controlled his head, I got a hold of the bird's feet.

Once we got him completely under control, Dr. Douglass cut the bandages on the broken wing. The wing bones crunched and ground in a sickening fashion as I felt the eagle try to flap the injured limb. Doc had me put the eagle on its back so he could more closely examine the wing. Dr. Douglass discovered a hole in the wing where the broken humerus had poked through the skin. He also found a groove in the outer wing where it looked like a .22 caliber bullet had grazed the wing near the wrist. This was similar to a mark that the eagle, Chief Joseph, had a few years earlier. Doc speculated that the grazing bullet caused this eagle to spiral out of control until he hit the ground. He said by the sight of the wound, the injury and break may have been a week old. We did a quick x-ray to check the extent of the damage.

The film revealed a fairly clean break, but time was working against the eagle. Doc decided to do surgery to put a pin in the wing. After the eagle was sedated, Mike was able to get a closer look at the wing. He mentioned that the blood flow to the lower part of the wing seemed to be compromised. As we got further into the surgery, it became apparent that the lower part of the humerus was not in good shape. Mike made a decision to try to fuse the eagle's wing. His plan was to cut the humerus back until he was sure it had a vascular supply, in other words, blood flow in the bone. He clipped the upper part of the humerus until it was about three inches from the shoulder. The lower humerus was cut until an inch above the elbow. He said that he wasn't sure that there was enough of a blood supply to the lower wing, but he was going to give it a try. The humerus ends were pinned and wired together and everything was sewn up and wrapped. He was given an injection of strong antibiotics to try to arrest an infection. Eventually, the young eagle awoke from the surgery and was placed in an inside hospital enclosure.

I placed several herring in with the eagle and a later check revealed that all the fish were gone. The next day, we gave him antibiotics and several more herring. He looked fairly alert and his bandages were all intact. He ate about six fish that day and that was a good sign. He had an appetite and I felt good about this bird.

The third day, however, was not a banner day. When I got to the zoo, I immediately went to the hospital to check the eagle. What I saw wasn't good. He was fluffed up with his eyes partially closed and obviously wasn't feeling too good. I moved around in front of him, hoping to get him to react to my presence. He didn't respond as I had hoped. It was still an hour before Mike got in, so I made my morning rounds to make sure everything in the bird section was okay. As soon as Dr. Douglass arrived, he went to check the eagle. In fact, he was at the bird's enclosure when I went back to the hospital.

"John, we need to catch him so I can check his wing. I have a feeling what we're going to find isn't going to be good!"

Mike understated the seriousness of the situation. Doc went into the exam room and got several things ready to check the wing. I easily caught the eagle and he didn't offer much resistance. At this point, I began to worry about his survival.

I brought him into the exam room and Mike un-wrapped the wing. A sickening smell greeted us as we got the bird on the table. The skin of the wing below the elbow had a greenish hue. It didn't take long for Mike to come to a decision,

"Gangrene has set in. In order to try to save him, I am going to have to amputate his wing!"

There was some sadness to Mike's words.

"Do you have anything to do for the next twenty minutes or so? If not, I'll need your help". Doc asked.

"No, I am free", I replied.

He told his Vet Tech Kathy to get everything prepped for surgery.

"I hope we can save him", I muttered as I handed the eagle to Kathy so that I could put on a surgical apron, gloves and a mask.

"Yeah, me, too!" Kathy remarked as she handed the bird back to me.

Kathy got all the surgical stuff ready and put on her apron, gloves and mask. We placed the bird on his back on the table and put the anesthesia mask over his head. Kathy dialed in the mixture of oxygen and halothane and the eagle slowly went to sleep. My job during surgery was to monitor the bird's breathing. Kathy plucked the area that was to be the amputation site.

Mike put on his surgical garb and opened surgical packs that contained scalpels, scissors and a tool to remove the pin. The first order was to remove the pin and wires. Next, the main blood vessels were clamped off that carried blood to the lower wing. There were not a whole lot of these. Dr. Douglass believed that a lot of the vessels were severed when the bone went compound. This resulted in the gangrene which led to this amputation. The vessels were clamped, the area was scrubbed and the only thing left to do was remove the wing. It is always a sad occasion when a bird loses its wing.

Mike started at the patagium part of the wing. This is the skin that runs from the shoulder to the wrist. I held the wing up where Mike could get to it. Kathy sponged the small amount of blood as Mike began to cut. The removal went fairly fast and there was little bleeding. I set the lifeless wing aside. It almost didn't look real. Dr. Douglass pulled skin over the remaining humerus and sewed the end to seal the site. It was coated with a topical antibiotic salve to protect the site from bacteria. Kathy handed Mike some gauze and Vet Wrap to bandage the nub. In a few moments, it was all done.

Kathy turned the dial on the oxygen to replace the halothane in the eagle's mask. I held his feet and prepared to scoop him off the table when the anesthesia wore off. It didn't take long. He was soon blinking and moving. Kathy pulled the mask and I gathered him into my arms. He was now a permanent resident of captivity. As I held him to make sure he was no longer groggy, I decided he needed a name. He was found near Spear Lake near the town of Lepanto. Lepanto wasn't a very catchy name for an eagle. Suddenly it hit me! Osceola! The town where we met the wildlife officer was named after the great Seminole leader. A fitting name for a Bald Eagle. I told Mike and Kathy that I had his name and they though it a good one. I put Osceola in his hospital enclosure and hoped he would survive the day. By the end of the day, he looked better. He was a lot more alert and had eaten a fish. The source of his discomfort, his toxic lower wing had been removed. He was looking a whole lot better than what he did this morning. It looked like Osceola was going to make it.

The next morning, I made a beeline to the hospital. I went to the enclosure where Osceola was kept. I didn't know what to expect when I peered inside, but he was very alert. He had eaten all of his food and seemed to be looking for more. Removing the dying wing really helped his physical state. Dr. Douglass was early that morning and he was quick to check Osceola's condition.

"Well, it looks as though he's going to make it", Mike wryly commented. "It seems that cutting his wing off was the best thing we could do for him!" Mike continued.

Sad to say, it was true. At least now, Osceola had a chance to live. We kept Osceola in the indoor enclosure for another week and I set up an outside cage next to Kalopin's.

The local Audubon Society Chapter President, Maury Radin, called me to inform me that they were putting up a $3000 reward for information that lead to the arrest of Osceola's gunman.

USF&WS Agent Joe Forrester was on the case already. The local media was alerted and Osceola's story along with the reward information was covered on TV and in the local paper. There was a picture of Osceola in the *Commercial Appeal* newspaper with the caption "Lost to a Hunter", referring to Osceola's wing. It also mentioned the reward money. Of course, a good hunter wouldn't shoot an eagle or any other non-game animal. The two rabbit hunters who found Osceola saved his life. An idiot with a gun was the person who shot the young eagle. Several weeks went by and no one came forward with any information. Joe Forrester said he had a few leads but nothing panned out in the case. It seems that the shooter was going to go unpunished. The Feds keep an eagle shooting case open for ten years. No one was ever prosecuted in Osceola's case.

After a month, Osceola's wing nub had healed enough where I could start handling him. I had several birds in my small outreach program, including Satch, but I didn't have a bird of Rock Star status like a Bald Eagle. I put some traditional jesses on Osceola and tried to get him to sit on my gloved hand. He was a little frightened of the whole procedure and refused to stay on the glove for longer than a few seconds. It wasn't a natural thing for an eagle to do. However, I did take him on some programs.

The first program where he was used was at Ford Elementary School in New Albany, Mississippi. My aunt, Elsie Stokes, was the librarian at the school and I had been doing an annual program there for about five years. I told her that I had a special bird this day. After I flew Satch over the children several times, I had the kids excited to see the last bird. I slowly extracted Osceola out of his travel kennel and cradled him with his feet down. This allowed me to show his good wing and this was comfortable for Osceola. The children were impressed. Even though he didn't have the signature white head and tail, they realized that they were seeing our National Symbol. Osceola was fairly calm throughout his time and when we were finished, he returned to his travel kennel without any problems. For the next few weeks, I used Osceola on several more school programs. I cradled him in the same way and the children's reactions were the same. Once again, this was 1983 and the Bald Eagle was still coming back. So to see any Bald Eagle up close was truly a treat.

Throughout the summer, I worked more with Osceola, focusing on getting him to stand on my glove. He gradually got used to the idea of standing on this foreign perch. I had to be careful not to move too quickly or he would bate, or jump off my glove. He wouldn't hit the ground, but dangled from his leather jesses. I rapidly helped him back on my glove, but sometimes he would jump off as quickly as he was upright again. I also had to get him used to going into his travel kennel. I really worried about stressing him during this period. I avoided working with him on hot days and also had to avoid working with him while I was on Menigar's "Whipping Boy" list. This really limited my handling time to weekend mornings and some days later in the afternoon.

I really limited the information I told Menigar. People were already calling the zoo asking about Osceola and when he might be seen. Whenever he asked me about training the eagle, I usually said, with some truth, I didn't have a lot of time work with him due to my other zoo duties. I didn't want him to focus on my activities with Osceola or Satch, for that matter.

Menigar was really checking into the rehab project as well. He demanded that I put together the number of birds that had entered the rehab project versus how many we had released. He also wanted to know how much food the rehab project was using. The raptor rehab project had always gotten a lot of publicity. People were very interested in raptors and every bird we released had almost celebrity status. The local TV and newspapers usually sent

211

someone to cover the release of a hawk or owl. Kalopin was still a local celebrity even though she didn't make it back to the wild. This publicity seemed to irk Menigar. It shouldn't have. It was positive for the zoo at a time when people were questioning a zoo's worth. This was something we could point to as a beneficial thing the zoo did.

I got the figures together and over a five year period, we had a 56% success rate. Some years were better than others. We did use some zoo food in the form of birds of prey diet, but we also had some local sources of donated rats and mice. The Memphis Audubon Society had donated several thousand dollars for enclosures and needed equipment. Dr. Douglass used the experience gained on the raptors to help in his treatment of the non-raptorial birds in the zoo's collection. All in all, the Raptor Rehab Project didn't drain the zoo's resources too greatly and brought better public awareness. It should have been part of the Zoo's showcased activities, but because it was my project, it was becoming more scrutinized and was increasingly in danger of being canceled.

I did my best to downplay my raptor activities. I started doing more of the free birds of prey programs on my days off, even though public education was part of my job description. I didn't want Menigar to have more ammo or evidence to use against to rehab project. Osceola was becoming the public face of the zoo's raptor outreach efforts. I didn't want Menigar to make a move against using Osceola in these programs. Even though everything was moving in a positive direction for the rehab program, the pressure was building on me. My "Whipping Boy" periods were becoming longer and more frequent. Sometime in the future, something had to give.

Chapter 28

Let's have a party Zoo-style
(By the way, make sure no one gets killed!)

Over the course of working at the Zoo, we had a number of parties. Most of them were very fun. They ranged from Zoo Grass, where the public was invited to listen to bluegrass music while enjoying free beer, popcorn and peanuts to zoo personnel only parties for Halloween or Christmas. Most of these parties were well organized and without too many problems.

Well, it was about time for an early summer party. The zoo staff had worked very hard all year and they were demanding to let off a little steam. The only problem was that none of the Senior Staff wanted to stay for the entire event. In order to have a party, a Curator or Assistant Curator had to be there to monitor the party and keep things in line. I was willing to be that staff member so I went to the Assistant Zoo Director, Duane Able, to tell him I would be the Designated Party Monitor. He said,

"Alright, if you want to do this, it's okay to have a party".

I told him, "Thank you!"

Before I left his office, Duane added,

"By the way, Stokes, make sure no one gets killed!"

I laughed and said "I'll do my best to make sure that doesn't happen".

Duane was being funny, but there was a slight twinge of truth to his statement. People who care for animals are cut from a different cloth and we had some interesting characters employed at the zoo.

With official permission, we started making plans on when the party would be, what food we would have and what beverages would be available. With everything falling in place, we finally decided on a Friday in mid-June. The zoo's American Association of Zookeepers chapter (AAZK) provided funding for most of the food and a couple of kegs of beer. The other food and refreshments were purchased though the Education Department and we used the education building, a converted Elephant Barn, for the party. We set up a volleyball net outside of the building, for many of the keepers played volleyball in the park after work. We had all the fixings for a great party. Friday arrived and all the last minute preparations were done, including cleaning the hippo pool for some late night keeper aquatics. After work, I went home to change clothes and to get my girlfriend Cindy.

We arrived at the zoo around seven and help set up the tables of finger food and beverages and helped tap the keg. People started coming in soon after seven o'clock and a few of the guests were in swimming attire. They dropped by to get some beer and some food before heading down to the hippo pool. They were braver than me and even though they assured everyone that the pool was clean, I couldn't help to think they may have missed a few "floaters". If you've ever seen an old style hippo exhibit you might know what I'm talking about; the pool water is clean until the hippo "releases ballast". Then, it looks like a sewage treatment pond with a couple of very large turds floating around. I opted to skip the swimming.

Most everybody that came went for the food and beverages first and had the usual small talk. We had some music as well in the form of a cassette stereo. It was a good atmosphere. Then things slowly began to change. After about an hour, Rob Nathum showed up. Rob was one of the Reptile Keepers and was a very intelligent fellow. In high school, Rob was a straight "A" student and was a model of good behavior. One day after school, Rob went

214

home and discovered that his mother had committed suicide. This was a terrible thing for anyone to discover, especially if the person was your parent. It was traumatic for a seventeen year old and Rob's life was never the same. He was an excellent zookeeper and there was never any trouble at work. However, at some of our parties, Rob was a live wire. Tonight was no exception.

At first, there wasn't any indication that Rob was going to be any trouble. I noticed something was amiss when I was standing in beer line behind him. Before he got his beer cup, he went over to the snack table and smeared french onion dip on both of his arms. He then returned to the tap and washed both his arms off with beer. To be sure, in any culture, this was an interesting form of hygiene. I asked him if he needed a cup and he turned and looked at me with an unusual smile and a faraway look in his eyes. He then picked up a cup and filled it with beer and walked outside.

I got my beer and found Richard Weeks, the Education Curator (the same guy that had the pet roach, Cheech). I asked him if he had noticed Rob. He said that he had. I told him that I thought Rob was stoned. He replied,

"I don't think he's high on marijuana, just look at his eyes. I think he's on something else, maybe PCP. I'll keep an eye on him, too!"

"What does PCP do to a person?" I asked and Richard said,

"It puts one in an altered state of mind, gives that person a lot of energy and makes them somewhat impervious to pain".

"Oh, great!" was my response. Richard nodded.

I thanked him for his help and continued on with the party. Cindy and I went outside and started watching the volleyball game. I heard a commotion inside and said,

"Oh no, I hope it's not Rob!"

Well, it was. It seems that he was over bathing in the beer again when one of the zoo's secretaries bent over to put some food

215

on her plate. Rob apparently liked what he saw and decided to grope the unsuspecting woman. She turned, saw who it was and said,

"Rob, you're a nasty boy!"

She didn't make too much of it, but hastily got her plate and found a seat. I asked her if she was okay and she said she was fine.

"Rob's pretty weird tonight and I figured it was best not to make anything of it. Have you seen his eyes?" she asked.

I told her that we thought he was on PCP and we were watching him to make sure he didn't get too out of hand. To this, she replied,

"I think you have your hands full. Good luck!"

I saw Richard and he added, "This could get interesting".

Rob wandered back outside. At least there wasn't much he could hurt out there. A little bit later, Cindy and I got to play volleyball. We had been at it for about fifteen minutes when Rob came charging onto the court shouting,

"I'm LSU, I'm LSU!" referring to Louisiana State University and Rob was obviously a fan of the football team.

He then ran full speed into the volleyball net and with every action, there's an equal and opposite reaction. Rob went flying backwards with almost as much speed as with he had hit the net. He sprawled out on the ground laughing and said,

"Nice tackle!"

We all thought he was trying to be funny and laughed along with him. He then jumped straight up with his arms in the air and said,

"I'm LSU!" and took off running into the zoo.

We resumed our game and about ten minutes later, Rob came back again, running at full speed and once again shouting,

"I'm LSU, I'm LSU!" and, you guessed it, right into the volleyball net.

This time he hit it slightly lower and the resulting impact flipped Rob into a partial somersault. He lay there for a second and jumped up and said,

"Yeeeaaah!!! I've gotta pee".

This time, everyone was a little more concerned. I decided to follow Rob inside to make sure he didn't destroy anything. I saw him go into the front part of the building by the restroom. A female keeper had gone in right before him and everything seemed to be civilized. I stepped back into the other room to get a snack. Apparently Rob believed that there was a time limit to use the restroom. The next thing I heard was a woman's scream. I ran back to the restroom area and there was the previous occupant sprawled out on the floor, pants still around her ankles. I looked away as she pulled up her pants and she said that Rob had opened the door, pulled her off the toilet and slung her on the floor. Rob emerged from the restroom and said,

"Whooooo Boy!" and went running back outside.

The lady was okay, but now I was concerned that Rob might hurt someone other than himself. There was no telling where he went when he ran out into the zoo. I looked around but didn't see him anywhere. In fact, nobody saw Rob for almost an hour. We all thought he had left the zoo which was great for us, but he was possibly out terrorizing the nearby neighborhood.

It was now close to 11:00 p.m. Eleven o'clock was the time we usually ended our parties. There was still about half a keg left over and one of the keepers, David O'Brien, volunteered to take it to his house. Anyone that wanted to continue partying could go to David's. We located a "float", a flat cart with wheels, on which to load the keg to wheel to David's truck. The easiest way to get the float into the building was through the back doors. So, we opened both back doors as wide as they could go. As David wheeled the float through the doors, Rob came running through the room from the opposite direction. He never saw the cart and hit it full speed and shin-high. He had so much momentum that his feet were completely knocked out from under him. He looked like a bizarre super hero as he flew through the air towards the volleyball net. He may have flown ten yards or so and impacted with a breathtaking thud. I thought he was seriously hurt. He lay on the ground for a few seconds and then hopped up, rubbed both shins a little and took off running again, emitting a "War Whoop" as he vanished into the darkness.

Everyone who witnessed this was a little stunned. I was now concerned because we were almost ready to shut everything down and go home. We helped David load the keg onto the float and then into his truck. He drove his truck out into the parking lot and returned to get a few other items. Everyone else started to leave. There were still about ten of us left.

Once again, I sought Richard. He had a degree in Psychology and had been a high school teacher before coming to the zoo. I asked,

"What are we going to do about Rob?"

His plan was genius! He calmly replied,

"He thinks he's an LSU football player. Let's see if we can use that to our advantage."

Most everyone now was near the main gate. Richard said,

"We need your help getting Rob out of here. He thinks he's a football player, and now, so are all of you!"

I heard several people saying, "What?!?"

"No really, if we can make Rob think he is part of a football play, maybe we can get him out of the zoo and close the gate behind him", Richard explained.

Everybody started shaking their heads in agreement. The next thing Richard did was almost so ridiculous that you would think that it wouldn't work.

"Alright team, let's huddle up! Let's huddle up, huddle up!" each time his voice got louder. As if by magic, Rob suddenly came running up to our makeshift huddle.

"What's the play coach? Gimme me the ball cause I want to score". Rob responded.

We all looked at each other with the looks of "You're kidding me! This may actually work!" Rob was running in place when Richard grabbed both his shoulders, looked him in the eyes and said,

"I want you to run through the front gate and execute a post pattern to the left. Do you know what a post pattern is?" Rob said,

"Yeah Coach, just get me the ball!"

Richard said, "I'll throw it to you when you're open, can I count on you to score?"

Rob yelled, "Yes coach, get me the ball, I want to make a touchdown!"

"Alright, the snap will be after 3 on hike. Everybody line up. Let's win this game!"

So, there we were, lined up in our formation, no football or even anything that looked like a ball. Rob lined up on the right hand side. Richard got in the quarterback position...

"Everybody set, 91, 72, 45, 38, 3 hut, hut hike!"

At this, the imaginary ball was hiked to Richard. He dropped back as Rob ran through the front gate and really did run a post pattern.

"I'm open", he yelled at which point Richard hurled the imaginary pigskin in his direction. Rob jumped up, "caught" the ball and yelled,

"Touchdown! LSU wins the game!"

As he spiked the imaginary football into the bus lane in front of the zoo, one of the keepers slammed the front gate with a resounding "Clang" that reverberated for several seconds. We all cheered! First for Rob and then for the fact we got him out of the zoo. Instead of running back into the zoo, Rob ran off, hooting and hollering, into the great expanse of Overton Park. We all went out there to see if we could locate him, but he was gone. Everybody patted Richard on his back and gave him "high fives". He just calmly said,

"That was, strangely enough, easier than I thought!"

He had saved the day, or rather, the night. I figured Rob would eventually run out of steam and just sleep it off somewhere. Cindy and I went home. We had had enough excitement for the evening.

The next day, something unexpected happened; Rob showed up for work, albeit two hours late. After we all left the zoo, Rob returned about an hour later to get his jacket. Since he was locked out of the zoo, he tried to climb over one of the gates. A new night guard had seen this "wild man" trying to get into the zoo and being a little unnerved, called the police. The police responded, captured Rob and took him to the "drunk tank" to sleep off the effects. When Rob came to work, he claimed that the police had beaten him since he had bruises all over his arms and legs. One of his co-workers asked,

"Do you remember anything about the party last night?"

To this he said that he didn't. His co-worker said,

"It wasn't the police that beat you, you did this to yourself!"

Rob seemed a little bewildered, but as more of the night was recounted to him, he was embarrassed more than anything else. He apologized to everyone that he knew was at the party. Everyone basically said to him that they were glad that he didn't hurt himself more and that he didn't hurt anybody. He especially apologized to me since he knew I was in charge. I told him to not worry about it and that everything was okay. Rob eventually went into rehab and got clean. But for that one evening in June, he had given the partygoers more than a night of entertainment. I was just happy that no one was killed!

Chapter 29

Eagle Hacking and Restoration

During the early 1980's, I participated in the State of Tennessee's Bald Eagle Restoration Program. The Bald Eagle was slowly coming back, but to the areas that had birds that were already nesting. There were large areas in the East and South that previously had nesting eagles, but those birds disappeared, either through direct persecution or habitat loss or through the slow process of attrition caused by DDT. The adult birds were not being replaced and local populations eventually vanished. We had birds that wintered in the region, but returned to the upper Midwest and southern Canada to nest. There were a few restoration programs underway and most, if not all, were modeled after Peter Nye's program in New York State. Bob Hatcher, Head Non-Game and Endangered Species Coordinator of the Tennessee Wildlife Resources Agency (TWRA), decided to bring such a "hacking" program to Tennessee.

Despite the sinister sounding term, hacking isn't what it sounds like it should be; no one's breaking into a computer file or is wielding an axe. Hacking is an old falconry term that refers to the practice of tying a young captive hawk's food on a hack board. This usually occurs before the bird fledges or flies for the first time. The idea is where the bird is liberated for its first flight is the general area it will return to if lost. Food is left on the hack board for the hawk in case its hunting skills are not up to speed. It can go to the hack board for food. Eventually, the young hawk starts to catch prey and is ultimately recaptured to continue its training. In a

222

restoration program, the same idea applies, but the bird is obviously not recaptured after the release.

Hacking has been used to restore many depleted or extirpated species including the Bald Eagle, Peregrine Falcon and Osprey. The Bald Eagle had not nested successfully in Tennessee since 1962. The last known nest was at Reelfoot Lake. Not surprisingly, the first eagle hacking/release program in Tennessee was scheduled to begin at Reelfoot in 1981. It made sense, the last wild eagles nested here and why not a new generation? There was also a release project at Land Between the Lakes, about 70 miles away from Reelfoot. This project was in Tennessee just south of the Kentucky border, The Tennessee Valley Authority at LBL learned of TWRA's plans and said they had the resources to build and operate a hack site, beginning in 1980 and received the blessings of Bob Hatcher, who provided hacking guidelines. He had received them from the Georgia DNR which was the first SE state to begin bald eagle hacking in 1979, and patterned after New York's original eagle hacking that began in 1976. Volunteers of the Tennessee Conservation League assisted as hack site attendants at LBL during the first two or three years of the 9-year LBL project. Bald Eagle hacking at Reelfoot started in 1981, as originally planned. The location chosen for the Reelfoot release site was on the edge of Ronaldson's Slough. This slough, located on the northwest side of the lake, is an area isolated from the main lake. This fact precluded the general public from wandering into the area and disturbing the eagles.

The hacking cage or enclosure was 8' by 8' by 8' high built in a 65 foot Bald Cypress tree. The artificial nest was at the 48' level of the tree and had a bunch of sticks arranged to look like an eagle's nest. There was a trap door in the bottom of the hack enclosure so young birds could be placed and ultimately fitted with leg bands and transmitters. The enclosure had conduit metal bars which kept the young eagles in and other predators out. One wall of the bars had a drop away feature. A string was connected to a board at the bottom which allowed the bars to be pulled out and dropped to the swamp below the cage. The hack cage was large enough to accommodate several eaglets at once.

The 8 by 12 foot observation platform, where the volunteers watched and fed the eagles, was in another cypress tree about 90 feet from the hack tree. The trees were aligned where the sun would generally be to the rear of the observers. It looked like something from the Swiss Family Robinson movie. To get to the observation tree, a boardwalk was built at the edge of the swamp. This boardwalk led to the base of the observation tree and to a ladder. To get to the observation platform, one had to climb a triangle-shaped ladder (this ladder's rungs were nailed to the tree). Rough cut lumber was used to make a safety cage to prevent one from falling all the way to the ground. This was a sixty-foot climb and it was best not to look down. Once you got to the platform, you had to open a trap door, all the time being careful not to konk your head with the door. Once safely on the platform, the occupants of the treehouse were shielded from view of the eagles with burlap bags on the side facing the release enclosure.

There was a cable and trolley system which ran from the observation tree to the hack enclosure. This trolley was essentially a feeding tray where a day's worth of partially frozen fish, mostly shad, drum and the occasional gar, were ferried across to the eaglets. They were fed without human contact via this system. We also provided water from the observation tower to the hack tower by gravity flow through a hose.

The observation tree was, perhaps, the ultimate kid's fantasy. It was also a great place to observe the wildlife that lived in and around Ronaldson's Slough. Across the slough was a heron/egret rookery. There were several species that nested here including

Great Blue and Little Blue Herons, Snowy Egrets and Yellow-crowned Night Herons. In addition, there were a couple of pairs of Anhingas, a primitive bird also known as the Water Turkey. This area was the northern extent of the Anhinga's range. So, there was a lot of bird activity to take one's attention away from the eagles. This was okay though, because like the young of many species, including humans, a young eagle sleeps a lot in its early stages.

About half a mile or so from the hack tower was the base camp. The base camp consisted of a small travel trailer I nicknamed "Keep". Someone had written "Keep" on it and I am sure that "out" was to follow, but apparently the person was either distracted or ran out of spray paint. The trailer had a generator connected to it, so on the really hot nights, one could crank the generator and retreat to the air conditioned trailer. There was also a screen tent that adjoined the trailer. This tent had a couple of army cots and was the place I preferred to sleep. I liked sleeping in here because I could listen to all of the night sounds. Being close to a swamp, one could hear a cacophony of sounds ranging from insects to frogs, herons to owls and the occasional bobcat, fox or coyote.

The screen tent and trailer were situated in a small grove of trees. Every night about 11 p.m., a Barred Owl screamed from a tree right next to the tent. This scream was so scary that it would cause a person to bolt upright to ponder, A) "What the F*#k was that?!?" and B) "Did I crap myself?!?" The owl was so consistent with its scream, you could almost set your watch by it.

The whole hack project was manned by volunteers from the Memphis Chapters of the Audubon Society and the Tennessee Ornithological Society. We got together before the hacking season and divided the shifts/day among the volunteers. The weekends were always points of contention, so I usually took weekdays for my shifts. I always had plenty of vacation and holidays that I used for my volunteer time. On one of my shifts, a couple of ladies from the Zoological Society had relieved me. I was to return in a couple of days to relieve them. Before leaving I went over what was going on with the birds at the hack tower and anything else they needed to know. I mentioned, too, that there was a Barred Owl that screamed every night at 11. They thanked me for the heads up on the owl and the other stuff.

A few days later, I returned to base camp to relieve them. I noticed in the screen tent was a tear in the screen that had been repaired. It looked like something out of a cartoon where the character gets so frightened that it runs through a wall, leaving an outline of the character. This repair looked something like that. I couldn't help but ask the two ladies Susan and Sharon, how the tear happened to appear in the tent. Susan replied,

"Well, we had been drinking a little last night and were feeling a little tipsy. We had forgotten completely about the screaming owl and lost track of time, as well. All of a sudden, the owl screamed and without hesitating, Sharon freaked out and ran through the side of the tent! The hardest part about the whole thing was finding something to sew up the tent!"

I got a chuckle out of all this and Sharon looked a little embarrassed.

"Next time, I'll listen for the owl!"

Part of the adventure of the eagle hacking experience was going from the base camp to the towers. The mode of getting there was either to walk or ride ATVs. About a ¼ was around and through a soybean field. The other ¾ of the trip was through a swampy area. After a good thunderstorm, part of a heavily rutted area filled with gumboot mud. I dubbed this area the Panama Canal. It was quite fun to drive the balloon-tired ATV through the muck. The trick was not to go too fast or too slow. Too fast and you found yourself covered in mud. Too slow and you're stuck in the goo. The mud had the consistency somewhere between quicksand and Play Dough. It took a lot of effort along with plenty of cursing to extract oneself from the muck. Later in the summer, the deer flies waited for you to either emerge from the swamp or go into it. If you've never experienced deer flies, mosquitoes seem like a minor annoyance, even like a vacation. The bite is painful as well. The deer fly must have gigantic mandibles for its size. To put it in perspective, picture a Chihuahua with the bite of a Pit Bull. The deer flies pursue their victims in a swarm, biting any exposed flesh. One of the TWRA guys, Corkey, was so hounded by a swarm that he drove his three-wheeler off the road into a stand of river cane, only to be feasted upon once his vehicle had lost its forward momentum. Needless to say, Corkey came running out of the cane thicket, slapping any fly with what hand was not being used to keep them off his face.

I had a situation where I decided to walk to the towers. I drove my car to the edge of the soybean field and parked it at the edge of the woods. It had not rained in a while, so the path in wasn't muddy. I wanted to do a little bird watching en route to the towers. At the end of the day, I walked back to the car. About fifty yards before getting to my car, a very persistent deer fly began hounding me. It was trying its best to bite me in the face. Despite my best efforts to shoo it away, including several solid hits with my hand, the fly kept up its assault. I finally cleared the trees and as I neared my car, I noticed a dragonfly sitting on the antenna of my car. The deer fly was still orbiting my head. When I got close to my car, the dragonfly zipped over and caught the pesky deer fly and took it back to the antenna for consumption. I let out a cheer and said to the dragonfly,

"Thanks!" and to the deer fly, "serves you right!"

The birds for the release program came from two sources. The bulk of them came from wild southeast Alaskan nests, where the

227

Bald Eagle population was doing very well. The State of Tennessee got permission from the State of Alaska to selectively remove six week old youngsters for shipment to the hack towers. A team of nest climbers from Tennessee went usually in late June to get the birds. Up to eight per year were sent to Tennessee. The other sources of young eagles were several zoos that had eagle breeding programs. Eagles from Cincinnati, Columbus and John Ball Zoos were released in Tennessee. These birds were generally available about a month before the Alaskan birds. So, the hacking season ran from early June to late August.

The important age for the young birds was six to eight weeks old. At this age, the young eagle could feed itself and it stayed in the hacking enclosure for a month, at this point, it was fully grown. This period of time allowed the bird to imprint on the area. This is critical if the bird survives to breeding age. The area where the bird is released is the area the bird will hopefully return to nest. In 1983, Tennessee had its first successful nest since 1962. The nest was about 20 miles south of the LBL site near Dover, Tennessee. In 1984, a male that was released at Land Between the Lakes hacking site in 1981 returned to the area. He nested about eight miles south of the LBL release site near Dover, Tennessee. Two astonishing things occurred with this nesting. He had survived and was only three years old! He was just beginning to molt in a few white head feathers, but produced one young that year and several more over the following years. One of his male offspring of a later year returned to the Kentucky side of LBL and produced young when he was also three years old. This return of these, and many more hacked birds and the nesting of their offspring proved that hacking worked!

The eagle release program eventually spread across the State. In addition to the hack site at Reelfoot and LBL, release sites were set up at Dale Hollow Lake, Bell's Bend on the Cumberland River near Nashville, Chickamauga Lake near Dayton, South Holston Lake near Bristol and the final hack site was at Douglas Lake near Dandridge. To date, the eagle hack program has been proven to produce eagles that have continued nesting in Tennessee. As of 2012, Tennessee had 185 occupied nests. At least 123 successful nests fledged about 215 young in 2012. Many, if not most of the nest can be traced to birds that were released in Tennessee, their offspring and the progeny of the offspring. I have been proud to have been involved in the release programs at Reelfoot, Bell's Bend, Chickamauga and Douglas Lake, where the eagles we produced at the facilities at Dollywood, have been released. The Bald Eagle continues to rebound and all that was needed was a little help from humans.

Chapter 30

THE IDEA and the Beginning of the End, Part 1

Osceola was doing better as a program bird. He was starting to stay on the glove for longer periods of time, thus making it easier to use him in presentations. When he stood upright on my glove, he was a very regal looking specimen. He still did not have his white head or tail yet, but was majestic. I did a program at the Memphis Audubon Society and after the show a lady came up to me and said,

"That Bald Eagle you have is very pretty, but is a shame that he will never fly again!"

I shook my head in agreement. After the program, I was driving the birds back to the Zoo and an idea came to me. Maybe there was a way to get Osceola in the air once again. There was a guy in California named Burke Ewing. He was a hang glider pilot and had a dog named Curtis. Curtis was a shepherd mix and was Burke's companion on his hang gliding trips. Most of Burke's flying took place at Torrey Pines, a coastal soaring site in San Diego. Whenever Burke launched his glider from the cliff, Curtis usually ran behind him until he got to the cliff edge. 99 % of the time, he stopped before going over the edge. However, one time he did not and went over, luckily landing on a ledge. However, the impact broke his left front leg. After Curtis was safely extracted from the ledge, the break was repaired and the leg healed. Burke thought,

"If he wants to go with me that badly, maybe I can make him a harness so he can fly with me."

So, for several years after this, Burke and Curtis could be seen soaring the cliffs of Torrey Pines. The duo had celebrity status for a while and even appeared on the "To Tell the Truth" TV show. Burke and Curtis flew together for several years until Curtis passed away after a long life.

I had the thought that if a man could fly with a dog, why can't someone construct a harness and fly with an eagle? So, from this moment in April 1984, I had the idea to fly with Osceola. I needed to design a harness and find someone to construct it. However, my future at the Memphis Zoo was starting to look uncertain. Great plans don't always go smoothly.

As I mentioned before, my "Whipping Boy" sessions became more frequent. Director Menigar had me under the magnifying glass, noting every little thing I did, or from his point of view, didn't do. I had to make sure that any report due from me was turned in well ahead of time. Many of my reports came back like so many graded term papers. I asked several of the Curators and Assistant Curators if Menigar marked and corrected their reports and everyone said "No". He checked my bi-weekly employee attendance/time logs. He even checked my Inbox and started opening my mail! I went to the local post office and asked about the legality of this. I got conflicting answers. One person said if the mail was addressed to me in care of the Memphis Zoo, he could open anything he wanted. Another postal employee said that if was addressed to me regardless if it said Memphis Zoo or not, it was my private business. He also said that if I wanted, I could file an official complaint.

My situation with Menigar had gotten so bad that one day I was going to my office and I was met by Charles Brady, the Mammal Curator. He stopped me saying,

"Johnny, don't go in there. Menigar's in a pissy mood and wanting someone's head. He specifically asked if anyone knew where you were! Tell you what, go somewhere away from the office and I'll page you when the coast is clear."

"Thanks for the warning," I replied and I wandered to the other end of the zoo to check the Ostrich nesting on the African Veldt.

Nearly an hour went by before Brady paged me. It seems that Menigar had a speaking engagement and was gone from the zoo for the rest of the day. It was ashamed that I had to lie low, especially since I had not done anything recently to draw Menigar's ire. However, this was the slow beginning of the end of my zoo career.

I was doing a lot of outside the zoo programs, with nearly all of them now either on my days off or at night. I didn't want anything more that Menigar could use against me. One evening, I had done a program for a local outdoor club's annual banquet and an outdoor writer with the local paper was in attendance. He really liked my presentation and sent a letter to Menigar commending my program and praising the Memphis Zoo. I received a courtesy copy. I was in the bird department office a week or so after the program and Menigar poked his head in the door. He mentioned that he got a letter from the outdoor writer. I didn't know where he was going with this. I thought he might say something like, "Good job" or something like that. I didn't receive any praise from him, only the mention that I had done this program on the clock as a representative of the zoo. I made mention that I did this program in the evening on my own time. He countered that since I was on salary that I was always on the clock. He seemed angry that I did this program! I knew this argument was fruitless and I just shut my mouth. No matter what I did, I couldn't win.

The next day Menigar called me into his office. What have I done this time? I knocked on his office door and he motioned me

232

in to sit down in the chair in front of his desk. Without saying so much as a "Hello" or "What's going on?" he simply said,

"You have got to surplus Osceola. You need to find another zoo or nature center to send him to."

I was very stunned and said, "Well, he has been doing great in programs and really adds a lot to the presentations..." before I could further plead my case he interrupted me with,

"We don't have room at this Zoo for four eagles. This eagle is taking up a rehab enclosure that is badly needed for incoming birds."

Since when did he care about the rehab program? I countered with,

"I can get some money from the local Audubon Society for an enclosure for Osceola and.." I was interrupted again,

"I am ordering you to move this eagle out of this zoo, so you had better start calling around to find him a home. End of discussion and there is no negotiating this! We're finished, so you can go now!"

I got up and a looked him in the eyes. Menigar saw that I was hurt and angry and said to me, as if I were a child,

"Go on, I've got stuff to do!"

I turned and wandered out of his office and mumbled "As$hole" under my breath. Menigar must have heard me and said,

"I'm sorry, I didn't hear what you said. Did you want to add something?"

Boy, did I, but I said that I was clearing my throat. I turned and walked away, but I really wanted was to break a chair over his freaking head!

I was stunned by Menigar's order. He knew how to get me! I guess in a normal situation, zoo management would be happy to have an employee who was willing to do extracurricular beneficial activities, all without cost to the zoo. Nope, not this time! I couldn't move one way or another without scrutiny. My immediate supervisor, Cliff, had told me a week earlier that he couldn't do anything more for me. He had exhausted all of his excuses defending me and that I was on my own. He said that Menigar seemed to have a vendetta against me and to be careful. I did my best to toe the line. I tried to stay within the confines of my zoo time, even though I gave the zoo 20-30 extra hours per week. All of my raptor training and programs were conducted after my regular work hours. I wasn't ready to change. I had to come up with a solution to be able to keep Osceola.

Later that same day, we had a senior staff meeting. Whoopie! More time with my favorite zoo director. The thing I hated about these meetings was that most of the curators smoked during the meeting. The only non-smokers were Chuck Beckson and me. I decided that I didn't want to breathe the unfiltered smoke any longer, so I got a particle mask from the maintenance department. I put on the mask and found a seat. As the meeting started, several of the regular smokers apologized for smoking and put out their cigarettes. Unfortunately there was an open chair next to me and Menigar came into the room and sat in the chair. Great! He looked at me and asked what the mask was for and I simply replied,

"To filter some of the smoke."

He gave a slight chuckle and reached into his pocket, pulled out a pack of cigarettes, extracted a Marlboro and lit it. He began the meeting and took a drag off the cigarette and blew the smoke in my direction. I thought, at first, that he really wasn't thinking about where his exhaled smoke went. But with each inhale and following exhale, he purposely blew smoke at my face! Several people, including Assistant Director Able, noticed this. Each time Menigar did this, I saw Able getting madder and madder. I was perturbed, but I kept my cool. The meeting finally ended, but not without Menigar blowing two cigarette's worth of smoke in my direction!

Outside the room, Able came up to me and said how angry that made him.

"I don't see how you didn't curse him out or punch him in the goddamn face!"

I simply replied, "Because, that's what he wanted me to do! If I had reacted, he knew that he was successful. Also, if I would have cursed him, he could have gotten me for insubordination or something like that. I'm not going to give him that satisfaction!"

"Well, you're a bigger man than me. I wanted to hit him for you!" Duane exclaimed.

I thanked him for his sentiment. At this, Menigar came out of the meeting room. As he looked at me, I pulled off my mask, held it up to the light, shook my head, and threw it in the trash. Without saying a word, I left the zoo office.

I spent the next several days trying to find a solution for the Osceola situation. Menigar asked me almost on a daily basis if I had any takers for Osceola. I lied to him and told him that there were several places interested in the eagle and I was awaiting word from any of them. Meanwhile, I had a eureka moment. Why couldn't I get a permit for Osceola? I didn't have the proper space where I lived, but one of our local rehabbers, Martha Waldron, had room at her house. I talked at length with her about my situation and that I desperately wanted to keep Osceola in Memphis. She was agreeable to house Osceola. Armed with the fact that I now had a place, I contacted Burma Campbell of the U.S. Fish and Wildlife Service and asked to apply for an Eagle Exhibition Permit. Burma was familiar with Osceola and knew that I was using him a lot in educational programs. She simply stated that when I had the facility ready, she would issue a permit. Wow! That was easier than I thought!

During this period, Menigar also forbade me to pick up injured birds, even after work or on my off days. He told me to tell the

235

person that found an injured bird to bring it to the zoo. If the finder couldn't bring the bird to the zoo then have them contact a local wildlife officer for retrieval. If a wildlife officer couldn't be reached or couldn't pick up the bird, then I was to tell the Good Samaritan to "throw the bird in a ditch". I wasn't about to tell a member of the public to throw an injured bird in a ditch! So, I arranged to get a Rehabilitation Permit of my own. I could, as a private citizen, pick up an injured bird on my off time and turn it into the zoo's rehab program. Once again, I found a way to get around Menigar's asinine directives. I adopted a mantra of sorts: If something gets in the way, be like water and find a way around it! If someone couldn't bring a bird to the zoo, I could now pick it up on my off time.

I did acquire a rehab permit and began picking up injured birds on my off time. Everything went well until a snowy day in January. Some people called me about an injured American Kestrel. I told them that I would pick up the bird after I got off work at 5 p.m. They lived about 30 minutes from the zoo. As I left the zoo, it began snowing at a pretty good clip and it slowed my driving down considerably. I didn't arrive at the people's house for nearly an hour after I left the zoo. To make things worse, they were not at home! I waited for nearly an hour, but the occupants were nowhere to be found. This was in the days before cell phones, so I drove to a nearby pay phone and called their number. No answer, but I did leave a message. I returned to the house, but no one answered the door. I decided to go back home and tried several more times to reach them by phone.

The next morning, I arrive at work early to check all of the birds. By the time my co-workers arrived I heard my name yelled over the Zoo's loudspeaker,

"John Stokes, come to the zoo office immediately! Immediately!!!" It was Menigar. When I got to the office, people are looking at me like I was a dead man. Chuck Beckson said,

"Man is he mad at you! I've never seen him this mad, even at me and I have seen him spitting mad!"

I said, "Really!"

I walked into Menigar's office and he snarled,

"Get in here and shut the goddamn door and sit down!"

I didn't sit and I saw Duane Able in attendance. I knew it was serious when Duane was here. Menigar interrogated me with,

"I just spoke to some people who called and said they had an injured bird you were supposed to pick up but didn't. They were very irritated that you didn't get the bird. Explain to me why you were trying to get this bird, dammit?!?"

I glanced at Able; he was shaking his head and rolling his eyes out of contempt. I replied,

"I have my own Rehab Permit and I can pick up an injured bird as a private citizen".

Before I could finish my defense, Menigar slammed his hand on his desk and pointed his right index finger at me and said,

"I forbid you to have your own permits. You are not a private citizen! You are on salary which means that you are a zoo employee twenty-four hours a day!"

I interrupted him during his rant, "I am a private citizen as soon as I step out the zoo's front gate and I can have my own permits!" At this point, I was yelling at him and I didn't care if he fired me on the spot. This seemed to catch him off guard and I saw a slight smile on Able's face. Menigar countered,

"You, you've given the zoo a black eye. This isn't over! Consider yourself on notice! Now get out of my office and go do your goddamn job!"

Wow, I wasn't fired! As I walked down the hall, Beckson pulled me aside and said,

"He kinda grows on you doesn't he?!?"

I laughed and left the office and went to the hospital to call Martha. She was off from school due to the snow and volunteered to collect the injured falcon. Later, she arrived at the zoo with the female kestrel. The wing was badly broken and had been for some time. Her wing was not repairable and I eventually sent her to the Lichterman Nature Center as an education bird.

Meanwhile, I made plans to move Osceola to Martha's house. We finally had an enclosure ready. I had a permit in hand and informed Cliff of my intentions to move him to Martha's place.

"You might not want to do that", Cliff replied. I asked him why and he said, "Well, if you do, Menigar wants you fired!"

"What?! Why?!" was the only thing I could say.

I was very puzzled. I found a solution to get Osceola off zoo grounds, but would still be able to use him.

"He plans to get you on insubordination if you do this and I don't have any defense for you!" Cliff replied.

"Insubordination?!? How is this insubordination?" Cliff shook his head and tried to explain,

"He says that you cannot have personal Federal Permits as a Zoo employee and although I don't agree with him there is nothing I can do! If you move Osceola to Martha's place, I have been told to fire you! I'm sorry, John. He's looking for anything to get you. If I were you, I'd try to find Osceola a new home soon. The longer he is here, the more friction you are going to have! It is now a personal thing between you and Menigar and you keep challenging him, he is going to win!"

I thanked Cliff for the warning. I guess I didn't have any choice. I'd have to give up Osceola.

Chapter 31

The Beginning of the End, Part 2

A few weeks had gone by since the kestrel incident. I informed Martha that I would not be moving Osceola to her house. She was disappointed but understood the situation. She made a comment that Menigar really seemed to be harassing me more than anybody normally should. I agreed with her wholeheartedly but commented that there was nothing I could do. I was on the bubble right now and Menigar had a sharp needle!

"Well, watch yourself and I'll see what we can do."

I didn't exactly know what Martha was referring to when she said "I'll see what we can do" but as far as the Osceola situation, I was out of options.

It was now the end of February, 1985. Menigar had been exceptionally quiet with me. I was also avoiding him whenever possible. I stayed out of the office as much as I could and went in early to do any of my needed office work. I felt like a refugee and in staff meetings, where I normally kidded around with the other curators, I was very silent. I didn't want Menigar to misconstrue anything I said. However, at the last staff meeting in February, Menigar asked that Cliff and I stay after the meeting. I looked over at Cliff and he shrugged his shoulders. After Menigar dismissed everyone, he got up, closed the door, lit a cigarette and reached into a file folder. He sat back at the table and pulled a piece of paper out of the folder that looked like official Memphis Park Commission letterhead. It was! Menigar began,

"You're probably wondering why I asked you to stay?"

Cliff shook his head and I just stared straight ahead. I figured it had something to do with me and that the official looking document wasn't a letter praising my good work. At that point, I believed that I was going to be fired. I was almost right.

"We are here to try to correct a situation that has gone on for far too long. We have got to change course here and get on the right path."

I thought Menigar was trying to make a new start in our relationship so I perked up a little. Maybe I wasn't going to be fired after all!

"John, I'm here with Cliff as a witness to issue you a Written Reprimand for Insubordination. The kestrel incident gave the zoo a black eye and you violated a direct order whereas I forbade you to pick up injured birds on your off time. I understand that you got your own rehab permit to get around this. As a City of Memphis employee, I forbid you to have any personal Federal or State permits, which include rehab permits and in regards to eagle #5035 (Osceola), no Eagle permits. I have ordered you to find that bird a new home and I expect you to do so soon. If you continue along this path, I will have no choice other than terminate your employment. There will be no 3 or 10 day suspensions and I will skip directly to termination! You have spent far too much time doing rehab related activities, when you could have spent your time more wisely improving the bird section. Do you understand the gravity of the situation?"

I nodded my head in agreement and looked straight ahead.

"Are you sure you understand that any future violations will be dealt with swiftly and completely?!?"

Menigar's tone bordered on anger, I guess because he expected me to protest. I just nodded again and looked straight ahead. With this, he signed my Written Reprimand and passed the copy to me.

"Remember this is a very serious situation you are in and I expect you to adjust your behavior so there will not be any need to continue to the next and final step. Do you have any questions?"

I looked over the reprimand and simply replied,

"No."

"Well. If neither of you have any questions, then we are finished here. Thank you!"

Menigar concluded our meeting. I walked out of the office a little relieved. Cliff asked me if I were okay and I said,

"Yeah, 'cause I thought I was going to be fired!"

"Well, please watch yourself 'cause he's serious", Cliff concluded.

"I will, thanks!"

The rest of the day, I felt a little relieved. I now had a piece of paper which indicated to me that I was doing the right thing. Even though I had been disciplined for what was considered "bad" behavior, it wasn't going to keep me from doing what I felt was best. I was off the next day and went down to the Memphis Park Commission office to see Frank Fogel. Frank's position included overseeing the functions of the Zoo and was Menigar's boss. Luckily for me, Frank wasn't busy that afternoon. I went into his office, he greeted me with,

"Hey John, I got a copy of your Written Reprimand. What have you been doing right to deserve it?!?"

He knew of my troubles with Menigar and frequently called me to let me know that I was doing a good job.

"Well, Frank, I can't deny that I have violated his direct order to not pick up injured birds as a zoo employee, but I have my own Rehab Permit and I believe as a private citizen, I can have my own permits and can pick up birds on my off time and days off. I feel that he is totally wrong when he says I can't have my own permits". Frank agreed with me,

"He can't tell you what you can and cannot do on your free time. It would be like someone telling me that as a Park Commission employee that I couldn't play tennis on my off day at a Memphis Park Commission tennis court. He has no right, legal or otherwise, to tell you that you can't have permits!" I continued,

"Menigar's argument is that since I am on salary that I am a zoo employee 24 hours a day".

At this Fogel began adamantly shaking his head and said,

"No, you are a private citizen who works for the Park Commission. This isn't the military and you are not an indentured servant! You can do what you want with your free time. If he has an argument with that, tell him to give me a call and I'll be glad to straighten him out! I'll be keeping a close eye on the situation and if you feel it's getting out of hand, let me know."

I thanked Frank for his time and as I was leaving he said,

"By the way John, everybody here is happy with the job you are doing representing the Zoo and the Park Commission with all the great work with the raptors!"

With this, I shook his hand and told him,

"Thanks! It's nice to hear that!"

I returned to work after my day off and I felt a little on edge. Cliff had taken off for a few days and I felt pretty vulnerable. I got to work extra early to go into the office to check daily reports from the keepers in my section. To my dismay, Menigar was already there. I was surprised by him at the coffee urn. I got my coffee and turned around and gasped as if I had seen Satan himself. I uttered,

"Ga-go-good Morning, Hal!" He asked,

"What are you doing here so early?!?"

I felt liked asking him the same question and delayed my answer for a second. I feared that any answer might have been used against me.

"I am, um, checking daily reports to see if anything unusual has taken place or if any of the keepers need any supplies…" my voice trailed off.

I expected him to jump on me for being in too early or even worse, retaliate for going to see his boss about my reprimand. I didn't expect Frank to say anything to Menigar, but things have a way of making it back to the zoo.

"Well, good, carry on! I have to go do a presentation at a breakfast meeting at a local men's club." Menigar's reply almost shocked me and I simply said,

"Enjoy your breakfast!"

He said "Thanks!" and went into his office to get some stuff for his talk.

I sat back at my desk, looked over the reports and as soon as I heard Menigar leave, I went out to check the bird collection. At this point, calm came over me. I somehow realized that perhaps I needed to search to find a new way, a new situation. It is funny how things work. One door begins to close and another starts to open.

Chapter 32

Osceola's New Home and Heading for the Exit

Unfortunately I had to find a new home for Osceola. I started calling some nearby zoos to see if they needed a Bald Eagle for education or exhibit. None of the zoos I contacted in the region had room for an eagle. I wanted to find a place within a few hours drive so I could go see Osceola. But, it appeared as though I was going to have to start calling outside of the area. I didn't know what else to do, but I soon got an unexpected option.

Bob Hatcher of the Tennessee Wildlife Resources Agency called to inform me of several people in Nashville who were trying to start an eagle rehab, breeding and education facility. He mentioned that I needed to get to know these people as there might be some funding for future employment for me. I immediately asked him more. He told me that one fellow, Al Louis Cecere, was a fundraiser who was interested in eagles. The two other fellows involved were Tom Nolan, a falconer and research scientist at Vanderbilt, and Kevin Schutt, a raptor rehabber. These two would be the main decision makers. Kevin headed the Cumberland Wildlife Foundation and already had enclosures at his home. Bob asked me if I might be interested in helping this group. I tried to control my enthusiasm and told him that I was definitely interested. He gave me contact information for Kevin and Tom and before too long, I gave Kevin a call. I introduced myself and he said that Bob had highly recommended me for future employment. I told Kevin that I was interested in working for them. He said that it was looking as though they would have money to hire me in early 1986.

I told Kevin about my situation with Menigar and Osceola and that I needed to place him somewhere soon. Kevin said that he could put together an enclosure pretty quickly and would apply for a permit for Osceola. I called Burma Campbell of the USF&WS and told her that I wanted to transfer Osceola to the Cumberland Wildlife Foundation in Mt. Juliet, Tennessee. I told her that Kevin would contact her soon about the necessary details. She said that she would await the information from Kevin before she could okay the transfer. Within a week, Kevin had his Eagle Permit and I had a way out with Osceola. I had a real chance of working with him again if I sent him to Kevin. We worked out a time and date to transfer Osceola and I informed Cliff and Menigar that I had a home for Osceola. I gave Menigar copies of Kevin's permits and he said,

"Very good, when is he picking him up?"

I told him the next week. He smirked, I'm sure thinking that he had defeated me. He won the battle but I found a solution that involved a future reunion with Osceola.

In early April, Kevin Schutt came to Memphis and picked up Osceola. I had an instant rapport with him and I had a good feeling about Osceola's new situation. I helped load the kennel into Kevin's truck and took one more peek at him.

"I'll take good care of him until you start working for us next year", Kevin assured me.

"Do you have any timeline when funding might be available?" I curiously inquired.

Kevin replied, "Well, it looks like we might get some good funding early next year. If this happens, then we'll hire you at that point, if you are still interested."

"If you get the money tomorrow, I'll be there in two weeks!" I exclaimed.

Kevin and I had a good laugh.

"You can come up to Mt. Juliet anytime to see Osceola and before you know it, you'll be back working with him again." I added to Kevin's statement,

"Yeah, I'd like that!"

With this, we shook hands, Kevin got in his truck and Osceola and he departed toward Nashville.

Now that Osceola was gone, one would think things would now improve for me at the Zoo. However, this was not the case. I was in Menigar's office just as frequently as before, most of my "meetings" were on Friday when Cliff was on his days off. I was continually harassed for minor things; bird department keepers on break for fifteen minutes instead of ten, a drink cup in between the fences of the Eagle Aviary, animal feed buckets in front of the zoo commissary; things that I normally addressed in my daily rounds.

During this time, I had heard a gorilla joke from which I was able to use the punch line in my sessions with Menigar. The punch line had a gorilla placing its index finger in the corner of its eye. Then, with wiping motion, as one would remove a teardrop, the gorilla responds to a human act in the joke. This motion meant "screw you" in gorilla language!

I got called into Menigar's office again, with Able as a witness. I can't remember what I was there for this time, but each time Menigar asked if I understood what he was talking about, I put my finger to my eye and wiped, much like the gorilla did. At first Able didn't see me do this. He had heard the joke as well. But he quickly caught on and every time Menigar asked if I understood, Able looked at me. As soon as I answered "Yes" and put my finger under my eye, Able just about laughed. I was doing this so much that Menigar asked me if I had something wrong with my eye. At this point, Able began to laugh but quickly disguised it as a cough. I said that I had a new pair of contact lenses and one of them was bothering me.

He said, "Well, this meeting is over, so you can go do something about it".

"Yeah, that would be great!" I replied and Able and I got up and left the office. As soon as we got outside the room, Able burst into laughter,

"I got to where I couldn't look at you! I'll have to start doing that the next time I'm in a meeting with him!"

As a note to all of the above, during this period the curators were all placed on a Performance Appraisal System. The appraisal system judged the person on several criteria. Annual raises were given according to a score derived from adding up the sum of the points of all the criteria. An evaluation was conducted twice a year and Cliff did mine. He gave me high scores in all categories and recommended me for a raise. Menigar had the final say and it was no secret that he devalued all of my scores. If Cliff gave me a 95 score, Menigar devalued my total to 80. One needed a 90 or better to be considered for a raise. Not surprisingly, I didn't get a raise the last two years I worked at the zoo.

The summer of 1985 was winding down. My girlfriend Cindy, a hang gliding buddy of mine, Butch Pritchett and I went on a hang gliding trip to Arizona. Butch and Cindy got along about as well as a mongoose and a cobra and I was in the middle of them. The flying was great, but the verbal fights between Cindy and Butch led me to declare that this was the worse vacation I had ever had. After ten days, we finally left for home and I couldn't wait to get those two back in their respective enclosures.

Osceola was doing fine at his new home and Kevin was able to take him to a few events where he was able to meet some country stars. In August, Cindy, had decided to go back to college for her Master's Degree in English. She had been attending Memphis State University, but she felt that the Master's Degree program was not as good as she would have liked. She instead chose to return to the University of Arkansas at Fayetteville, some three hundred miles away from Memphis. She really didn't tell me of her plans to go to Fayetteville until about a week before she left. Needless to say, I was a little shocked at her decision and a little saddened as well. She moved in mid-August and I didn't get to see her for nearly a month. Our relationship had become one of phone calls and letters. She was now in a new phase of her life and was looking forward to being a full-time college student again. It was a lot more difficult for me. I was in a precarious situation at the zoo and was now in a long distance relationship.

In September, I finally drove to Fayetteville to see Cindy in her new home and situation. She seemed to be truly happy and this calmed a lot of my fears. I had been a little jealous of this whole situation. But seeing her new life and that I was still part of it made me feel better. Still, it was a five hour drive to see her. I had just recently purchase a fairly new minivan and soon would be putting a lot of miles on it. Things were still as precarious with Menigar as ever, but at least now, I was more at ease with my relationship.

In September, I moved out of the house Cindy and I were renting together. I didn't have to move far and in fact, right around the corner into a house owned by a fellow named Danny Moore. Danny was friends with Assistant Mammal Curator Houston Winbigler and he knew that Danny was looking for a roommate. This all worked out well. However, I now had a young orphaned Turkey Vulture that Kevin had sent to me to hold until I moved to Mt. Juliet. I contacted Martha Waldron to see if she had space for the bird and she did. I transferred the bird to Martha's care and named him Paddington. So that situation was nicely solved.

The raptor rehab program now had an official assistant. His name was Dave Hill and he was a Vet Tech at the zoo hospital. Dave had returned to the zoo after a few years of being away. He was an intern during the Williford House days in 1980 and was a roommate of mine for a few months . He was very interested in raptors and made a great addition to the rehab team. He had already been helping with rehab anyway, but now had the official title of Assistant Coordinator of the Memphis Zoo Raptor Rehab Program. This took some of the pressure off of me, but also was a good thing since I was probably going to leave soon.

In October, I got a call from Kevin Schutt. He said that I should be making plans to move to Mt. Juliet early next year. He said that funding would be available in February for Cumberland to hire me. He asked if I still wanted the job and I told him most assuredly that I did.

"Well, come February, pack up your stuff and head this way!" Kevin said.

"Are you sure the money will be there?" I inquired.

Kevin answered, "Yeah, everything should be in place by the end of January. We should be getting a good sized check from Miller Brewing Company. With the money, we'll be able to hire you and start building more of our facility. You'll be in on the ground floor. You'll be the Director of Wildlife and will be in charge of rehab, breeding and education programs. Does this all sound alright to you?"

"Well yeah, I can hardly wait!" I replied with excitement in my voice.

Kevin replied, "Well, plan on February and we will start getting everything ready for you. We look forward to having you here."

Finally, I could see the exit door for this portion of my life. It would be bittersweet to leave, but with Menigar eagerly wanting to scratch the itch to fire me, I didn't have too many options left. I did take advantage of one final perk. The Zoological Society funded a trip to an annual meeting of the Raptor Research Foundation. The ten day meeting was in Sacramento, California and was attended by the best raptor minds from the U.S., Canada, Europe and the Middle East. There were seminars and field trips and I learned a lot and made many contacts from this meeting. I returned to Memphis and gave the Zoological Society a full report. I did feel a little guilty, however, knowing that I was leaving soon, but the Society people felt that it was money well spent.

When I got back from California, an astonishing thing happened; Menigar became very nice to me! I had gotten used to the sometimes twice a week meetings in his office, or him ignoring me when I passed him on the zoo grounds. For example, I would see him coming and as soon as we got close I would say,

"Good Morning (or afternoon) Hal!"

At this, he would usually turn his head skyward as if he were looking for something up in the trees. On my return, I saw Menigar walking in front of the zoo office and said my usual,

"Good Morning, Hal". I expected the usual snub, but this time, he ambushed me with,

"Hey John, Good morning to you! How was your trip to California?"

Somewhat stunned, I answered, "Oh it was great! I learned a lot and got to see a lot of good stuff and scenery."

"Well, you'll have to tell me more about it later. Glad you're back!"

I felt like I had just witness a scene from Dicken's *A Christmas Carol* where Scrooge had awoken Christmas Day after being visited by the three ghosts. The only thing missing was Tiny Tim exclaiming,

"God Bless us everyone!"

250

I really didn't know how to act. I watched Menigar as he went into his office and he waved to me as he went inside the building.

"What the Hell is he up to?!?" I said out loud.

Was he trying to set me up so I would finally step high enough to put the noose around my neck? Then, once I was in position "Kapow", kick the stool out from under me? I was very cautious about what had just taken place. But as the weeks went on, Menigar was unwavering in his pleasantry; he was almost too nice! It was a total and complete turnaround in his attitude to me. Maybe he was on some sort of medication that made him happy with the world. Still, I was very careful. To me, the stool on which I was standing had one leg shorter than the other three. I later discovered why he was so chummy.

Chapter 33

Good-Bye Memphis, Hello Mount Juliet!

New Year's Day, 1986. For the first time in a couple of years, I had a totally new outlook on my life's situation. The chapter on my Memphis Zoo career was now about to close. Kevin called me at the end of December and told me that they would be ready for me to start full time in February. So, I turned in my two week notice which made January 10th, 1986, my last day of employment. Some people were surprised, others relieved. A few of my co-workers thought that I would retire from the Memphis Zoo. My future didn't lie here. Sometimes one is almost forced upon a different path, a different timeline. Had Menigar not been so tough on me, I might have stayed there, but I really wouldn't have had the real raptor opportunities that I eventually had. Change for the good is not always recognized for what it is at first. It's like standing in front of a painting, only you're standing with your nose pressed against the canvas. You can see some colors and make out some shapes, but you really can't tell what the artwork is about. Only when you pull back and get a different perspective, can you really see the entire work. That's the way life is sometimes.

My last day was an emotional one for me. I went through the bird department and said my farewells to all of the birds I had the pleasure of working with for so many years. I looked at the bird house exhibits I had a hand in creating. I reflected upon some of the bird species I had a part in their successful breeding. I took a last look at the zoo hospital and the raptor enclosures, the eagle exhibit, the waterfowl area. All had been a part of me for eight and a half years. I had a place for Satch where I was living at the time, so he was already off zoo grounds. He was a part of the zoo that was going with me to Mt. Juliet. At the end of the day, I went to the employees lounge and said good-bye to all of my co-workers. It was tough leaving my human friends as well. I turned in my keys to Cliff Ross and thanked him for giving me the chance to work with birds. I thanked him for making a dream come true. I thanked him for defending me all of these years. I was nearly in tears as I shook Cliff's hand. He wished me well and thanked me for what I did there at the zoo.

"I'm sure you'll be back to see us, won't you?" Cliff asked in a sentimental tone.

"Yeah, I'll come back from time to time. You know, my daughter's here and my sisters live here, so I'll be back around if you don't mind me dropping by." I said while clearing my throat.

"Yeah, you're welcome anytime, John." Cliff replied. Chuck Beckson was in the lounge as well and I gave the gentle giant a big hug.

"Yeah, good luck, John. Mike (his son who helped me with Satch in the early days) is gonna miss you being here. Thanks for letting him help you with the birds." Chuck added.

I said proudly,

"Mike was a good student and helper. He's a great kid!"

"Anyway, keep in touch and we'll see you around", Beckson concluded.

"Alright, I think I've got everything", I said as I carried a box of my stuff out the door. I headed to the zoo office to say good-bye to Duane Able. I looked for Dr. Mike Douglass earlier while I was at the zoo hospital, but he wasn't there. He was in Able's office and as I said good-bye and thanked him for all of his work with the raptor program, he simply said…

"What poor bastard is Menigar gonna pick on now that you're leaving?"

"I don't know, but it's not my problem anymore!" I quickly shot back.

"Well, good luck to you and go over there and mount Juliet 'cause that what Romeo wanted to do!" Mike added.

I had to think about it for a few seconds and I laughed and said,

"I'll look for Juliet." With this Duane Able joined in and wished me good luck as well and shook my hand. As I was headed out his door, Able said to me,

"And Stokes, one more thing…." as he said this he held his index finger up to his eye near his tear duct and did a wiping motion. I laughed and did the same thing back to him. With this, I took my box of stuff and headed out of the zoo office and out towards the gate. I said good-bye to the cashiers and guards and they all wished me well. As I walked through the gate for the last time as an employee, I turned and gave a final scan. The zoo had been a good place for me. I learned a lot about birds and a lot about me. I had made a lot of friends and one main adversary. All and all, it was a great experience.

That night, a few people from the zoo had a going away party for me at a mid-town bar. It was quite fun and embarrassing as well, but it was a nice send off. I was required by common law to give a speech at the end of the night. What was originally a small gathering of zoo friends, had swelled to a larger crowd of people who had dropped in off the street. I thanked everyone for coming out and that Memphis would always be special to me. Toward the end of my impromptu speech someone yelled from the back,

"At least you're getting out of Memphis. Tell the world about us, the forgotten ones!" With this, everyone roared. I said,

"I will, I promise you! Good night and thanks!" I stayed until just about everyone was gone. I finally left the bar at about one in the morning. The next day I woke up a different man and not too quickly after I got up, I received a phone call from Martha Waldron.

"Hey John, how was your last day?" she inquired

"Oh, it was bittersweet, but great!" I answered.

"How was Menigar with you?"

"Well, he wasn't there, but he has been extremely nice to me, I guess because he knew I was leaving".

To this Martha replied, "Well, that might have had a little to do with it but he got really nice to you because he had to".

I asked, "What are you talking about? I thought someone had slipped him some happy pills for the last six weeks or so. It was kinda strange because I thought he was up to some ploy to trip me up so he could fire me."

Martha continued, "Well, I heard a rumor that your buddy Menigar was actually summoned to the Mayor of Memphis office for a little discussion about his relationship with you. It seems that word had gotten to the Mayor's office about your situation with Menigar and his treatment of you. He was pretty well told to leave you alone and to let you do your job. He was warned that if he continued to harass you that he would be making more visits to the Mayor's office to look into his job performance and how well he is doing at the zoo. So, in a sense, he was told to back off or else!"

"Wow! The Mayor's office, huh?!? How did they know about all of this?" I asked.

"Apparently, the information came from several sources including the Park Commission and someone that I know." Martha said wryly.

Apparently, Martha was friends with the Mayor and maybe Frank Fogle had talked to him as well.

255

"Well, I thank all of you for your help. This certainly clears up that mystery for me."

Martha concluded by saying, "The situation went on for far too long and it was a shame that it forced you to leave. We're going to miss you here and thanks for the work that you did!"

I thanked Martha as well and told her I'd be picking up Paddington when I got an enclosure for him. She assured me that there was no rush getting him out and I could take my time getting him.

My last few days in Memphis were spent tying up the usual loose ends and building a portable temporary enclosure for Satch. I packed most of my stuff and paid my roommate, Danny, for my last month's part of the rent. I had made plans to spend a few weeks with Cindy in Fayetteville before I moved to Mt. Juliet. Danny said that my stuff was safe there until I needed to get it. I still had my cat, Denver, and my sister Susie agreed to care for her until I got settled in Mt. Juliet. Everything was now in order and in the middle of January, I drove to Fayetteville to spend a few free weeks with Satch and Cindy. Satch adjusted well to his new, temporary home. Cindy was happy to have us both there. It was an enjoyable time and things, for once, seemed to be in balance. I was about to enter a whole new phase of my life. Things were to get a whole lot better.

Chapter 34

My New Home

After spending a few weeks in Arkansas, it was time to start my new job. Kevin called me to see if I wanted to go to Florida to visit a few bird facilities and to go see a space shuttle launch. I thought, "Why not?" and said "Okay". I drove to Mount Juliet and met Kevin. He loaded his travel bags and southward we went. It was the 26th of January and our itinerary took us to the Orlando area to see the bird and rehab facilities in the area. The next day we visited the Florida Audubon Society's facility in Maitland and then went to a few smaller places around the area. Our plan was to be around Cape Canaveral early the next morning. Everyone who had been to a shuttle launch advised us to get there early. They also said that restroom facilities were limited and suggested to locate the nearest porta potty.

On the 28th, I woke up with some gastro-intestinal problems. I took Kaopectate and hoped that the problem would go away. By breakfast, it was apparent that this problem would not abate soon and a decision was made to scrub seeing the shuttle launch and instead, go to Tampa. There were a few facilities we wanted to see around there and we also wanted to go to Busch Gardens. I also had an option of having a restroom nearby in case I had an emergency. We got to Busch Gardens around 11:00 a.m. and viewed a number of exhibits. By 11:30, we got in line to ride the tram that toured around the African Veldt. We were in line for about ten minutes and were getting close to our turn to board the tram. I noticed a few of the tram workers talking and shaking their heads. I saw one of the female employees crying and it was apparent that something was wrong. Maybe one of their co-workers had been injured or something had happened to one of the animals on the Veldt. The tram pulled up and it was time for us to board. As we were boarding, one of the tram attendants came over the intercom and announced,

"Ladies and gentlemen, we regret to inform you that, ah, umm (his voice breaking as he continued) the Space Shuttle Challenger has just exploded after liftoff! We don't know any more details at this time and we're sorry that we had to share this with you, we're very sorry..." his voiced trailed off.

Kevin and I found a seat on the tram and looked at each other with looks of disbelief. It didn't seem real. As the tram left the station, the tracks took us out into the open African Veldt exhibit. We could see as we looked toward the east the results of the explosion. We saw the main smoke and debris cloud and also saw the paths of the solid rocket boosters. I couldn't believe what I was seeing and I couldn't even take my focus away from the horrible sight to even look at the animals on exhibit. I glanced at Kevin and he had his gaze fixed skyward as well. I felt a lump in my throat and I noticed that several other passengers were staring skyward and a few had tears in their eyes. I looked again at Kevin and he just shook his head and fought back the tears. This made me start to well up as I pondered what we were seeing. The tram finally brought us back to the station and Kevin asked where the Beer Garden was. We were pointed in the appropriate direction and found our way in line. Everybody was talking about the space shuttle. How could you not?!? We saw the results of a national tragedy. We were starting to hear whispers that the crew had not survived which made the mood even worse. Kevin and I got a beer and sat down,

"If there was ever a good day to have diarrhea, this was it!" Kevin quietly proclaimed.

"Yeah, you're right! That would have been a terrible thing to witness in person…I'm glad I had the runs!" I replied.

He was right. My "problem" made us change our plans and took us to the opposite coast. To have seen that disaster live would have made it impossible to erase from my memory. We left Busch Garden and went to a nearby seabird sanctuary. We found a motel and were transfixed by the TV news. The next day, we decided to cut our trip short and headed back to Tennessee. We had had enough of Florida and the terrible event that had transpired. I later named a Bald Eagle "Challenger" in honor of the crew.

After the Florida trip, it was time to officially move to Mt. Juliet. Kevin had money for my salary and a place to stay. He arranged a storage unit for my limited amount of furniture and even met me in Memphis with a moving van. He brought along a fellow who became one of my best friends, Eric Thibault. Eric's first words were,

"Damn, I was expecting someone older. Kevin kept calling you the "Doctor" and we were going to move the "Doctor" to Mount Juliet. Are you indeed a doctor?"

"No, I don't know where he came up with that, maybe it's a nickname he wants to call me. Don't call me "Doctor", just call me John," I replied.

"Okay, John it is. Some people call me T-Bone since my last name sounds like this. My name should actually be pronounced "Ta-beau". You can call me anything you want except late for dinner!" he jokingly said.

"Well, Eric, it is nice to meet you. I look forward to working with you!" I added.

I shook his hand and introduced him to Satch, who was in the back of my mini-van. We then went into Danny's house and started carrying my stuff out and into the moving truck. This didn't take too long and before I knew it, we were finished. I closed the back of the truck and then gave my house key, along with a handshake and hug, to Danny. With this, I was ready to go. I told Kevin that I'd lead him to a shortcut to I-40. As we pulled away, I had mixed feelings. I had lived in Memphis for twenty years. I had a lot of memories, some of them bad, but most of them good. But now I was heading to my new life. I was looking forward to a whole new experience. I was going to work more with raptors and I was in on the ground floor.

We completed the three and one half hour drive to Mt. Juliet and drove to the storage facility to unload my stuff. I didn't have an official place to live as yet. Kevin had bought a mobile home in a trailer park for me, but it wasn't ready to occupy. I had arranged to stay with my cousin, Alan Ray, in a garage apartment in the west side of Nashville. I had about a thirty minute drive to Mt. Juliet, but it didn't matter. I also got to spend time with Alan, who is like an older brother to me. I was also enthused to be back in the Nashville area and looked forward to going to work.

One of the first tasks that Kevin, Eric and I set out to do was to build more enclosures at the "Site" as we called the location that was to house our education, breeding and rehab birds. The land was owned by Kevin's cousin, Billy Clinnard. Billy had bought the land to eventually build a house, but at this time, it was an unimproved lot. The area was fenced with a gate across the road. Kevin had already built a four enclosure building on the land. In here, he had a few birds that were in rehab; a couple of Red-tailed Hawks, A Great Horned Owl and a few Turkey Vultures. Osceola was still in an enclosure at Kevin's house some five miles away in Mt. Juliet. Billy's land was about a mile north of Long Hunter State Park, part of which borders Percy Priest Lake. We needed to build Osceola and Satch enclosures on the Site. During the day,

Satch stayed in his temporary enclosure that I made for him and used while I was in Fayetteville. At night, he stayed in my van, something he was very used to doing. Osceola was fine where he was, but it would be nice to have all of the birds together.

Before long, we had purchased some lumber and began building new homes for Satch and Osceola. Within two weeks, we had both of them at the Site. We started building two more enclosures for the Great Horned Owl named Owl-X (Alex) and another on the back side of Owl-X's new home. Even though Owl-X was already at the Site, we wanted to have him in his own enclosure and use the one he was in for other birds. I got to where I could wield a hammer fairly well and Eric and I were a pretty good construction team.

It was really nice to be involved in a totally new situation. I was thrilled to go to work every day. For the first time, I was totally relaxed in my life. I had money in the bank since I got my pension back, or at least what I had contributed over eight and one half years. I was having fun at work and I was working full time with raptors. The only real drawback to my new situation was I was now three hours away from my daughter, Lendi and eight hours away from my girlfriend Cindy. So I was now in a long distance relationship with my daughter and an even longer distance with Cindy. Still, I couldn't complain. I didn't have to worry about Menigar anymore and whether or not I would be employed at the end of the day.

Chapter 35

My "New" Digs

I was commuting from my cousin Alan's house some 25 miles one way. He lived on the west side of Nashville and Mount Juliet was on the eastern side of Davidson County, just inside the western boundary of Wilson County. I had been making this daily trip for about three weeks, but my commuting days were soon to be finished. One day at the Site, Kevin told me that the mobile home he bought for me would be ready in a few days and that it was "real nice!" Those few days went by and Kevin announced that the trailer was ready. I followed him to Mt. Juliet and to Page's Mobile Home Community. He pulled into the driveway and stopped at the first trailer past Mr. Page's house. I thought to myself, "I hope this isn't it!" Sure enough, it was. Kevin got out of his truck, opened the front door and motioned for me to come inside. I reluctantly obliged.

"Whaddaya think? Is it nice or what?!?" Kevin exclaimed.

In my mind, I voted for the "or what" portion of his statement. All I could reply was,

"Yeah, it's something alright!"

Kevin's definition of "nice" and mine were completely different. The mobile home had seen its better days. The exterior was brown and white and looked like something that survived re-entry from Space. From its style and meticulous construction I guessed that it was built in the early 1970's. A placard next to the front door confirmed this; "*Proudly built in 1972*". Inside, the walls throughout had a dark, simulated wood grain paneling. The floors were covered with badly worn brown and gold shag carpeting.

The kitchen was a world of delight all its own. The floor was rolled linoleum that had a quilted pattern of brown and gold, complete with a large speed bump-like bubble dead center. This was capped by an incredibly sturdy, very much out of place, solid wood table accompanied by two matching naugahyde-covered benches. From the ceiling hung a wagon wheel light fixture, with a light bulb and globe at the perimeter of each spoke. The cabinets were dark brown and constructed of the finest particleboard covered with a rich wood grain appliqué. A few of the doors were askew and when I tried to close them, they automatically went back to their previous positions. The sink was missing a knob for the "Hot" water and under the sink was particleboard that obviously had gotten wet repeatedly. The stove however looked good and the refrigerator was clean and functional.

I followed Kevin on the tour of the palace, I mean place. I noticed that the drapery matched the Western motif, I think. Surrounding each window were lovely, floor length drab yellow drapes complete with yellow valances trimmed in brown. Each valance had a row of brown dingle balls. As we went down the hall that connected the two bedrooms and the bathroom, I stepped on what I thought was solid floor only to get a trampoline-like effect. The particleboard flooring in this area had apparently rotted away and left the shag carpeting as the sole means of support. Luckily, the rest of the floor wasn't this way.

Past this spot o' fun was the first tiny bedroom. It was about the size of a walk-in closet and was eventually used as such. The bathroom was another sight to behold. It was decked out in yellowish wallpaper and its floor was covered, not with the swanky shag, but with a low pile indoor/outdoor carpet (which was brown, of course). The cabinet holding the sink had two drawers on the

263

left that didn't close properly. Hell, they didn't even match! Under the sink was also collapsed particleboard. The mirror above the sink was in pretty good shape, but was probably ashamed to reflect all this ugliness. The toilet was yellow-gold molded plastic and listed about 30 degrees to the right. The bathtub was also of the same high quality material from which the toilet was formed and it too, like the kitchen sink, was missing the "Hot" knob handle. It fact, upon closer inspection, the threads were stripped. Why have a knob when one can use pliers?!

Completing the tour was the Master Bedroom. It took all of the previously mentioned fashion elements and put them on lavish display; shag carpeting, wood grain paneling, shady drapes and a smaller wagon wheel light fixture. The closet had mirror-covered sliding doors that didn't close all the way. To top it all, was a window unit air conditioner held in place by a window frame with a cracked window. This was corrected by the use of a small piece of plywood. All in all, it was a pretty depressing place. I almost felt sorry for it, if one can feel sorrow for an inanimate object.

Kevin commented, "We'll get your stuff out of storage and move you in tomorrow".

I must have looked less than enthusiastic because he then said,

"This is only a temporary place for you to live. We will find you an apartment and we will move this trailer down to the site and use it as an office."

I had serious doubts that this trailer could survive the five mile move to the south but I said,

"Yeah, that would be nice!"

At least I wasn't paying to live here. The next day, I got what belongings I had at my cousin's place and thanked him for his support. Kevin kept good on his promise and got my stuff out of storage. I spent most of the afternoon unpacking and by nightfall, I had my belongings in place. I had an uneventful night in my 70's retro party place and the next day I went down to the Mt. Juliet Post Office and filed a change of address card. I was now an official resident. The final act to make my move complete was to get my cat Denver from my sister Susie. So the next weekend I went to Memphis, saw Lendi, got Denver and my accumulated mail from my former roommate Danny. After a three hour drive back, I brought Denver into the Casa de la Oeste. She, too, was unimpressed. But at least now, all of my worldly possessions and my cat companion were all in one place. I had finally completed my transition. My "temporary" stay in this trailer lasted five years.

Chapter 36

Building the Cumberland Wildlife Foundation

We continued to build enclosures at our site. Kevin was in contact with several other wildlife rehab facilities in the region. One of which, The Raptor Research and Propagation Project (now known as The World Bird Sanctuary), was headed by Walter "Stormy" Crawford. I had met Walter a few years back at the Raptor Research Foundation's annual meeting in Sacramento. Walter is a colorful character and has been working with raptors since the late 1960s. He is one of those people one either likes or really dislikes. I happen to like Walter. He also had a number of birds that he needed to surplus. Kevin had told Walter that we would take a Mountain Caracara, an old pair of Red-tailed Hawks, an old Swainson's Hawk and an Imperial Eagle, a rarer cousin of the Golden Eagle. The only problem was, we only had room for the eagle and not the other birds. To make matters worse, Kevin was on his way to get the birds the next day. His plan was to stay overnight in St. Louis get the birds early the next morning. Eric and I were determined to have enclosures constructed for all of the birds by the time Kevin arrived back in Mt. Juliet that evening.

Kevin departed early Tuesday morning and Eric and I met at the site at dawn. We already had our materials ready, so upon arrival, we were able to get at the task at hand. We needed three additional cages so we ended making a four roomed building with shared common walls. This cut down on the needed materials and also allowed us to work faster. We worked throughout the day, without a break for lunch, and by the time the sun had set, we had a four room building, albeit unpainted, ready for the birds. Kevin arrived later that evening and by flashlight, we unloaded the birds into their new homes. The next morning, I got a good look at our new charges. The birds were mostly, in human terms, retirees. Walter had the Red-tailed Hawk pair, Swainson's Hawk and the Imperial Eagle as display birds and these birds were essentially taking up space. The Mountain Caracara, however, was a very interesting specimen! She was given the name of P.I.T.A. by bird trainer Steve Martin. P.I.T.A. stood for "pain in the ass" and was deemed "untrainable" by Steve. Walter didn't have a need for this bird, so we got her in the deal.

The Mountain Caracara is native to the high foothills of the Andes and in the wild, is doing fairly well. Pita, however, was the only Mountain Caracara in captivity in the U.S. and we had her. She was hatched at Busch Garden in Florida in 1974. Her parents were apparently deceased (or may have been deported). This bird's North American cousin, the Crested Caracara, sports a bushy crest and looks like it was made from a box of bird parts that included samples from a chicken, vulture and hawk. The Mountain Caracara, by comparison, looks rather dapper. Pita was black and white and had a flat top type of "hairdo". In fact, she looked as though she was wearing a tuxedo. She had yellow legs with toes tipped with white talons. She had amber eyes and the skin on her face varied in color depending on her mood; from rooster-comb red when she was disturbed, to yellow when she was calm. She, by far, was one of the most interesting birds I had seen. That is saying a lot, since I worked with a variety of birds at the Memphis Zoo.

We had a number of other enclosures to build as well. Kevin had purchased plenty of lumber to build more units. We had money from Miller Beer to help purchase materials, equipment and provide salaries. Eric and I stayed busy throughout the spring and early summer with construction. Despite the fact we were busy building cages, we still had time in the afternoon for other activities. At nearby Long Hunter State Park, we got involved with a group of locals who played volleyball several times a week. I also got to fly a few times a week as well. I was less than two hours away from the Henson Gap and Whitwell flying sites. Whitwell was the site I had the pleasure of hitchhiking up a few years back where I met Happy Go Lucky Slim. Eric was interested in learning how to hang glide and went with me on these flying excursions. I accumulated several hours of airtime each week and really expanded my knowledge of flight. I also purchased a glider on which I could train Eric. We started looking for nearby hills to aid in Eric's quest to become a manbird.

Within a few weeks we had found several hills that we had permission to use. The glider, a 229 Raven, was a little large for Eric, but it would be easier for him to launch and land since the glider's stall speed was lower with a lighter pilot. Eric was a quick study and was getting the "hang" of flying. He was soon executing 90 degree turns and was landing on his feet. Before long, he would be ready to make his first flight off something higher.

On one of my trips to Lookout Mountain, I learned a lesson about being extra careful when choosing people to help me with my glider in windy conditions. When the wind velocity exceeds 10-12 m.p.h., it is wise and necessary to have assistance with one's glider. While moving a glider to the launch, a high wing could result in a somersault. I got my glider in line behind the launch and Eric helped me do a hang check to make sure all of my lines were straight and that I was hooked to the glider via the carabiner. Also, on our trip that day was Brian Grelen. He was the son of a Tennessee Wildlife Resources Agency Officer named Tom Grelen. Brian was interested in hang gliding and was a pretty good photographer. He was here to document hang gliding from launch to landing and was shooting many photos as I readied my craft and harness for flight. I was now ready and simply had to wait until the person in front of me launched. The winds this day were 15-18 m.p.h. and required a full complement of launch assistants. A person was on each side wire, one on the tail, and back then, we usually had someone on the nose wires as well (we later discovered that a nose man wasn't needed, so in the 21st Century, we no longer have to pick our nose...man). The guy in front of me scooted up to launch and all of the launch assistants helped him steady his glider. He picked up his craft and moved it into the airflow.

"I've got up!" The guy on the left wire called out.

"I've got neutral!" The guy on the right wire replied, but I could clearly see that his right wing was down more than his right.

"I've got up!" once again the left wireman said.

"I've got neutral!"(meaning the wing was neither up or down) the right wireman sang.

But in this case, the right wing was down again. I yelled to the pilot,

"Your right wing is low!!!"

He looked back at me, nodded, leveled his wings and yelled "Clear!" Away he went to an uneventful launch and started his climb into the soarable air.

It was now my turn. The wind was a steady 18 m.p.h. and I had the same crew of people that had launched the previous pilot. I did another visual check of my glider and harness and asked what the windsock was indicating. It was straight in and I picked up my glider and the crew helped me ease it into the airflow. I heard "Up" from both the side wiremen and I yelled "Clear!" as I leaned forward and stepped into the rising air. What happened next was that time began to slow. The glider was rolling in the direction of my right wing and it was rapidly getting lower. I shifted my weight hard to the left to counter the drop, but it didn't respond. Did I blunder into a strong thermal that just happened to be at the launch when I cleared the takeoff? Something caused my unintentional right turn and I was now heading back towards the cliff. With time in the molasses mode, I was able to assess the predicament to which I was currently a party. I saw a few trees near the edge of the cliff and I was able to flare my glider and landed perfectly in the top of one of the small Chestnut Oaks. At this point, time rapidly returned to its normal pace. I was secure in the treetop without any worry of the glider falling. The next thing I heard was Eric's voice,

"Are you alright? Are you okay?" Eric asked with concern in his voice.

"Yeah, I'm good and I am safely in this tree! I probably scared the heck out of a few squirrels, though!" I responded.

As Eric climbed the tree to help me, he said,

"This crash wasn't your fault!"

"Whaddaya mean?" I inquired.

"The guy helping on your right flying wire held on too long and caused your glider to go into a severe right turn. He looked like he was shooting a bow. Brian probably has pictures of it!"

Eric continued, "The first thing the guy said was that everybody had let go at the same time. To me, in so many words, he admitted his guilt. That idiot could have got you killed!"

"Well, I'm glad it didn't result in that!" I said with a sigh of relief.

Eric helped me unclip from my glider and in the finest primate style, climbed the small tree and helped extract my glider. It was essentially undamaged, with the exception of a few bent battens. These were easy to get back to their regular configurations with some creative bending and a batten chart. It took us about an hour to get the glider back to the top. Eric looked around for the guy that caused my crash. Somebody told him that Robin Hood had left.

"Good thing, Eric said, cause I was going to whip his as$!"

"Violence begats violence!" I replied

"Yeah, he'd begatting his as$ whipped! Eric countered.

I couldn't help but laugh. Besides, I was alive and unharmed and learned a valuable lesson of whom I chose to help me with my glider in windy conditions. Eric and I returned to Mt. Juliet and I felt almost fortunate to drive up to my broken down mobile home.

In the meantime, Kevin told me that we were going to Tucson, Arizona for a week for the annual meeting of the Raptor Research Foundation. I had attended this group's meeting the previous year's meeting in Sacramento. Kevin felt it important to attend this conference in order to make more connections in the raptor world. Tom Nolan, the Vice President of CWFA, also planned to go with us. The only catch was that I had to use my van for the trip. I didn't mind too much since the vehicle was still fairly new. My stipulation was that I could take my hang glider with me, since Arizona had a number of flying sites. Tucson, in fact, had a site within its city limits known as "A" Mountain. Kevin agreed to my terms and even expressed that he wanted to learn to fly as well.

This was to be my second trip to Arizona in a year. The previous year had been the vacation from Hell with Cindy and Butch. This year, there would not be the tension of two people who totally disliked each other. Eric had to stay behind and care for the birds, but he had help in the form of a couple of volunteers named Marty Rush and Linda Bowman. These women had helped Kevin some over the last couple of years and I began to utilize them in care and handling of the birds. Both learned very quickly what needed to be done to care for the birds and were pretty good at treating the rehab patients we had.

271

The trip out to Tucson was uneventful and I got to see a lot of the same people I saw in Sacramento. Dr. Tom Cade, the head of the Peregrine Fund, was there. As were many of the same people that were influential in restoring many raptor species. We looked at the schedule of event for the week and chose seminars we thought would help us in our efforts at Cumberland. Kevin and I also checked some of the local sites for hang gliding. We found "A" mountain, I guessed named because it had an "A" on it for the University of Arizona. It was a smallish hill and this day was awash with dust devils and other assorted turbulence. I decided to keep my glider on the van.

The conference concluded the next day and we decided to drive to Flagstaff to spend the night. The following morning, we went to the South Rim of the Grand Canyon for a little sightseeing and then headed back to Tennessee. We learned a lot in Arizona and made plenty of contacts. It was a worthwhile trip.

During this time Kevin and a fellow named Al Louis Cecere, a man who had found the Miller Brewing Company sponsorship for the Cumberland Wildlife Foundation and the Save the Eagle Project (STEP), decided that CWF needed a high profile publicity "gimmick" to draw attention to CWF and STEP. What they came up with was a replica river flatboat like the one used by Col. John Donelson as he floated down the Cumberland River with a number of other flatboats. Colonel Donelson headed the flotilla that carried women and children and eventually helped in the founding and the settlement of Nashville.

The flatboat was built near Gallatin, Tennessee and Eric and I had to go up for several evenings for several weeks to help with its construction. The idea was to float this boat down the Cumberland River, thus re-creating Colonel Donelson's trip. The boat would make stops at several river towns, where the locals could board the boat and were told of the historical journey. At these stops, Eric

272

and I were to do bird programs at a nearby park. Kevin and Al were certain this trip was going to raise thousands and thousands of dollars. Eric and I thought this whole flatboat idea was pretty ridiculous especially since, in the end, the flatboat (and its backup outboard motors) cost well over ten thousand dollars to build. This same ten thousand dollars could have been used to buy more bird enclosure materials or give Eric a raise from his measly seventy-five dollars a week.

The flatboat trip finally happened with Kevin in his authentic "Long Hunter" garb and Eric and me meeting the flatboat along the way. The riverbank dwellers were only moderately supportive of the event and the whole idea only raised about three thousand dollars in donations. So, even though the flatboat excursion was more like Gilligan's Island and less like the Titanic in that no one was hurt or died, it still sunk! It was a waste of time and resources.

Chapter 37

1987-Cumberland Comes of Age

January, 1987. The previous year had been a great one with many advances and adventures. One thing that helped me see my now fiancé Cindy at least twice a month was that we were now getting food donated to us by Pel-Freeze out of Rogers, Arkansas, about twenty miles from Fayetteville. Tom Nolan, Vice President of the Cumberland Wildlife Foundation, was a research scientist at Vanderbilt University. He had used some of the Pel-Freeze provided mice for some of his work at the university. He contacted Pel-Freeze about possibly acquiring some of the culled surplus rodents. They were very willing to help us and donated the animal carcasses to us. All we had to do was go pick them up in Rogers. It worked great for me in that CWF paid for my gas to Rogers and back. I got to stay with Cindy and even took my hang glider along with me and I had the opportunity to fly on several of these trips. So I was now going to northwest Arkansas twice a month. Not a bad deal, but just a lot of driving.

Cumberland was the "go to" rehab facility in Middle Tennessee and worked closely with the Tennessee Wildlife Resources Agency. We even housed a number of confiscated animals for the State of Tennessee including a young female cougar named Miss Kitty, a Coyote named Wiley and two alligators named Stump and Godzilla. We also had a great Veterinarian, Dr. Scott Thomas, and his staff to do the surgery and initial care. We had more enclosures built to handle the extra rehab birds. At this point, the Cumberland Wildlife Foundation was now becoming a well-oiled machine.

The Cumberland Wildlife Foundation was involved in a number of different education scenarios. We conducted a lot of school programs, state park programs, displays at state and local fairs, garden clubs, Boy Scout and Cub Scout programs. At one particular cub scout program, I was at the portion of the program that I brought out Osceola and talked about the Bald Eagle. I had Osceola on my glove and was a little distracted as he bated or jumped off my hand. This doesn't hurt a bird as long as it has two leather jesse straps, one on each leg. I continued talking to the cubs and as I helped Osceola back on my glove, I didn't notice that Osceola's left foot was pawing the air. As I put my right arm down to boost him back on my glove, his left foot grabbed my right arm. Instantly, I felt a pain, not unlike the combination of a wasp sting and stepping on a nail. My initial reaction was to pull my arm away, but when I did, I threw Osceola off balance and off into a dangling position. He didn't let go of my arm, but held on, thrusting his talon deeper into my arm. I could feel one of his talons grating along my ulna. I finally got him back on my glove and I'm sure I was a lighter shade of pale and queasy. I tried to keep my composure and did my best not to grimace when a little scout blurted,

"Excuse me Mister, but that looked like that hurt!"

Taking about an understatement!!! I had Osceola safely back on my glove and a nice, deep puncture wound. I continued my speech about the Bald Eagle and at the end, put Osceola back in his travel kennel. I then went to the nearest restroom and washed my arm. The wound was barely bleeding and I did my best to flush the hole. I finished loading the birds, took them back to the Site and went home to my trailer. My hand and wrist were throbbing. I took a couple of aspirin, hoped for the best and went to bed. Sleep was difficult as I accidently rolled over on my wounded wrist several times during the night. The next morning, I awoke to a swollen hand and wrist. In fact, my hand had a greenish hue to it and looked like a Nerf football. It was a little difficult to do my job that day, but within two days, my hand was back to normal.

Since that time, I have been "footed" as it is called by a number of different birds. It rather goes with the job. Hopefully it doesn't result in a severe injury. Charger, the first Red-tailed Hawk I trained, grabbed my right thumb and drove her back talon into my joint nearest my thumbnail. She saw a remnant of a piece of the meat I was feeding her and tried to grab it. I had to hold her foot with my gloved hand and slowly extracted the talon from my thumb.

Probably the worse time I ever got footed was actually two times, by two different birds, two days in a row. One of the Bald Eagles in our care, a huge female from the Aleutian Islands in Alaska, had impacted with the wall of her enclosure and had dinged her wing. The injury was such that I decided to take her to Doctor Thomas. I took the eagle into the clinic in a large sky kennel and when Dr. Thomas was ready, I reached into the kennel to extract the bird. In a situation with an untrained bird, the best way to control the bird is to grab both the bird's legs at the same time just above the feet. I had on two welder's gloves that came to my mid forearm. When I reached in to grab this large bird, she was faster than me. Instead of grabbing her feet, she grabbed my left arm at my elbow. She immediately sunk her two and one-half inch long back talon into my elbow. She released her grip, but her talon was still imbedded in my arm. In fact, I could see the tip of the talon just below the surface of my arm. I slowly extracted the talon, readjusted my grip and removed the eagle out for examination. As I was holding the eagle, one of the Vet Techs named Judie saw the blood on my elbow and asked what happened. She then flushed the puncture wound with peroxide and everything was fine. The eagle's wing was not as bad as it looked and Dr. Thomas cleaned the area and put some Neosporin on the scrape. I returned the eagle to the Site and put her back in her enclosure. For several days I kept a close eye on her wound and it quickly healed.

A day after I was grabbed by the eagle, a large female Red-tailed Hawk was brought to us. She had been struck by a vehicle on one of the local highways and had a broken wing. I put a wrap on her left wing and took her to the animal clinic. I had her in a smaller transport kennel and when Doc was ready, I used the same gloves and same technique as the day before with the eagle. Unfortunately, I got the same results. This Red-tail had back talons that were an inch and one half long. She jumped as I went to grab her and sunk her back talon of her right foot into my left elbow. Unfortunately for me, her talon went precisely into the previous day's talon wound. My arm was already swollen and was painful, so this event was excruciating. The hawk would not let go.

I tried several tricks to make her release her grasp, but each attempt caused her to increase her grip. I got the bird and sat down on a stool and a Vet Tech named Phyllis Crawford, who was a body builder, saw my dilemma. She slowly and carefully pried the talons out of my arm. At this point, I was getting a little light-headed and asked her to hold the bird for a minute so I could regain my composure. Afterwards, Dr. Thomas looked over my arm and cleaned it with Betadine. The hawk was finally x-rayed, her wing was wrapped and I returned her to our facility. A few weeks later, she was released. I now have a ¼ scar near my left elbow to remind me of these "footings" and to be careful when I go to grab a bird.

Chapter 38

Some Changes are afoot

Even though things were humming along at Cumberland, there was some internal strife. Kevin and Tom had an association with Al Louis Cecere. Recall that Al was the fundraiser who brought in the Miller Brewing Company support. It was his efforts that supported what we were doing at the Cumberland Wildlife Foundation. I didn't have a whole lot of contact with Al and knew him from a distance. But apparently, Tom, Kevin and Al had a meeting and a big decision was made. The next thing I knew was that Kevin told me that Al was no longer associated with our group. I was never told of the details or reason why, just that Al was not part of us anymore. I didn't ask too many questions since it really didn't concern me. Little did I know that this decision did affect how CWF would operate in the future.

Later in the summer, I had some internal strife of my own. My fiancé Cindy with whom I had been involved for nearly five years, broke up with me. The physical distance that separated us finally killed our relationship. She had met someone in college and she wanted to explore where that new relationship would take her. Despite my pleading and lobbying on my behalf, she wasn't convinced to stay. I was devastated. I wrote Cindy several letters hoping to change her mind. I actually talked to her a few times over the following weeks, but it was apparent that nothing I did would make a difference. It was a sad time for me, but I had to accept it.

The first part of September, I had to go back to Rogers, Arkansas to Pel-Freez to pick up a load of rodents. I normally stayed with Cindy, but obviously I couldn't now. I did take my hang glider with me on that weekend and went to a place to fly near Atkins, Arkansas. The winds were not very strong and as I waited on the launch for the winds to increase, a young Red-tailed Hawk flew past and looked me directly in the eyes. He "kee-yarred" as he went by, caught a thermal and began circling right over the launch, all the while looking down at me. At that point, something in me changed! I had been sad about losing my relationship with Cindy, but at that moment, I found symbolism in that young hawk's flight. He was free! I made the decision to let go. I released my hold on the relationship that was and said my farewells.

I suited up in my harness and after a quick check, I launched and followed that young raptor skyward. As I climbed, I was reminded that life is a journey and I was on a new path. The young hawk beckoned me to come along and participate in what life had in store. I climbed well over several thousand feet in that hawk's thermal and saw the young bird as he set out on his own path. I looked over the mountain and surveyed the Earth below and looked at the horizon. I chose a new path as well. Life was gently tugging me along on this new course, this new track and from that lofty vantage, I knew was going to be okay! Several years later, I realized that Cindy had been in my life to be a teacher. I did learn a lot of things from her, especially when it came to relationships. We eventually became friends again and I called her from time to time when I had relationship questions. It was always nice to talk to her. She always had a good answer and it is great to know that I was still her friend.

I also continued to teach Eric to hang glide. He finally made his mountain flight off Henson's Gap near Dunlap, Tennessee. He had flown off a smaller hill with an elevation of 250 feet and did very well. He was ready for the big flight. Everything went well with the exception that someone had accidently turned down his radio. This almost proved to be costly since I was at the landing field with my radio. He launched successfully and was doing well until he went to turn and slipped his turn. He had plenty of altitude, but the slip scared him. I didn't know he couldn't hear me as I calmly radioed instruction to him. We had gone over his flight with the scenario of radio failure. He continued on towards the landing zone and as he flew overhead, he yelled,

"I'm going in! My radio's dead and I'm doing my best!"

At this point, I went from calm to worried. Eric headed toward a tree line and I was running along yelling,

"Turn, turn, turn!!!"

I am sure Eric didn't hear me, but at the last possible moment, just before he was to impact some trees, he pulled off a low 180 degree turn. He leveled the glider, but dragged a wingtip and spun to a stop. The onboard wheels dissipated most of the energy of the crash, but he still bent his downtubes. Eric was shaken but okay and his first mountain flight was also his last. I did get his glider repaired and Eric seemed interested in flying again, but he met a woman who took up most of his time. They eventually married and she was not too keen on the idea of him hang gliding.

I also reinvigorated my idea and desire to fly with Osceola. I got Eric to help me measure Osceola to get a harness made. I knew a hang glider pilot in Arkansas named Mark Stump who built harness for flying. I gave him a call to discuss with him my idea to get Osceola in the air again and I send him some harness plans and materials for Osceola's harness. Within two weeks, I had the harness in hand. One problem; it was too small. It would carry a Red-tailed Hawk, but not an eagle. In my plans, I forgot to leave room for Mark to sew the zippers. I re-drew the plans, bought some new material and zippers and sent it all to Mark, again. Two weeks passed and I had Osceola's new rig. For some reason, I didn't fit Osceola in the harness. I guess I figured that I'll fly with him the next year.

Chapter 39

The Loon, Iron Eyes and 1989

The following year at Cumberland was pretty much the same. We continued to do a lot of educational programs. Eric eventually got a job with the Corps of Engineers as a Ranger at Cordell Hull Lake in upper middle Tennessee. Kevin simply wasn't paying him enough and he needed more money in his married life. We rehabilitated quite a number of animals as well. One memorable bird that came in was a Common Loon. I got a call from a local supermarket about a "duck" that was stranded in the parking lot. I had a feeling what this "duck" was. The previous night had been clear with a full moon. When the moon is full, a parking lot looks like a body of water to a night migrating bird. To a loon, the parking lot was an inviting place to rest. A loon's feet are so far back on its body that it can't walk on solid ground. When a loon lands on a parking lot, it cannot takeoff. If it were on a body of water, it could run along on the water while flapping its wings, thus becoming airborne.

As soon as I pulled into the parking lot, I saw a few people standing around this bird. I got out and sure enough it was a Common Loon. One man thought that the duck had broken both its legs since it couldn't take off from the parking lot. I explained what was going on with this wayward bird. It wasn't too unusual for a loon to do this, except it was early Spring. We usually got a loon or two in the Fall. Nearby Percy Priest and Old Hickory Lakes had wintering loons and perhaps this was one from nearby that got a little confused. I gathered the loon, all the while avoiding its dagger-like bill. It had a small scrape on its keel and no doubt had bruised its pectoral muscles.

I took the loon back to our office and set up a pen with a kiddie pool in it. I put the loon in the filled pool and it immediately started drinking and bathing. I went to the local bait shop and bought three dozen minnows. I placed the minnows in the pool and within an hour, all were gone. I repeated this procedure everyday for the next week and at that point, the loon was ready to be released. I took the bird to nearby Couchville Lake at Long Hunter State Park and placed it in the water near the boat dock. It immediately started running across the water as if it were going to takeoff. Suddenly, it stopped, turned around and looked directly at me. It then bowed its head and vocalized a low flute-like whistle. Slowly it turned back around and paddled across the lake. I didn't know what to think of the loon's vocalization; some may have interpreted it as a "Thank You". Others may have viewed it as "get back". At any rate, it was satisfying to see the bird return to the wild.

Later in the year, we got a new Golden Eagle from the World Bird Sanctuary in Eureka, Missouri. She was a large female from Alaska and was found floating in a glacial pool. She was taken to a local rehab center where it was determined that she had severe cataracts in both eyes. She may have tried to catch a duck or goose and failed. The bird apparently was old and return to the wild was not in her best interest. She turned out to be a great bird and was given the name "Tashina" by Eric. She was easy to handle and had a seven and one half foot wingspan and made quite an impression when we used her in programs.

We also got a young male Golden Eagle in our rehab program. The bird was found in near Columbia, Tennessee and had been shot in the left wing. The wing had a carpal break near the wingtip from a shotgun pellet. Dr. Thomas was optimistic about the bird's

283

recovery and placed a light wrap on the wing. I named him "Iron Eyes" after the famous Native American actor, Iron Eyes Cody. Iron Eyes was famous for the anti-litter commercial of the 70's where someone threw garbage at his feet as he stood by a roadside. As he turned to the camera, a single tear ran down his cheek. I met Iron Eyes Cody earlier in the year at a pow wow and he held Osceola for several pictures. He had been a falconer earlier in his life and was comfortable handling him. Osceola behaved splendidly and quite a number of people got a picture of the two.

Meanwhile, the local media ran stories about the eagle Iron Eyes. This was in hopes we could find who shot him. Even though there was a reward for information that would lead to an arrest, no one responded. The eagle was doing well for a week or so, but I noticed that his appetite had decreased and he appeared more listless. I took him to Dr. Thomas for an exam. He was concerned that the eagle had an infection in his wing. An x-ray confirmed his suspicions; the carpal bone was infected. Instead of the break healing, the bone was actually deteriorating. Dr. Thomas placed him on a strong antibiotic to try to combat the infection. Iron Eyes continued to struggle despite the antibiotics and I had to force feed him. This seemed to perk him up a little but the infection to not respond to the treatment. I found him dead one morning. It was hard to believe that a small infection could kill a mighty bird as he. I contacted the local media and follow up stories were aired and printed about Iron Eyes passing.

It's funny how rumors get started. Apparently someone or enough some bodies heard part of the Iron Eyes (the Golden Eagle) story and that he had died and didn't realize it was a bird. The rumor then circulated that Iron Eyes Cody had died! We heard this rumor too and upon checking that the real actor was still alive, we understood what had happened. We had to put out several little brushfires to stop the spread of the falsehood. It was a good thing that Wikipedia didn't exist back then!

1989 proved to be a year of flux. We continued to operate as we had over the last few years, but this year, the last of the Miller Brewing Company donation started to fizzle. We had a fundraiser in 1988, but it was only moderately successful. I still had some money left from my pension refund from the City of Memphis. We had money coming in from our programs, which we were now doing over 200 per year, but it was not keeping up with our bills. Kevin contacted a local public relations firm to help raise some money. The President of the firm reassured Kevin with,

"Yeah, I can raise $10,000 for you with one phone call!"

Kevin placed a lot of stock in what he said and believed that this PR firm was our financial salvation. He said that they had a lot of ideas to bring in donations which required very little effort on our part. One idea the firm came up with was to put donation canisters by cash registers at a few local convenience stores. All we had to do was collect the money from the canister once a week. The first week Kevin went to the ten or so stores to collect the loot only to be highly disappointed at the amount. The ten canisters had less than $20 in change. He made the decision to collect the money every other week. After two weeks, Kevin made the rounds again; less than $30 was raised. So far, the canisters had made less than $50. True, there was little effort on our part, but $50 in three weeks wasn't going to pay too many bills. A Boy or Girl Scout troop could have done a better job fundraising!

Kevin called the PR firm's President to see if he had any luck getting donors and he was told that a few guys with deep pockets were "Thinking about it." Meanwhile, my pay started to become somewhat sporadic. Kevin began skipping paydays so I could get a paycheck. He was able to pick up so extra income by working with his father-in-law. By early summer, I was starting to wonder if we were going to get any "big" money donations.

After being involved with the PR firm for a few months, CWF received a bill for $20,000! Kevin called the President and asked him why the bill was so high,

"It's just business baby. Sometimes ideas work, sometimes they don't. We tried a few things and I made a few calls, but I guess people just aren't that much into helping birds. Sorry!"

Kevin suggested that we owe them less than half of that amount and that is what we will pay them. The Firm refused the offer. Kevin and Tom discussed what to do about the bill. They refused to be robbed by this PR group and decide not pay them. The PR Firm took the Cumberland Wildlife Foundation to court. To everyone's amazement, the judge ruled on behalf of the PR Firm! I had nothing to do with all of the proceedings but was directly affected by the outcome. In order to keep the Firm from winning anything in a settlement, Kevin and Tom decided to dissolve the Cumberland Wildlife Foundation. What had been a fairly blissful existence for me for a few years now had a dark cloud hanging over the future. A new organization was formed to replace CWF.

The Wildlife Preservation Corps was chosen as the new name. Tom Noland did not accept the position of Vice President, so I was designated the acting VP. We were pretty much the same organization with the same staff and the same problem; we were running low on cash. At this point, I had nearly depleted my pension fund refund from the City of Memphis. I had $10,000 when I started with CWF a little over three years previous and now I was down to less than $1000. We were heading into summer which had been our slow time for funding. We did some state park programs which brought in some money, but not enough to pay all of the bills. Kevin began work with the new Nashville Zoo. He was doing some concrete rockwork on some of the large exhibits, so he took himself off WPC's payroll. He was still the President and was still trying to find funding for us, but he was also working more or less full time at the zoo.

I had several volunteers that helped me. Marty Rush, who had been a volunteer for several years, was the coordinator. There were several more that helped including Kim Kincaid, Charlotte Sturm, Tina Crenshaw, Joe Degrauuw, Bart and Renee Leonard. There were also two teenage fellows who were like my adopted sons; Jim Hendel a seventeen year old with three children and Brad Huff, another seventeen year old "Rebel Without A Car". All of these people and several more helped whenever they could and proved to be invaluable over the next few months.

Brad and Jim would go with me on some of the programs. Brad went with me to do a program in Jackson, Tennessee. On the return home, the company van began smoking. It was just a little smoke at first, but the closer we got to Nashville, the more it began to billow. Apparently, one of the rings had gone bad and was allowing oil to seep into the engine. By the time we got to the city limits, one would have thought the van was on fire. I was so embarrassed to be driving this rolling, noxious death fog machine that I pulled into a convenience store. I asked Brad to go in and ask the clerk for two medium sized paper bags.

"What for?" Brad asked.

"You'll see!" I replied.

Brad went in and got the bags and came out and asked,

"Here are the bags. What are you going to do with them?"

"Alright, give me one bag and you keep the other. Take your bag and tear two 50 cent sized holes here (pointing ten inches down from the top) and tear a single hole about two inches below those two holes." I instructed.

While Brad tore the holes, I did the same with my bag.

"Now take your bag and roll the top down about four to five inches", I continued.

Brad was a little puzzled, but complied. When he had his finished, I then said,

"Take your bag and do this", while saying this I put my bag over my head and aligned the eye holes. Brad started laughing and did the same as I had done.

"Alright, I think we are ready for the drive through Nashville", I said as I started the van.

I got back on the interstate and as we drove next to someone, either Brad or I would look at the driver who usually laughed, that is, until we passed. The next thing the poor driver knew that he or she was engulfed by a thick, fragrant cloud of oil smoke. Several people were seen fanning their faces or switching to the next lane. Of course, Brad and I were laughing all the way back to the facility. It was an embarrassing situation that at least, for this short while, we were able to make light of. Kevin quickly found someone to do the ring job for a very low price and the van returned to its relatively smoke free status.

In early June, I received a call from Al Louis Cecere. He wanted to know if we had an eagle available for an event in Texas. Recall that Al was the original fundraiser for the Cumberland Wildlife Foundation, but was released from any association with CWF. I told Al that Osceola was available and that I could help him with his event. He said he would donate $200 to WPC for my efforts. My schedule was clear and Al and I went to the Kwik Copy Annual Convention in Houston. The keynote speaker for the event was Ronald Reagan. We had Osceola on display for the conventioneers to see. The convention went well for us and it was the first of several events Osceola and I did with Al.

This small donation from Al helped but even with Kevin not being paid, I was only getting paid sporadically. As the summer progressed, like the water in a farm pond in a Texas drought, the money started to evaporate. My saving account was pretty well drained. I used a lot of what I had left to pay child support, my van payment and to buy food for the birds. My van was having transmission problems and the Company's van, which previously had oil ring problems, now had extreme brake problems; so much that I had to put it in reverse to stop (usually scaring the person half to death who was stopped at the light in front of me)! To save wear on both vehicles and money on gas, I rode my ten speed bicycle from Mt. Juliet where I lived to our office and bird facility five miles down a very busy highway. I went on a forced diet. About six months previously, as a bit of a joke, one of our volunteers gave me two cases of dented canned green beans and green peas he bought from a salvage store. I was getting so low on cash that these became my staples.

Kevin had been trying to find funding but had met with little success. One day at our "Site", Kevin stopped by for a visit. Kevin asked, "How are things going?" I answered,

"Well, other than risking my life riding my bike ten miles a day, being virtually out of money and wondering what I am going to do with all of these birds, my wife hounding me for child support and the bank threatening to re-possess my barely running van and add to this, a steady diet of green beans and peas which have given me a very regular digestive system, I'd say things are going great!"

Kevin replied, "Damn, son, I didn't realize things are going that poorly. I am still trying to find some money for you!"

I countered with, "Well, you had better do so soon, because I have probably a month to go before I have to find homes for all of these sixty birds! If you can somehow get the brakes repaired on the big van that would really help!"

Kevin answered, "I'll see what I can do!"

He got in his truck and began to pull away. He suddenly stopped, put his truck in reverse and motioned me to come over.

Kevin said, "By the way, I got officially hired at the Zoo to do the rockwork for all of the new exhibits so I guess that means that you are now in charge. I'll be in touch!"

With this, he drove away. I felt like someone had given me a car with an engine that was blown. If I would repair the engine, I could drive it around.

It was now August; I hadn't been paid in three weeks. To help with our situation, Doug Markham, Public Relations Officer with the Tennessee Wildlife Resources Agency interviewed me for an article about the Wildlife Preservation Corps. He knew about our dire circumstances and wrote an article as a possible way to get funding for us. His article was distributed in a number of local papers around Nashville. I continued to ride my bike to work. One morning, while enroute to the facility, an un-opened soda can whizzed past my head and directly afterwards, three boys in a Corvette passed uncomfortably close. One of the boys looked back at me and laughed. I was lucky that he had poor aim! I arrived at work and gave my recently divorced mother a call. I asked her about the possibility of moving in with her in Mississippi. She was agreeable but hoped that it didn't come to that. Maria said,

"Sometimes miracles happen, but if for some reason one doesn't, you can certainly stay with me."

She was always an optimist. I thanked her and afterwards, I called several bird facilities to see if they could take some of the birds. With a full backpack of chicken leg quarters, I pedaled to the Site to feed the birds. Osceola looked at me as I arrived and I walked up to his enclosure. I said,

"Well, buddy, it's starting to look like I'm not going to get you back in the air. I had hoped that things were going to improve for us, but it is not looking too good. I may have to send you to a new home. I am sorry that I have let you down."

Osceola cocked his head and looked at me, maybe he understood, maybe not.

I finished feeding the birds and went to the back of the Site and sat beside a tree-lined limestone sinkhole. This had become my recent place of meditation. I said out loud,

"God... Universe... somebody out there...if you can hear me, I need a little help here. I am out of money and just about out of time and if I don't get some help soon, I've got to do something with all of these birds and get out of here! I'm pretty desperate! Please, can you all do something for me?!?"

In my head, I got a message that help was on its way. I responded, "Yeah, if that's true, it had better be within the next two weeks. I have set a deadline. I thank you for anything you can do!"

Off in the distance, I heard thunder and it sounded like it was getting closer. I finished my rant and my plea and hopped on my bike for the five mile ride to Mt. Juliet. It was starting to get dark and about halfway home, the storm arrived. Soon the sky opened and I felt like I was pedaling in a carwash. I didn't have my raincoat, lightning was striking nearby and the passing cars splashed water all over me. This morning it was a soda can, this afternoon, the storm. Somehow, it all just seemed fitting and only enhanced my gloomy mood.

A week passed and there was no good news. I drove the van with the bad brakes to the local processed chicken distributor. I spent my last thirty-five dollars; ten going to gas and twenty-five purchased enough chicken leg quarters to feed the birds for another two weeks. As I drove to the office to put the chicken in the freezer, I felt that I was watching this dream job die. I was watching my hopes to fly with Osceola fade and everything

291

seemed to be falling apart. I felt like I, too, had lost a wing and the ability to soar. Even though I had Marty and the other volunteers to help me, I felt alone in my struggle with each day less promising than the day before. I went to my desk and looked at the calendar. Two weeks ago, I circled Friday as being the Decision Day. That Friday was four days away. It looked like I must admit defeat and accept my fate. I had never been one to give up easily, but it looked like logic was about to trump hope.

I went to my desk looked at my phone. I noticed that there were three messages. I hit the play button and the first message was from someone with an injured owl. The second one was from Walter Crawford of the Raptor Research and Propagation Project in Missouri. He said that he could take back some of the birds he had previously sent us. The last message was from James Norris. He was very soft spoken and sounded like an elderly man. He mentioned that he recently read an article in his local weekly paper about the Wildlife Preservation Corps and that we needed money to care for the birds. He said that his mother "Birdie" had recently passed away and left a small amount of money to be used to help birds. He said that the WPC might be a place for his mother's money and would like to speak to someone about this. He left his phone number. I replayed the message several times to make sure I had the right number. I gave him a call, but there was no answer.

I decided to go to the Site to feed the birds and after doing so, I returned to the office. I called Mr. Norris' number again. This time he answered. I introduced myself and he expressed a desire to come to see our facility. We agreed to Wednesday for his visit. I spent the next day spiffing up the place. I figured that he may have a few hundred dollars to donate, but at least this amount would help pay the shipping costs to send the birds to new homes with maybe enough left over for gas money to drive to my mother's house.

Wednesday I met Mr. Norris at our site. I toured him around the enclosures and got out Osceola for him to see. He was impressed with him and commented that he had never been this close to an eagle before in his seventy-six years. Osceola was as regal as ever and perhaps sensed the importance of this man.

Mr. Norris said, "I believe that your organization is worthy of my mother's money. However, I cannot make this decision alone. I'll need to get my sister and two brothers here to see your place. They all live out of town and it'll be Saturday before I can round them up for a visit. Is this okay with you?"

I replied "Well sure, Saturday's fine with me and I look forward to meeting them."

Mr. Norris asked, "Is Saturday at noon, okay?"

"Yes sir, that is a great time!" I responded.

With this, we shook hands and Mr. Norris got in his Oldsmobile and drove away.

Saturday: Noon. The Norris family arrived at our Site. The two brothers and sister appeared to all be in their seventies. Birdie must have been very old when she died. James introduced me to his siblings as we began the facility tour. Once again, I brought Osceola out of his enclosure and everyone in the family took a photo with him. About halfway through the tour, Eric Thibault, my former co-worker, stopped by to pick up a Great Horned Owl that he had rescued after a car collision. The bird has been in our care for a few weeks and was ready to be released. I introduced Eric to the Norrises and they all followed Eric and me to the Great Horned Owl enclosure. There were several birds in the pen and while Eric waited outside, I went in to extract the bird. It was a warm late August day and I was sweating from the heat and humidity. As I attempted to catch the owl, one of its enclosure mates flew over my head and grazed me with one of its talons. I didn't think much of it. I caught Eric's bird and walked out of the cage to put in a kennel. Everyone, including Eric, had a look of shock on their faces.

Eric whispered to me: "John, you've got blood streaming down the right side of your face!"

I touched my right cheek and looked at my hand; it was crimson! I just thought it was sweat. Eric found a towel and after placing the owl in the transport kennel, I pressed the towel to my scalp. After Eric insured that the scrape wasn't too bad, he said his good-byes to the Norris clan and departed.

Mr. Norris pulled me aside and half-jokingly said: "John, you didn't need the theatrics! We were going to give you the money!"

With this, we both laughed.

All of the Norris family seemed satisfied that Birdie's donation would be used to help the birds. They all thanked me and got back in the car. James reached into his coat pocket, pulled out a check and handed it to me. I glanced at it quickly to see a four with a couple of zeros: $400. I thanked the family and shook all their hands. I insured them that their mother's money will be well used.

James Norris said, "All we need is a receipt from your organization for the lawyers and you can mail it to the address on the check".

I replied, "I'll get that to you tomorrow and thank you all again!"

With this James got in his car and closed the door. I glanced at the check again for the address and noticed the writing; *Four thousand dollars*. I looked at the numbers; $4000.00! I ran to Mr. Norris' window and as he rolled it down,

I exclaimed, "Four thousand dollars! You have saved us! You have all saved us! I can't begin to thank you all enough!"

James said, "You're welcome, but it isn't us, it was our mother's wish and I believe that she would have been proud to help. Thanks for the tour, son!" With this, I again shook his hand and watch as they drove away.

I looked at the check again and held it skyward saying,

"Thanks, Birdie! We won't disappoint you! Thank you, God, Thank you, Universe!" I was so excited that I even showed it to Osceola and said,

"We've gotten a break, Buddy! We don't have to move after all! Maybe now I can keep my promise to you and one day, we will go flying!"

I went back to the office and called my mother and told her that I won't have to move in with her. I also let Walter Crawford know that he would not have to take any birds. He was relieved. I called Kevin and informed him of the donation. He was happy that we wouldn't have to close our doors. I called Doug Markham of the Tennessee Wildlife Resources Agency…

"Doug, this is John Stokes and I am calling to tell you that your article has saved us!"

Doug replied, "What? Really? How?"

I explained the whole Norris situation and how the WPC was given $4000.

Doug stated, "Well, I am glad that it worked!"

"No Doug, what you did with your article has rescued us. I was just a few days from closing the doors and moving in with my mother, but now we have a new lease on the life of WPC!"

Doug humbly stated, "The Norrises are the ones you owe that to, not me. I just wrote an article.

I exclaimed, "Doug, without that article, James Norris would not have known about us, so all credit goes to you!"

Doug continued, "Well, I am glad it helped! Maybe a few more people will donate to help you."

A few more people did. With the money, we were able to catch up on some overdue bills and my ex-wife and car loan people had something to smile about as well. Autumn arrived and with it, a new start.

Chapter 40

Merger Time and I have something in common with Osceola

October 1989. The funding was not going as well as I had hoped. The donation from the Norris Family saved the Wildlife Preservation Corp from extinction, but we were close to again being on the Endangered List. I had been doing a few appearances with Osceola in cooperative work with Al Louis Cecere. Bob Hatcher of the Tennessee Wildlife Resources Agency suggested that Al and I join forces. He pointed out that we were working toward a common goal so why not combine our efforts. Al was a fundraiser. I was not. Al had little to no bird handling experience and I did. In November, we did just that. Kevin was still the President of the Wildlife Preservation Corp, so he met with Al and signed over all the Cumberland Wildlife Foundation/WPC assets. WPC was officially dissolved and all of its material possessions, and its bills, were now the responsibility of the National Foundation to Protect America's Eagles.

Unfortunately, Al and NFPAE were just as broke as WPC was. I felt like I was in a pre-arranged marriage, only this situation had more the feel of a shotgun wedding. Al and I had a shaky relationship at first. We didn't know each other very well. I'm sure he still had bad feelings towards Kevin and Tom Noland. As earlier mentioned, I had nothing to do with the decision of Tom and Kevin, but I was probably guilty by association. Things did get better!

Since both parties were low on cash, we needed to raise money. We spent a lot of weekends with the birds on perches and donation buckets in front of some local Wal-mart stores. On a good weekend, we managed to raise $800-1000 in donations and tee-shirt sales. Al was determined to pay off all of the old WPC debt. Several weeks passed with good donations on the weekends and no paycheck for me. We still had too many bills for me to get paid. I was desperate again. One of our volunteers, Kim Kincaid, was dating a fellow who owned a bar in Nashville. She talked to him about a part-time bartending job for me. I met Mike McNinch at Cagney's Bar and after a quick interview, I was hired on the spot. I worked my first 7 to 4 shift that night. I worked three to four nights a week and worked my "real" job every day. This made for some long days. Some days, I'd leave my bar job, go home, take a shower, and go to my bird job. Afterwards, I'd go back home for a quick nap and then back to the bar. At least I was getting money for food and gas, but not enough to pay my child support and car note.

On one of my workdays with the birds, I finished soon enough to go hang gliding. I picked up two of my flying buddies, brothers Tim and David Wood and one of our bird volunteers, Marianne Adcock. It looked like a great day for flying. Tim, David and I were looking forward to some extended flights, while Marianne hoped to get a tandem ride with one of the local pilots, Clark Harlow. The winds were blowing straight into the Henson's Gap launch near Dunlap, Tennessee. We all set up our gliders quickly and were soon off into the thermally air. Marianne and Clark launched as well. After Marianne's flight, she drove the van down to the landing field and waited for us to land.

My goal was to fly up the valley from the Henson's Gap to Pikeville, some twenty miles away. I only made it about five miles when the winds aloft got increasingly stronger. After twenty minutes, I had to abandon my plan. The winds got so strong that I couldn't make much forward progress. I made a decision to land. I climbed in any available thermal updrafts and converted altitude for forward progress and distance. Even so, I had to battle some serious headwinds just to make it to a landable field. Finally, at lower levels, the wind abated enough to allow me make it to a large field. There was a fellow out washing his car and I yelled down,

"Is is okay to land here?"

He waved and yelled, "Yeah, sure!"

I set up a textbook landing pattern. With my feet out of my harness and about ten above the ground, I bled off my excess speed. However, my right wing flew into a small, but strong thermal that was lifting off and this caused my left wing to contact the ground. I started a slow uncontrollable turn to the left. I shifted my weight as far as I could to the right to counteract the turn. I had just about had the glider leveled when the corner of my control frame contacted the ground. A second prior to impact, the Voice said very plainly,

"You're going to break your arm".

One second later, a small impact. I slid through the control frame and along the ground with my right arm extended. My left hand still clutched the left upright tube of the frame. As a result, all of the energy of the crash transferred to my left humerus. The outcome was a spiral fracture of the bone. I felt it snap. Since it was a cool February day, I had a flight suit on so I couldn't readily assess the damage. I was lying on my right side so I thought,

"I know my arm is broken, but where is it?"

I moved my left arm and at that point, it flailed toward my chest. It was broken, alright. I felt crunching as the arm came to a stop. I moved my fingers, so I knew I hadn't damaged the brachial nerve. My next concern was whether or not the break was compound; did I have a section of bone sticking through my skin? I needed to get upright, so I took my left arm and moved my hand towards my mouth. I was wearing gloves, so I secured my hand to my mouth by biting the glove between my thumb and index finger. I was then able to push up with my right arm enough to unclip my harness from the glider.

Once I was standing, I unzipped my flight suit enough to reach into my left sleeve near the break. I didn't feel any blood but I started counting, eventually to sixty, to give any blood a chance to soak though my sleeve. Thankfully, no blood. However, I got the first of many painful muscle spasms. My unsupported muscles we trying to align themselves. Each time I thought about my arm, a spasm occurred. I had to stop thinking about my arm, but the spasms, like aftershocks following the initial quake, continued for the next hour. I looked at my glider and was expecting to see a damaged control frame or more. The glider had a grass stain on the nose and that was it.

I needed to get to a hospital, so I walked to where the guy was washing his car. He saw me, still in my harness and cradling my left arm and asked,

"Are you okay?!?"

I told him that I had broken my arm and needed to go to the nearest emergency room. He quickly responded. The car he was washing was a small four door Ford Tempo. Since I still had on my harness, the easiest way for me to fit it in was to stretch out on the back seat. He helped load me in and away we went. I suddenly remembered that I had traveled down with Tim, David, and Marianne. I needed to go by the landing field to let them know I was on the way to the hospital. I told my temporary ambulance driver about this and he obliged by stopping at the LZ. He pulled up to the parking area where pilots were disassembling their gliders. He got out of his car and yelled,

"Does anybody here know John Stokes?"

Tim, David and Marianne came to the car and peered into the back seat. Tim had a look of fear and I quickly said,

"I'm not dead, I've just broken my arm."

Tim replied, "Whew!"

I told them I was on the way to the hospital. The driver told Tim where to find my glider. He and brother David set out to retrieve my downed craft. The driver said he was taking me to the Sequatchie County Hospital. Marianne got in the car and went to the hospital with us.

Upon arrival at the ER, Marianne took control of the situation. The nurses took me into a room where they proceeded to remove my harness. They were going to cut it off, but Marianne explained how expensive it was. I was able to wiggle out of the top. They did have to cut the sleeve off the flight suit and underlying sweat shirt. As they did this, I had the worse spasm of them all. They quickly alleviated this with an injection of synthetic morphine. Within a minute, the jerking and twitching was over and I began to feel very relaxed.

My arm was then x-rayed and the resulting film showed very clearly the spiral fracture along with a fragment that had broken away from the main bone. They were concerned about the break becoming compound and were about to admit me for surgery in the morning. Due to my economic situation (I didn't have any insurance), Marianne told me not to let them admit me to the hospital. She said that her mother worked for an orthopedic surgeon and he might be able to take care of my injury for a low cost. She found a phone and called her mother. Within a few minutes Marianne returned and said that Dr. Laughlin would take care of me. This info was relayed to the Sequatchie hospital staff and before I knew it, I had a temporary cast. Tim and David had arrived at that point and told me they had my glider and were ready to go back to Nashville. Tim said,

"Your glider, except for a grass stain on the nose, is undamaged. You took all of the impact."

I nodded to acknowledge the fact. Had I had some larger wheels on my control frame, I probably would have rolled to stop and I wouldn't have been there with my arm in a cast. This was a painful lesson to learn.

I signed my release papers, gathered my bill and x-rays and headed back to Nashville. I had an 8 a.m. appointment with Dr. Laughlin, so Marianne insisted I stay at her apartment while Tim and David returned my glider and van to my trailer. They even fed my cat! I had a restless night trying to sleep upright on the Marianne's couch. During the night, I inevitably leaned several times to my left to be rudely awakened by crunching bones and muscle spasms. During one of the few times I actually slept, I dreamed of Osceola. I didn't know why until I awoke. My subconscious mind was trying to show me that I had broken the same bone as he! I didn't get much sleep after that and by daybreak, I was ready to see the doctor.

I met Dr. Laughlin that morning. He looked at the x-rays and decided to try a weighed cast to hold the bone ends in alignment. I didn't want to argue with him, but I had seen far too many breaks in bird bones that were similar to mine. All required a pin and/or wires to get them to heal. But, he was the doctor and he was trying to save me some money. So, a weighed cast it was. Doctor Laughlin wanted to try this for two weeks and then do another radiograph to check the progress. I thanked him for everything. Marianne drove me to my trailer, where I got out, thanked her and gave her a hug. I went in and got my keys, checked my cat and drove to the Site. There, I went to Osceola's enclosure and showed him my wrapped left arm and said,

"We now have something in common; I broke my left wing, too!"

He cocked his head and looked at my cast with his penetrating gaze. I doubt he understood what I said. I fed him and the other birds and afterwards, went home, and took a short nap. I was tired but had to go Cagney's Bar for my nightly shift. I showed everyone my new fashion accessory and told the story many times that night of how I broke my arm. At 4 a.m. I got to go home. It had been a long twenty-four hours.

I had to learn to do everything with limited mobility of my arm. Showering was interesting. Bird handling even more so. Nearly all of the bird handling gloves were left handed. I found an old right hand welder's glove and made do with it. The only bird that had trouble adjusting was Satch, but after a while, he adapted as well.

For the next two weeks, I did my daily routine at the bird facility and worked three nights a week at the bar. Sleep was still a challenge since I had to attempt slumber while sitting upright on my couch. Invariably, I still leaned to the left at night so my morning routine was to pull my humerus bone ends back in alignment and push the fragment back into place. The bone was not healing.

After two weeks, I again met with Dr. Laughlin. He took an x-ray. Doc came into the exam room with the film and stuck it on a viewer. He related,

"It doesn't look good, John. I'm afraid we're going to have to do some surgery to repair your break."

All I could respond was, "Sounds good to me!"

I was thinking that I didn't have the economic means to pay for such an endeavor when Dr. Laughlin continued,

"I have arranged for your operation to be a free "teaching" surgery for the medical students at Vanderbilt University."

I couldn't believe it and thanked him profusely. It was Friday and my repair was scheduled for the following Monday. I went into work Monday morning and cared for all of the birds. Marty Rush volunteered to feed them on Tuesday. The surgery went well. Dr. Laughlin put in a stainless steel plate to hold the humerus halves together and screwed the floating fragment back in place. I was in the hospital for one day and upon release, I went to the bird facility to work. Little did I know at the time, that Tuesday in the hospital was my last full day off for ten months. I again adapted to the limited use of my arm and within a few days, my temporary cast was removed. I began the slow path to recovery. My arm eventually healed to the point that Dr. Laughlin couldn't see a difference in mobility of either arm. He had done a terrific job! To this day, I owe a sincere debt of gratitude to Dr. Laughlin, Marianne Adcox and her mother for helping me during this trying time. Somehow, thank you just doesn't seem to be enough!

Chapter 41

Screw Disneyworld! We're going to Dollywood!

March 1990. My arm was three quarters back to full strength. One month later, when my arm was up to full strength, I took my first hang gliding flight since the break. Everything went well and I had a great landing. I also had some wheels on my control frame in case I stumbled on landing in the future. Spring was in full swing and I hadn't been paid by NFPAE in three months. The money from the bar job has bought food and gas, but I hadn't paid my car note or child support since 1989. Fortunately, the people at the bank were sympathetic; Debbie was not and threatened to take me to court. I told her that I wasn't trying to get out of my payments and since she worked at a bank, she was very welcome to look at my checking account. I assured both parties that I'd catch them up as soon as I could.

Obviously, the Foundation wasn't rolling in cash, either. The once reliable Wal-Mart weekends were starting to fizzle. With worsening funding problems, Al and I looked for a place to sponsor us. I mentioned to Al that we once had an eagle on display at Opryland. He contacted the local theme park and they were only mildly interested. One of the board members of NFPAE, James Rogers, was a big fan of the Bald Eagle and was an entertainer at Dollywood, Dolly Parton's theme park. He suggested that Dollywood might be a good location for our birds. He arranged a meeting with Dollywood President Ken Bell and Dave Anderson, Head of Attractions. We drove to Pigeon Forge to pitch some ideas to both men. The meeting went well. Later that week, we conducted one of our raptor programs at the elementary school where Ken's daughter was enrolled. Ken and Dave were in attendance and both were impressed. I introduced them to Osceola and photos were made with Dave, Ken and his daughter.

Ken queried, "Do you think you can adapt your show to a theme park setting?"

"No problem", I replied

Ken then said, "I believe that Dollywood can be the new home of the National Foundation to Protect America's Eagles. However, I do not have the final say. I'll have to contact the two principal owners of Dollywood, Jack Herschend and Dolly Parton."

Within a day, Ken had the approval of Mr. Herschend. It was now up to Dolly. She was on a concert tour so it took about a week before she responded. Ken called Al and told him that Dolly had given him an enthusiastic "Yes!" Al and I again traveled to Dollywood and met with Ken and Dave over proposals for an eagle exhibit, a stage for the bird show and an off-park facility. Everything went well. It was still hard for me to believe that this was happening! After we said our thanks and good-byes, Al and I returned to Mt. Juliet, but we'd soon have a new home!

I was hurting for cash. I came up with an idea and suggested to Al that perhaps Dollywood might be able to "front" us part of our next year's budget to help in our transition. Al was reluctant, but I said to him,

"It doesn't hurt to ask, all they can say is "Yes".

Al called Ken Bell who agreed to help us. In April we received a sizeable check that allowed us to operate until our move to East Tennessee. I was finally paid three months back pay, which made the bank and Debbie happy. However, I continued to work at the bar for extra income and I had grown to like the characters in this neighborhood pub.

Everything was turning around, but I noticed Osceola was acting differently. He had a tremendous appetite, but felt lighter and was losing weight. He also had what appeared to be a cold. I took him to Dr. Scott Thomas of the Airport Animal Clinic in Nashville. Scott ran a series of tests on him and told me,

"It doesn't look good, John. Osceola has aspergillosis, a fungal disease that attacks the lungs and air sacs of a bird".

I was shocked and distressed as well because the disease is usually fatal.

Dr. Thomas continued, "However, there is a new drug that has been used in Europe and Canada to treat this disease and has met with some success. It is now available in this country and I'll call the University of Tennessee Vet School to see if I can get some for Osce".

I heard Dr. Thomas on the phone and apparently the Vet School had the drug. He said,

"They're shipping a thirty day treatment today. Since this is an experimental drug in the U.S., the medication is free. I just hope it works soon enough to keep him from dying."

At least, there was a glimmer of hope for Osceola. Dr. Thomas advised me to put Osceola in a stress free environment.

The next day, I picked up capsules of Itraconazole. I opened each capsule and counted 40 beads of the medication to put on Osce's daily food. Osceola was one of the first birds in this country to be treated with this drug. For a week, I gave him the meds, but he was still losing weight and getting weaker. I had him in a pen inside our office with a heat lamp. He was still eating, but I had to feed him bits of food by hand. I checked him several times a day and by the second week of treatment, Osceola appeared very weak. The medication didn't seem to be working. He was able to stand and was still eating, but I feared the worse. There wasn't much more I could do for him. His situation was so dire that one particular evening, I said good-bye to him. I felt like I was saying farewell to my best friend and I asked God and the Universe for his quick passage. I wanted to stay with him through the night, but I had to work at the bar and I didn't have anyone to cover for me. I looked at Osceola one last time and with great reluctance, I left.

As I worked my shift I couldn't help but worry about Osceola. I was anxious for my night's work to be over and at 4:30 in the morning, I headed directly to the office. I got to the room where he was. I couldn't see directly into the heat lamp illuminated enclosure, but as I approached, I closed my eyes for the last few feet. As I slowly opened them, I was shocked and amazed! Osceola was very alert and even chirped when he saw me.

"Osceola!! You're alive!!!" I exclaimed with a lump in my throat.

I had never been happier to see an individual in my life! I went and got him some food. I handed him bits of beef and he immediately started eating. He finished all the initial offering and still looked hungry. I gave him more. I presented him a Gizzard Shad, his favorite fish, and he quickly devoured it and then another. Soon, he had a full crop of food. It appeared that a miracle had happened! I said out loud,

"I don't know what has taken place, but I thank everyone involved!"

For the next few weeks, Osceola rapidly improved and at the end of the treatment period, appeared to be cured. I took him back to Dr. Thomas and he did a battery of tests and the results showed the fungus was gone. I thanked Dr. Thomas for saving Osceola's life and he simply said,

"It would have been a shame to have lost him!"

I wholeheartedly agreed. I left the clinic and as I drove back to the facility, a passing shower had left a rainbow in front of me. It was a wonderful end to this great day.

In July, we met Dolly for some publicity photos. I introduced her to Osceola and while he was adjusting his balance, he flapped his right wing, and brushed Dolly's head in the process. Dolly said,

"Osceola is my biggest fan!"

The gathered press laughed. In late October, we returned to Dollywood to finalize all of the bird facility plans. As a preview for the spring, we did a bird show at one of the open air theatres. I met James Rogers for the first time and personally expressed my gratitude for arranging everything with Dollywood. He had become our second savior in so many months. James simply replied,

"I am glad I could help in some small way."

By mid-January, 1991, the Dollywood construction crew had converted an old cattle barn for our program birds and had built a breeding aviary for Bald and Golden Eagles. At the end of the month, we moved from Mt. Juliet to Pigeon Forge. This involved the purchase of over twenty extra large sky kennels and a number of medium sized ones as well. We needed all of these to transport our eagle population and the other birds as well. Al arranged to have a large stock trailer and someone to haul the birds for us. On moving day a number of volunteers, including Jim and Brad, showed up to capture the birds for placement in the kennels and then into the trailer. Within a few hours, we had loaded all of the raptors and were ready for our trip east. Al and I said our good-byes to Brad and the others while Jim accompanied us on the three hour drive to Pigeon Forge.

The drive to our new home was uneventful. We had already designated enclosures for each bird or group of birds, so we were able to unload them directly into their new homes. All of the non program eagles went temporarily into our breeding enclosures, with a pair of Bald Eagles and Golden Eagles, both of which had laid eggs the previous year, receiving their own cages. By the next morning, Osceola, Satch and all of the birds were in place. I, too, had a new home. A few weeks earlier, I had rented a two story seventy year old farm house about five miles from Dollywood. It was clean and the area was surrounded by lush green hills and clear mountain streams. Quite a step up from the dilapidated trailer I occupied in Mt. Juliet.

The Dollywood construction crew worked hard on the "on park" facilities. By March, the huge Eagle Mt. Sanctuary, the largest eagle aviary in the United States, was completed and the theatre for our shows was ready. We transferred most of the Bald Eagles to the multi section exhibit and one eagle was placed on display next to the gift shop. We had been getting the birds ready for our Wings of America show at our "off park" facility. But with the theatre completed, we began our rehearsals at Dollywood for our opening day in April.

Everything came together very quickly and before I knew it was two days before Dollywood's opening day. Eagle Mountain Sanctuary and the Wings of America Show were the featured attractions at Dollywood in 1991. We got word that Dolly was going to do a live remote for the Today Show from Eagle Mt. Sanctuary on Friday. She wanted an eagle behind her during the interview so Al asked me to stand behind her with Osceola. Friday morning I brought Osceola to the aviary and I saw the camera crew from NBC. I also saw Dolly getting some last minute touch-ups on her makeup. The Producer came over to me and went over the details of the interview. About one minute before air, I brought Osceola into position. Dolly, somewhat surprised, turned and said,

"Oh, hello, John. How is Osce-y today?"

I told her he's fine and ready for his close-up. The Producer yelled,

"Thirty seconds!"

Dolly again turned to me and said,

310

"John, don't let Osceola snatch my hair off on national TV!"

I laughed and told her that he wouldn't.

Dolly replied, "That's good, just make sure that he doesn't get a beak full of blonde!"

The live interview went well and Osceola was seen by millions of viewers. Afterwards, Dolly thanked Osceola and me for a great job and told me that she'll be at my first show with her friend Bob. I said okay. Dave Anderson was watching the proceedings and came over to compliment me. I asked,

"Who is Dolly's friend, Bob?"

Dave replied, "Bob Hope. Bob and his wife Delores are Dolly's special guests this year at the Grand Opening and they'll be at your first show".

"The Bob Hope?!?" I asked.

Dave stated, "The Bob Hope! Have a good show!" and with this, he walked away.

Opening Day I got to the park early. Our off park facility was about a mile from our theatre and aviary. We had to bring the birds over, unload them and have our transport van off the Park an hour before it opened. We got all of our equipment set up and we were ready. I was nervous, as were my workmates. Al even seemed a bit twitchy. We were set for our first show at 10:30. At 10:15, I glimpsed a horde of people headed towards the theatre. It was a crowd of visitors and reporters following Dolly, Bob and Delores. Al met the contingent and showed them the eagle aviary. Afterwards, they piled into the theatre and sat in the reserved section. I peeked through the curtains to see Dolly and Bob; these entertainment icons were in our audience! I grew up watching them on television and now, they were about to watch Osceola, the other birds and me do our first show. People were taking photos and asking for autographs. Someone said something funny and I heard both Dolly and Bob laugh. This was surreal. A year and a half before, I was risking my life riding my bike in the rain on a busy highway, eating hand-me-down canned green beans and getting ready to move in with my mother. Now this.

At 10:28, we started the opening music and at 10:29, raised the curtain. I had a stomach full of butterflies. 10:30. I walked out on stage, introduced myself and thanked our special guests Dolly Parton and Bob and Delores Hope. I looked directly at Dolly and she winked. Bob smiled as well. Somehow, this put me at ease and the show went well. I flew Satch, the Red-tailed Hawk, over Dolly and Bob's heads and I assured Dolly that Satch wouldn't snatch her hair off.

Dolly said, "That's okay, John, if he does though, you're fired!"

The crowd roared! Osceola was brought out for the shows finale and afterwards, Dolly and Bob came onstage for photos. Bob walked over and thanked everyone for a great show. He said to Osceola,

"Nice show, Mister, you did a great job and John, you weren't bad either!"

I shook his hand. Dolly came over and thanked everyone and said,

"Osce-y, you sure are a handsome fellow! You did good!"

Dolly and Bob waved their good-byes to everyone and continued their tour of the park. It was a memorable day and a memorable year. We conducted close to eight hundred shows at Dollywood that year with well over 500,000 people in attendance. Osceola was in every one. In addition, a pair of Bald Eagles and our pair of Golden Eagles produced young this year and those were released into the wild. The first of many. The next several years we presented shows at Dollywood and across the country. Osceola went to New York and Washington, where he had security clearance at the Pentagon. He was becoming known throughout the country. At this point, he was perhaps the most famous Bald Eagle in America. His fame was starting to fly high.

Chapter 42

Osceola flies again

Speaking of flying, for a few years, I didn't fly my hang glider much except off a few small hills and at Kitty Hawk, North Carolina. I was involved in a new relationship. I finally decided to fly the mountains around Chattanooga again and discovered that Lookout Mountain Flight Park offered a different way to become airborne. This method is called aerotowing. The hang glider is towed aloft by an ultralight aircraft in a similar manner as sailplanes are towed by small airplanes. The beauty of this mode is that a hang glider can be flown in flat lands. I decided to give aerotowing a try and quickly adapted. I was struck how relatively easy it was to tow and that even paraplegic people can learn to fly a hang glider in this manner. Wait a minute. I knew someone I could get in the air this way; Osceola! With aerotowing, I could be towed to 10,000 feet above the ground if so desired. I had a feasible way to take Osceola back to the sky.

After one of our weekend shows at Dollywood, I had Osceola on my glove close to edge of the stage so people could take pictures of him. There was quite a crowd gathered and as it gradually cleared, I saw a man in a wheelchair waiting to see Osceola. He came up and I noticed that he was wearing a cap that indicated that he was a Vietnam Vet. I also saw that he was missing his left arm and both legs. I brought Osceola down to eye level of the man. At that point, the Vet came to attention, snapped a salute, held it for about five seconds and slowly lowered his arm. He then said a tearful "Thank You!" and rolled away. As I watched the man leave, I became teary-eyed as well. If anyone on earth understood what Osceola has gone through, it was that man! This strengthened my desire to take Osceola back to the sky!

I mentioned to Al that I was ready to take Osceola flying.

Al said, "Well, you have been talking about this for years and you have my blessings!"

I described aerotowing to him and he seemed fascinated. I had one problem; I didn't have Osceola's harness. A year before, we loaned it to a wildlife rehab center in Virginia. They used it to suspend an eagle with a broken leg. I gave the center a call and after a little searching, they found the harness. Within a week, I had it. It was a little soiled but intact. I put Osceola in the harness for the first time and he seemed comfortable. I had him suspended about three feet above the floor and within a few minutes, I noticed a fatal flaw in the design; without much effort, Osceola could wiggle out of the back of the harness. If he did this at 2000 feet, he was dead!

I looked over the harness. I came up with some modifications such as adding an internal zipper, having the main support zippers close from the bottom to the top, and Velcro restraining straps in the key areas to keep Osceola in the harness. I took it to the sewing shop at Lookout Mountain Flight Park and explained to Alan Bloodworth the needed modifications. He suggested with the changes needed, it'd be cheaper to make a new harness than to modify the old. I agreed. I gathered materials for the new harness and returned in a few days. Alan said he can have it ready in two days and that he'd Fed-Ex it to me in Pigeon Forge.

Two days later, I got the new harness. I opened the box and I couldn't believe how good it looked; it was vivid blue with red restraining and support straps. I was ready to try Osceola in this new and improved design. I took it to work and carefully loaded Osceola. It fit him like a well-tailored jacket. I then suspended him from a rope connected to a beam in our bird barn and to my surprise, he did very well, even for periods of 25-30 minutes. He calmly looked around as if this is part of his daily routine.

For the next step, I climbed into my harness and connected Osceola beside me. He was hanging a little too close, so I devised an outrigger system to move him six inches out. This worked fine. Over the next several days, I worked with Osceola by hanging next to him for 15-20 minutes. This went well except he occasionally moved his feet and caught a talon on my harness. I had to somehow figure a way to isolate his talons from my harness and me.

Before long, we entered the ground testing phase. My friend and hang glider pilot, Tim Locke, helped the cause by loaning the use of his truck. We placed my assembled glider, in flying position, in the truck bed. I connected my harness to the glider and Osceola was connected to me. Tim proceeded to drive around one of Dollywood's huge parking lots. This gave Osceola the sensation of movement. However, when we began a turn, he moved his feet and snagged one of his talons on my harness. This caused him to panic. The solution was to attach Osceola's leather jesse straps to a bungee which was then connected to the end of my harness. This worked! On our next circuit, Osce calmly enjoyed everything, including the turns. I still needed a way to isolate his talons from my harness. I devised a foot shield out of thick plastic. I tried several versions and found a design I thought would work best. For the most part, I was satisfied with the overall tests. It was time to take Osceola flying!

I informed Al that I was ready. He reminded me that we still needed to get permission to fly with Osceola from the U.S. Fish and Wildlife Service. I wrote a letter that detailed my plans and sent a copy to Carmen Simonton of the regional permit office in Atlanta. She carefully guided us through the intricate permitting twists and turns. With her help, approval was finally given, especially since our flights were to be included in an educational special about eagles on the Disney Channel.

Flight day. Al, Osceola and I arrived at Lookout Mt. Flight Park in the morning to take our first flight before the Disney Crew arrived in ten days. I made the first tow flight with Osceola's harness. I wanted to see if the modified foot shield would cause any problems. Sure enough, the shield caught too much air causing the harness to turn sideways. I landed and looked for a solution. Al suggested that I take the shield off and wrap Osceola's feet and talons with Vet Wrap bandage. This would allow free movement of his feet without his talons scraping my harness. I would have flown with Osceola that day, but we didn't have anything with which to wrap his feet. We returned a week later. I discussed my plans with tow pilot Neil Harris. We rolled out a Falcon hang glider and I pre-flighted the glider for airworthiness. Neal helped me connect it to the ultralight. Al and I wrapped Osceola's feet. With this done, I climbed into my harness and connected to the glider. Al then attached Osceola to my harness. After twelve years of dreaming and delays, it was time.

I gave Neil the "all clear" sign. He revved the ultralight engine and we started rolling to a takeoff. The glider lifted off and I held my altitude at about twenty feet until the tug plane got into the air. I glanced over my shoulder and watched Osceola as he looked around, perhaps realizing that he was in the air again. After thirteen years, he was back in his element, albeit not exactly as he had known before, but as close as "humanly" possible. After ten minutes, we reached 2000 feet, our pre-determined release altitude. Neil waved me off and I pulled the release lever. We were now free flying. I almost couldn't believe this was occurring. For twelve years, I had dreamed of this moment and now it was here! After all that Osceola and I had been through and the times that it

317

looked like the dream was going to die, it was happening! I almost felt like I was removed from the scene and that I was an observer of someone else's life.

Although it felt otherworldly, I re-engaged reality and I looked back at Osceola. He was turning his head looking at the top of the mountain, the sky, the ground, the glider, and me. About 100 feet below us was a pair of Red-tailed Hawks. He immediately spotted them and watched as they passed below us. Perhaps, it was at this point that Osceola realized that he was in the sky again. For so many years, he could only look up at soaring hawks. Now, he was looking at the tops of their wings! I was overjoyed sharing flight with someone who totally understood. We were of different species, but were now of one soul. History was being made.

After about ten minutes of free flying, we landed. I was elated that the flight went so well. As I unhooked from the glider, Osceola had a different look in his eyes. There was a fire there that hasn't been there in a long time. I took him out of his harness and placed him on a perch. He kept looking up for he has been home. I shook Al and Neil's hands and thanked them for their help. I decided that one flight was enough for the day and drove back to Pigeon Forge. On the way home, I reviewed the flight. Something about it struck me; I had always felt bad for Osceola. But thinking about the way he watched the Red-tails made me sad and a little choked up. How he must miss flying! He no longer enjoys the freedom to go where he wants. He is an earthbound eagle. I had more freedom as a flying bird-man than he does. At least today, he again savored the sky.

One week later, we returned to the Flight Park, this time with a film crew from the Disney Channel. At sunset, we made a beautiful tow to feet. Flight Park Owner Matt Taber piloted the Dragonfly ultralight, with a cameraman to document the flight. The cameraman said that there wasn't enough light left for filming.

318

It didn't matter to Osceola, he was flying again. He got to see the sun setting behind Sand Mountain and a world painted with orange and rosy hues. After we landed, Al unclipped Osce from the glider and I put him in his sky kennel for the night. The film crew attached a digital video camera to the glider's left wing in preparation for the next morning's early flights.

Thursday dawned clear and cool. We got everything ready to take advantage of the calm morning air. The glider was set on the launch dolly and wheeled into place. Neil took the tug for a flight to check the morning air. He landed and announced "Smooth as glass!" Osceola was harnessed and his feet wrapped by Al. I suited up and clipped into the glider. Then Al hooked Osceola to the glider and latched him to my harness. Al checked and double checked to make sure everything was safe and secure. Then he laid his hand on the helmet on my head and said a prayer. This time, our flight plan was to go to 4000 feet. This would allow Matt and the cameraman in the chase ultralight to get plenty of shooting time. The tug was in position, the tow line was connected to the glider and me. A check was made of the release system. We were now ready. This would be the highest flight Osceola would have made in thirteen years. The takeoff was uneventful and we began our 10 minute climb to the designated altitude. The air was incredibly clear! I was amazed at how far I could see and how crisp and detailed everything appeared. By the time we reached release altitude, I could see the Tennessee River as it wound its way around Chattanooga and churned towards the northwest into Alabama. I could see the Smoky Mountains, some 70 miles in the distance and could recognize some of the familiar peaks. No telling what Osceola could see with his superior vision. Could he have possibly seen Atlanta some 100 miles to the south?

I was soaking in the view probably as much as Osceola. His head was in motion, looking one way and then the other. His eyes reflected a sense of fascination. The glide down didn't last as long as it normally would have. When the photo ultralight would come close by, I would increase my speed to match its speed, degrading my glide in the process. This time, Osceola didn't seem to mind the speed, maybe because we were higher. We made three more flights that day. With each flight, Osceola became calmer during the launch and landing procedures. We took our last flight, and since thermals starting to form, it was a little bumpier than the first three. We entered a small thermal and gained a small amount of altitude, once again something Osceola hadn't experienced in a while. Since the camera was moved to the front of the glider, our last landing was made on the wheels. It too, went well. Al unclipped Osceola from the glider and my harness, and I put him, minus his harness, on his traveling perch. This allowed him to cool off and get a well-deserved drink of water. He had a different look about him. Not one of fear, but possibly one of elation.

The footage was eventually aired on a segment of the Disney Channel's *Audubon's Animal Adventures*. Osceola and I flew again in October to get still shots for some publicity Al had in mind. For me, it was a good excuse to take him back to the sky. At this point, Osceola had made eight flights with a total of 2 hours and 10 minutes of airtime. Not bad for an eagle with one wing! The story of Osceola went around the world in various TV and news media. He even appeared on Good Morning America and had a featured story in *Reader's Digest* entitled *"The Bravest Eagle"*. Many people wrote letters and came from all over the world to Dollywood to see the hang gliding eagle. History had been made. Meanwhile…

My wing dips as we exit the thermal and jostles me from my daydream. I look back at Osceola and notice that he is looking down. A Turkey Vulture has joined us and is riding the same thermal. It glances up and sees a new creature; a symbiosis of eagle and man. The vulture turns downwind as Osceola and I head out over the valley. As I look back on our flights, it is almost hard for me to believe that this has happened. It has never been about garnering publicity, but about fulfilling a dream and a promise. The journey has been filled with obstacles, false starts and occasional disappointments, but it is a dream I have never given up. It has been about believing and perseverance. It has been about giving something back to my friend Osceola but in turn it has been about finding something in me. One can defy the odds and loose the shackles and make the seemingly impossible, possible. All you have to do is believe and you can truly soar!

Epilogue

As of this writing, July 2013, it has been 17 years since Osceola and I first flew together. In September, 2002, I left Osceola and the American Eagle Foundation and took a job as the Lead Keeper of Birds at the Santa Barbara Zoo in California. I didn't venture there alone. I developed a close relationship with one of my Foundation co-workers, Dale Kernahan. She became my girlfriend and eventually my wife. She also got a job at the zoo as the acting Lead Keeper of the Herpetology Department. We worked at a beautiful zoo, had some great co-workers, experienced some tremendous hang gliding and saw some wonderful scenery. Our great California experience only lasted two years. In June of 2004, legendary Eagle Lady, Doris Mager, asked Dale and me to join her organization, Save Our American Raptors, Inc. In July, we moved from Ventura to Trenton, Georgia, a small town 20 miles from Chattanooga. Lookout Mountain Flight Park www.hanglide.com where I took Osceola hang gliding, is only ten minutes from our house. In February of 2013, with Doris Mager's blessing, Dale and I formed Wings to Soar (www.soarsouth.org) and continue the work Doris started in the early 1960s.

In May of 2005, Dale and I began a partnership with See Rock City, Inc., www.seerockcity.com the famous natural attraction on Lookout Mountain above Chattanooga. Since 2005, we have conducted the Rock City Raptors Birds of Prey Show from Memorial Day Weekend to Labor Day. We also present a lot of programs at schools, state parks and civic groups.

I have visited Osceola many times since we have left the Foundation, but since the Spring of 2012, Al Cecere, American

Eagle Foundation President www.eagles.org and Carmen Simonton and Reecie Collins of the U.S, Fish and Wildlife Service have allowed me to use Osceola in a limited number of presentations. Thanks!!! It has been nice to become re-acquainted with my old friend, who is now 32 years old. I hope one day in the not too distant future, that Osceola with again be under my full time care. Who knows, maybe one day we will get to fly together again.

I want to thank a number of people who have helped in some way with the creation of this book. First, I want to thank my wife, Dale, for all of her encouragement, love and support not only for the book, but in our everyday lives together. She has spent many hours listening to different segments of this book and has offered some helpful suggestions. She has a wonderful, positive attitude and views life as an adventure. Thanks for sharing your precious time with me! You're wonderful and I love you!

I want to thank my parents, Gilbert and Maria, for their guidance and patience and for allowing me to do stuff that I am sure would make any parent nervous! While I am on the subject of family, I want to thank my sisters Susie and Mary for not killing me when we were younger and for purging the phrase, "You're just a girl", from my vocabulary. Thanks, too, to my daughter Lendi for her love and support. I would also like to thank my cousins for their encouragement, especially Alan Ray, who allowed me to live with him during my early days at the Cumberland Wildlife Foundation. Thanks, too, to my nephew Johnathan!

Special thanks to Cliff Ross, Kevin Schutt, Bob Hatcher, James Rogers and Al Cecere.

Thanks to all of my friends and volunteers who have helped me while I was at the Memphis Zoo (especially Martha Waldron and Wanda Elder), the Cumberland Wildlife Foundation, the

American Eagle Foundation and S.O.A.R (kudos to Karl Gumpright and Pam Carey). Thanks to Matt Taber of Lookout Mountain Flight Park for helping with the Osceola flights and to Neil Harris for being such a great tow pilot and helping get Osceola back in the air. And a special note of thanks to the free flight community; what a great, unique bunch of individuals! I especially want to thank Burke Ewing and Curtis for giving me the idea to take Osceola flying! If you want to learn more about hang gliding or paragliding, please visit www.ushpa.aero for more information.

Thanks to Cindy Simmons, Rhainne McRae and Rex Lilse for their many hours editing various phases of my book and for putting me on the right track.

A special note of gratitude goes to my fifth grade teacher, Dorothy Weight. The little field guide to birds she gave me as a going away present led to my career with birds. You never know who you may influence with a kind act. What we do in Life is only limited by a lack of imagination! Two things one needs to do while you are here; acquire knowledge and treat everyone you meet the way you would want to be treated; the Golden Rule.

Thank you for taking the time to read my book! If you would like to get in contact me, please e-mail me at johnstokes@hotmail.com

If you would like to learn more about Osceola the hang gliding eagle and video of us flying go to: www.osceolabaldeagle.com

For photos of some of the stuff and people in this book go to http://aneaglessky.blogspot.com . Also, look for us on Facebook under, Osceola, An Eagle's Sky.